The Day the King Died

A Terrible Miscarriage of Justice

Jim Morris

With a Foreword by Glyn Maddocks

❥ WATERSIDE PRESS

The Day the King Died
A Terrible Miscarriage of Justice

ISBN 978-1-909976-13-9 (Paperback)
ISBN 978-1-908162-86-1 (Epub ebook)
ISBN 978-1-908162-87-8 (Adobe ebook)

Copyright © 2015 This work is the copyright of Jim Morris. All intellectual property and associated rights are hereby asserted and reserved by him in full compliance with UK, European and international law. No part of this book may be copied, reproduced, stored in any retrieval system or transmitted in any form or by any means, including in hard copy or via the internet, without the prior written permission of the publishers to whom all such rights have been assigned. The Foreword is the copyright of Glyn Maddocks.

Cover design © 2015 Waterside Press. Design by www.gibgob.com. Main cover photograph reproduced by kind permission of the National Archives.

Main UK distributor Gardners Books, 1 Whittle Drive, Eastbourne, East Sussex, BN23 6QH. Tel: +44 (0)1323 521777; sales@gardners.com; www.gardners.com

North American distribution Ingram Book Company, One Ingram Blvd, La Vergne, TN 37086, USA. Tel: (+1) 615 793 5000; inquiry@ingramcontent.com

Cataloguing-In-Publication Data A catalogue record for this book can be obtained from the British Library.

Printed by CPI Group, Chippenham, UK.

e-book *The Day the King Died* is available as an ebook and also to subscribers of Myilibrary, Dawsonera, ebrary, and Ebscohost.

Published 2014 by
Waterside Press
Sherfield Gables
Sherfield-on-Loddon
Hook, Hampshire
United Kingdom RG27 0JG

Telephone +44(0)1256 882250
E-mail enquiries@watersidepress.co.uk
Online catalogue WatersidePress.co.uk

Contents

Acknowledgements *iv*
About the Author *v*
The Author of the Foreword *v*
Foreword *vii*

     Introduction 9
1. **Beginning** 15
2. **The Burglar** 23
3. **Police** 31
4. **Shooting**. 37
5. **Police Constable Jagger** 45
6. **Arrest** 49
7. **Hospital** 57
8. **Identification** 65
9. **Police Evidence** 69
10. **Consistency** 75
11. **Family** 81
12. **Evidence** 97
13. **The Farm** 107
14. **Mistakes**. 111
15. **Misdeeds** 119
16. **Doubt**. 125
17. **Saturday Night** 129
18. **On Remand** 139
19. **The Trial**. 149
20. **Defence Evidence** 175
21. **The Prosecution**. 193
22. **The Defence**. 203
23. **Withheld or Ignored Evidence** 211
24. **Some Thoughts on the Summing-up** 217
25. **The Run Up to the Appeal and its Aftermath** 223

Epilogue: The Rest of February 1952 and On *231*
Index *233*

Acknowledgements

I've often felt that 'Thank you' on a page loses it's vitality because you can't look the person in the eye. That said, it needn't be any the less sincere. Some folk have helped me greatly in the writing of this book, and, even though I kept it back for a good five years before I sent it to Waterside Press I will always feel a special warmth for it.

When I first went to Huddersfield to see the site of the tragedy I was enthused by Steve Lawson and the late Colin Van Bellen who turned out to meet me and were my guides for the day. When I returned Steve was ever eager and willing to help. These two men deserve a very special thank you.

Also Patrick Robertshaw joined us and like Steve has corresponded with me on and off ever since. Steve, an ex-policeman and Patrick a former barrister and judge both gave me little insights into the story that brought us all together.

As ever when starting the task of basic research it's all about the relevant documents and finding them — the staff at the National Archives in Kew are a bit special!

I also felt a bit in awe of Campbell Malone when I met him to discuss the case but when he'd read the book he was convinced by my points. That helped me team up with Glyn Maddocks and I felt just by Campbell reading the book that it gave me some credit.

But it's Bryan and Alex Gibson at Waterside Press who have made the publication a possibility and their hard work in editing and correcting the manuscript has been encouraging.

Thank you too to Jon Robins at the Justice Gap.

And the family. Not only mine but some of Alfred's too, 'we' won't give up until Alfred Moore can rest in peace.

About the Author

Jim Morris has taken a close interest in crime and punishment for many years, having written on subjects as diverse as unsolved murders, true crime and the Great Train Robbery. He lives and works in Ireland. His previous writings include *Unsolved Murders of the North* (2011); *More Unsolved Murders* (2012) *The Great Train Robbery: A New History* (2013) (all Amberley Publishing).

The Author of the Foreword

Glyn Maddocks is a consultant with Gabb and Co in South Wales and Scott Moncrieff in London and has been dealing with miscarriage of justice cases for over 25 years. In 2005 he was named Welsh Lawyer of the Year having dealt with the successful appeal of Paul Blackburn. He has almost unprecedented experience of appeal cases and making applications to the Criminal Cases Review Commission and has written widely on these subjects.

Foreword

The story of Alfred Moore, a Huddersfield poultry farmer and small time burglar, who was convicted of the murder of two Yorkshire police officers and hanged in Armley Prison, Leeds in early 1952, is one more sad if minor footnote in the long, dismal and inglorious history of the British criminal justice system.

Jim Morris tells the story of Alfred impressively, vividly, in forensic detail and in doing so he demolishes, brick by brick, the prosecution case, which the jury, no doubt, found so persuasive and, which inevitably led to an innocent man being sent to the gallows for a crime that he did not commit.

Following the meticulous path laid out chapter-by-chapter by Jim and looking at the evidence that was deployed against Alfred, it becomes immediately obvious that there was in this case no agnostic search for the truth; from the beginning there was one narrative and only one narrative, and that was the 'guilt' of Alfred Moore.

Jim makes it clear that the police decided even before the night of the murder was over that Alfred was the person responsible for shooting Police Constable Jagger and Detective Inspector Fraser, and every piece of evidence available was constructed, marshalled and manipulated to ensure that at Alfred's trial the jury were compelled to find him guilty of this heinous crime, and they did so.

In those immediate post-war days, which now seem so far away from our world, the legal system was used easily and effectively to despatch its failures and errors by means of the hangman's noose. From 1949 until February 1961 some one-hundred-and-twenty-three other men and women met the same fate as Alfred in consequence of their direct exposure to the full might and glory of the British criminal justice system — that is one execution on average every thirty seven days!

Fortunately, but not without protest we have, since the mid-1960s, not sent any more innocent men or women to the gallows. But the errors and mistakes still continue with depressing regularity and we should all pause for thought when anyone suggests that we should return to the very dark days of what used to be called, rather euphemistically, capital punishment.

There is nothing more barbaric than when a state executes one or more of its subjects, particularly when there are so many examples of it doing so on the basis of inaccurate or mistaken facts or of errors or omissions deliberate or innocent, and where it has been subsequently established that the evidence relied upon was incorrect or untrue.

The most chilling and haunting detail in Jim's book about the Alfred Moore case is at the end. Alfred's last letter—written a few hours before his execution—is quoted verbatim and in it Alfred impressively and with articulation protests his innocence. Cogently and persuasively he makes his case and sets down on paper, and for the future, the facts and the arguments that would and should have led to him being acquitted.

One can only speculate about what Alfred thought about how the British justice system had treated him. Although thankfully we no longer hang people in this country, I have to say that I would find it hard to argue that things have improved much in the last sixty or so years and that avoidable mistakes don't still occur too frequently and too regularly, and that the innocent are not still convicted day in and day out in our courts.

Glyn Maddocks
6 November 2014

Introduction

King George VI died on 6th February 1952. Alfred Moore also died that day. Both left grieving families. The king died peacefully in his sleep; Moore's death had been scheduled.

Alfred Moore was a thirty-six-year-old, married, father of four. The family lived at Whinney Close Farm, a smallholding in the parish of Kirkheaton, to the north-east of Huddersfield in the West Riding of Yorkshire. He was a poultry farmer, and his farm occupied just over eight acres — he also had a growing number of pigs. The Moore family had only been at the farm for a few months but he was a hard worker and had previous experience in poultry farming.

Up until the middle of February 1951, Moore supplemented his income as a 'part-time' burglar. At this he excelled, but the police were more than suspicious, and enquiries were being followed up. There had been a spate of burglaries where he'd previously lived, in Honley, on the other side of Huddersfield, but these stopped when the family moved.

Whinney Close Farmhouse had nice furniture and building work, that the previous owner had started, was re-commenced. The children were in a private school and taxis were often seen coming and going, and Alice Moore, Alfred's wife, liked to dress well. There are a few vague ideas recorded as to his criminal associates but he was always said to work alone. The local CID, under the leadership of Detective Inspector Duncan Alexander Fraser, had intensified the quest to catch Moore, and a group of policemen had been 'observing' him.

It was in the early hours of Sunday 15th July 1951, when a cordon of ten officers was in place around the farm, that a shooting occurred, which cost DI Fraser and Police Constable Arthur Gordon Jagger their lives. This led to the trial and subsequent conviction of Moore for murder, for which he was hanged on 6th February 1952.

The shooting occurred at approximately 1.55 am. The cordon around the farm was formed and in place by 11.45 pm on the Saturday night and the officers had been briefed to observe Moore's movements. If he was seen to leave the farm then they should wait about fifteen minutes before reporting to the senior officers and, if Moore was seen to approach the farm, suggesting he was returning from a possible burglary, he was to be intercepted. The police said they only had a brief and scanty description of him and the photograph they had was not a good likeness. It is possible therefore that they might well have observed the movements of someone else, but all of the officers present on that cordon stated that they saw no-one from the start of the observation until 1.55 am. They had also been observing the previous night and the Friday and Saturday night of the previous week and they had observed his former home in Gynn Lane in Honley, as well as 'staking-out' likely places they thought he might break into.

At about 1.55 am, PC Jagger, who was near an ash-tip to the south-west of the farm, saw a man on the footpath going in the direction of the farm whom he intercepted, and simultaneously he 'shouted'. DI Fraser, who was posted eighty-four yards away, went to assist. Meanwhile PC Jagger flashed his torch on 'The Man' and took hold of his left arm. DI Fraser approached and The Man was asked if he was Alfred Moore (they may have asked him if he was Alf or Albert Moore). The Man said 'Yes' and DI Fraser attempted to apprehend him. The Man was having nothing of it, he pulled out a gun and shot PC Jagger in the abdomen before shooting DI Fraser four times, although one shot misfired. The Man was then said to go in the direction of Whinney Close Farm. DI Fraser was dead. PC Jagger attempted to summon help in the agreed way by blowing his whistle, but as most of the other members of the cordon had heard the shots, they were already making their way towards the scene of the shooting.

None of the police officers were armed. They were all experienced officers, and although the cordon had been set up by DI Fraser, who had also undertaken the briefings and all the 'groundwork', it was Detective Chief Inspector Arthur Jenkins who was in operational command. He was a member of the cordon and had been on each of the three previous nights that the cordon had been formed.

DCI Jenkins gave the order to call an ambulance and to summon the Detective Chief Superintendent, George Metcalfe. There was a phone in the brickworks a few hundred yards to the south. DCI Jenkins made a sketch of the scene. Some lights were seen going on and off in the farmhouse and also smoke came from the chimney. Armed re-enforcements arrived with DCS Metcalfe, who was in charge of the entire CID for the West Riding Constabulary. At 4.40 am as dawn broke, DCS Metcalfe approached the farmhouse with an armed officer and arrested Moore.

Meanwhile, at the Huddersfield Royal Infirmary, DI Fraser was officially pronounced dead and PC Jagger was given treatment to attempt to save his life. He had a saline infusion and underwent surgery to try and repair the gunshot damage. He was given three pints of blood, painkillers and antibiotic drugs. Twelve hours after the operation he was deemed fit enough by one of the surgeons, and was conscious and alert and keen to assist his colleagues, so his side ward at the hospital was the scene of an identity parade on which Moore was a member. PC Jagger identified him as The Man he had stopped at 1.55 am that morning. A makeshift court was then convened in the ward where a series of depositions were sworn before a magistrate. This included a deposition from PC Jagger outlining the events of that morning and Moore, who was without legal representation, was able to cross-examine him. This was a futile exercise as he'd had no training in legal representation and asked probably the only question he could ask: 'Are you quite sure?' to which came the inevitable reply 'I am quite sure.'

Moore was charged with the murder of DI Fraser and, as PC Jagger died the following morning, he was charged with his murder too. His trial was at Leeds Assize Court the following December in front of Mr Justice Pearson. His defence was conducted by Harry Hylton-Foster KC and leading for the prosecution was George Raymond Hinchcliffe KC. The police provided the bulk of the prosecution evidence, but there was also Moore's brother who had spent the Saturday before the shootings with Moore doing construction work on the farm. His brother lived within walking distance of the farm and, as he had missed the last bus home, Moore walked part of the way home with him. Moore said he had returned to the farm by about midnight. The police said this was impossible as he would have been seen by a member of the cordon around his farm. The gun used in the shootings was agreed by ballistic experts to be a revolver and another witness, who had worked for the removals firm hired when the family moved to the farm, gave evidence that he had seen a Luger revolver in Moore's belongings. And in the farmhouse spent 9 mm cartridges were found when a wall was demolished. Although it could not be proved these were the cartridges of the bullets that had killed the two officers, a forensic expert said the bullets recovered from the dead police officers' bodies were also 9 mm. The gun was never found, but with all of this evidence, and the deposition of PC Jagger, the prosecution appeared to have a strong case.

The jury was only out for forty minutes before returning a verdict of guilty. The clerk of the court asked Moore if he had anything to say before he was sentenced to death, and he addressed the judge: 'My Lord, I protest my innocence. I am not guilty'. On went the black cap, out came the sentence. The only thing left to say was 'Amen'.

Moore appealed, the appeal was dismissed. The then Home Secretary, David Maxwell-Fyfe, could find nothing on which he could advise His Majesty to interfere with the due course of the law. Alfred Moore was hanged at Armley Prison in Leeds on 6th February 1952, at just about the same time as the Prime Minister, Winston Churchill, was informed of the death of King George VI.

Moore protested his innocence to the very end but the evidence was overwhelming, there could be no possibility of any doubt. But this assumes that the court, and jury in particular, knew all there was to know. And it assumes that the evidence was consistent. It also assumes the integrity of counsel and impartial accuracy from the judge; because there was doubt. Not the reasonable doubt that would have prevented the jury from convicting, but considerable doubt which should have meant that the case didn't go to court in the first place.

After it was all over, the rumour was that the family moved to Canada. It might be an idea to leave them there. There are all sorts of stories local folk in Huddersfield will tell about what happened to the rest of the family. But this story is about Moore and the trial; the family members survived, although one of the children (by now adult) passed away in 2003. In the course of writing this book I have had direct contact with some of them and indirect contact with the others. When Moore went into the witness box to give his evidence he asked Mr Justice Pearson if the names of his children could be withheld, I think it is fair to still honour that wish. But, for the rest, I would suggest that, as Moore was said to protest his innocence to the end, this book is simply an extension of his argument. I discuss subsequent events following Moore's death at the end of the book.

In criticising the outcome in Alfred Moore's case, it is my belief that a miscarriage of justice resulted from evidence that was embroidered, or concealed, or avoided, or simply lied about.

What cannot be done is to try and prove that the other likely suspect was the culprit, because he is long dead. As convictions are only made through the court system, with the examination of evidence, here it would merely be an allegation. This would detract from the main point of what follows — demonstrating that Alfred Moore did not murder DI Fraser and PC Jagger.

It is quite possible that this other individual was an associate of Moore's. It may well be that he did later exhibit a weapon, said to be the murder weapon, and there might be little doubt that the individual was cruel and ruthless and violent, none of which proves murder. Neither can it be proved that the gun he boasted was the gun that shot the two officers was in his possession at the material time. Nor can it be proved that he was in the vicinity of Whinney Close Farm when the shooting occurred.

It will be for the future to say that the murder of DI Fraser and PC Jagger is an unsolved crime. With this in mind, the murderer is known throughout as 'The Man'.

Chapter 1

Beginning

Just under a year before the start of the First World War, Mr and Mrs David Moore and their son, Harold, moved to the Longwood area of Huddersfield, which was about two miles to the east of the town centre, where their second child, a girl, Dorothy, was born. By 1915, Mr and Mrs Moore had moved a mile or two further east to Golcar when, on 6th June of that year, they had another son, Alfred. They lived in the Golcar area for the next twenty-odd years and had seven more children: Charles Henry was born in 1918; Gladys in 1920; John Franklyn in 1923; Edward in 1925; Alan in 1926; Alma in 1928 and Brenda completed the family in 1932.

At the age of five, Moore started school at the Bark Hill Council School, working steadily there until he was seven, when he moved on to Goitfield Council School, where he stayed until he was fourteen. He was a good scholar, and particularly good at handicrafts, for which he was awarded a certificate. He also won a certificate for swimming. Full-time education finished for him at the age of fourteen, which in the inter-war years was the norm. But he attended some further education classes later; his mother said he was always keen on learning. He was said to be keen on reading about subjects that interested him most: mechanics; the wireless; photography; gardening; and animals. He had a hobby of making mechanical models. Moore was blessed with an inquisitive mind with the patience and dexterity to use it to its potential.

According to his father, Moore had a terrible temper as a child; but, as in most other families, there are always two sides to a relationship. Moore's mother described the relationship between her son and his father as them just not seeing eye-to-eye. Moore was later to say that his father picked on him for little things. Overall, it sounds like the usual politics associated with any family. Moore's wife was later to say that, although his temper was very quick, he only lost his cool when provoked. His younger sister, Gladys, said he was '… always alright with me' but his father said he had struck Gladys across the face in a heated exchange about her husband. So, as well as the inter-family politics, it is also necessary to bear in mind that some family members might exaggerate others' traits; but other family members might play them down. Later, the police seemed to wish to record Moore's temper and violence from all and sundry.

Moore's tense relationship with his father came to a head one night over what sounds as though it was more of a misunderstanding, at any rate to begin with. There is some disagreement as to his age at the time, his father says he was sixteen, but Moore said the incident happened in July 1933 when he would have been eighteen. He worked late one evening, until about 8 pm, came home, had some tea and went out to the cinema. The second feature didn't particularly appeal to him, so he got home shortly before 10 pm — a time his father thought he should be home. It was July and it seems as though the weather was quite pleasant as the back door of the house was open. So, when Alfred opened the front door, the draft created made the back door bang to. He described his father as being in 'one of his moods' and the request not to 'bang the bloody door' was made and answered, but his father remonstrated 'not to bloody well answer him back'. Moore said his father then 'flew at me' (there was a claim that his father had broken Alfred's nose when he was sixteen, which may explain why both Mr Moore and his wife say this incident occurred two years previously). What followed was an ugly fight between father and son, until son managed to run out of a door his mother had opened, and made good his escape to the neighbours, and thence to his aunt's at Lockwood, where he stayed for about two years. His father describes the incident in these words:

> 'Alfred's temper was ruffling the whole family. He would fly into a temper at some trivial thing and the house was a hell-hole. This became so bad, particularly when he got bad-tempered with his mother, that I turned him out the house. He went to live with his aunt.'

His mother more or less agrees with his father. It is not wholly supported by Moore's siblings, though there is comment on his temper. Alfred seems to have left for his own safety, but his father said he put him out of the house. However, this might have something to do with who recorded the history—the above is based on statements later made to the police. Mrs Moore, his mother, was also to be interviewed by a doctor while Alfred was in the hospital wing of the prison on remand. It was noted:

> 'Mother later agrees, with reluctance, that the prisoner's father was a little jealous of him and was very nasty to his son at times. She says that [the] prisoner had cause to be terrified of his father at times when young, as his father had often struck him violently. She says [the] prisoner did have a temper but only when provoked and he would very quickly cool down and would say how sorry he was for what he had said in his temper.'

It is unfortunate that the information from the hospital was something the mother merely 'agrees' with rather than being something she could openly talk about—whatever her feelings—in a more active way, which would give a more vivid picture.

If the Moore family benefited from having some space from Alfred, then he certainly benefited from having space from them. Living with his aunt, uncle and his cousin he described as 'heaven on earth' and only returned to the parental home because his aunt became ill. His aunt spoke well of him, as did his cousin. And it might be worth considering the milieu at home where there were the two parents and ten children whose ages ranged from, roughly speaking, twenty-one years (Harold) to one year (Brenda). He then went to live with his aunt, her husband and Albert, his cousin, who was a year or two younger than him.

In November 1950, Mr and Mrs Moore moved to Harp Inge in Dalton, to the west of Huddersfield. By now Mr Moore was in his early-sixties and only Brenda was living at home with him and Mrs Moore. Alan was in the Royal Army Service Corps and Edward was in the King's Own Yorkshire Light Infantry. Harold, Dorothy, Alfred, Gladys, Charles, John and Alma had all married and settled around the Huddersfield area. Harold, Dorothy and Alma had remained in Golcar, Gladys had settled in Almondbury—with John next door and Charles just around the corner. In 1950, Moore and his family were living in Gynn Lane in the Honley area, which is about two and a half miles south of the town. And, by 1950, there was quite a collection of grandchildren.

Alice Cox was born in Saddleworth, which was then in the West Riding of Yorkshire. On 24th February 1940 she married Alfred Moore at the Huddersfield Registry Office, after a courtship of some eighteen months. She bore him four children. The eldest arrived in March 1941; their second child in July 1943; the third in October 1944 and the fourth child was born in August 1949.

Moore's employment record is a little sketchy; the bulk of the information now available comes mainly from police statements. It is understandable that a lad from the 'working class' of Huddersfield, who left school at fourteen, would have had few opportunities for higher education (though Moore did manage some further education). He, therefore, seemed stuck with 'dead-end' jobs, which would never allow him to realise his full potential.

He held his first job for several years—but accounts of the actual time span varies; his father at interview said four years, Moore said it was 'about six', and his manager suggested it was seven years—from September 1929 to September 1936. This was at Hirst and Mallinsons, a textile manufacturer of Longwood in Huddersfield. 'While he was at the firm he was a good worker and gave every satisfaction', was how his manager, Arnold Clay, was later to describe him. Interestingly, later, during his criminal career, his employer Mr Hirst was his one break-in to a private residence.

Moore started work at B & J Whitman's, of Brittania Mills in Golcar, where he was said to have begun rearing poultry at '… the side of the mill'. He secured a slightly higher salary and felt that he might have better prospects with this firm. But, after a while, B & J Whitman's was taken over and the new owners wished to cut down on staff, so Moore was laid off. He said he was with the firm for three years in total. As he left, it would have been difficult for him to keep his poultry there, so this venture also ceased.

When they married they took the tenancy of Bottoms Farm in Slaithwaite, and Moore moved the remainder of his stock from the small project next to the mill to there. During this time, he had a brief spell of employment with Mallinson's at the Linthwaite Mills, and it is also recorded that he worked in a chemical works in Milnsbridge but apparently the chemicals, or his proximity to them, upset his health. He commenced with the firm in April 1941 but was off sick from July, and finally left in the December. His work was said to be satisfactory but, again, it was a dead-end labouring job which must have been frustrating. Moore had tried to get his poultry farming business off the ground, but it hadn't gone well and, by early-1941, he had given it up, admitting he and Alice were in '… low water, financially'. However, there were also problems obtaining the foodstuffs necessary for the poultry. It was said his mother had helped them out financially during this time, and although his father knew of this, he hadn't interfered. Moore's relationship with his father hadn't improved; his father said he '… lost interest in him'. His father also said he didn't like Alice, Moore's wife, so hadn't attended their wedding.

When they gave up Bottoms Farm, the Moores made two house moves in fairly quick succession, the first to Scapegoat Hill and later Heath Hill, both in the Golcar area. At the same time he was employed with David Brown & Sons at their Park Works. In fact, he had two stints of employment with this firm—from April to November 1942—when his work was considered to be satisfactory. Following his 'service' with HM Forces he returned to this employer in October 1948, from which he was later dismissed for '… persistent absence'.

Moore made no secret of a reluctance to join the Army and, as an able-bodied man living in a country that had been at war for nearly two years, it was expected that he would be drafted for service in the armed forces at some stage. It was in the latter half of 1942 that he joined the Merchant Navy. He was prepared to serve either in this or the Royal Navy—it seems pure chance that the Merchant Navy got him first. This wouldn't have been an easier option because merchant ships were often unprotected. He based himself in the Hull/Grimsby area and remained as a merchant seaman until June 1946, when he was arrested for failing to report for military service. This arrest is notable because his behaviour during it is well documented.

It was on 19th June that he appeared before Huddersfield Magistrates Court, accused of breaking into the Honley branch of the Co-operative Society, but no evidence was offered, so he was discharged and walked free. But as he did so, a police sergeant told him he was about to be arrested on a military charge and two military policemen were waiting for him. The police sergeant later recorded that, at this time, Moore '… adopted a fighting attitude to resist arrest' and that he was '… very violent'. However, this is not the type of behaviour The Man was later said to show on the hillside as will be explained later in the book. Moore's days in the Merchant Navy were at an end, but the Military Court, sitting in Pontefract, found that as he had served in the Merchant Navy, then this was taken as 'service' and he spent just a few days in military detention. He was then deployed to the Pioneer Corps as a clerk and was demobbed in May 1947.

Moore worked for a cloth bleachers for a few months from May 1948, but mainly wanted to concentrate on his poultry business. The family were expanding too as, by this time, they had three children — the fourth was to appear a couple of years later. The marriage was said to be a happy one and, over the winter of 1948/49 he worked in the tool room of David Brown & Sons.

Alfred, Alice and the children lived in the bungalow in Gynn Lane in Honley for about four years before moving to Whinney Close Farm in May 1951. The police interviewed both neighbours in Gynn Lane. Mrs Jury, next door at number thirty-nine, said 'The Moores were always surrounded by mystery...appeared to have an enormous income...with no apparent source'. And, 'Mr and Mrs Moore did not make any friends in the neighbourhood and did not have any regular visitors to the house. In fact, I have spoken to them perhaps more than anyone else, and they were always noticeably careful not to disclose anything about their background.' One wonders if the latter statement was after four years of prying — it is not clear how Mrs Jury would have known whether or not they had few visitors.

During their time at Gynn Lane, a little discord was noted between Alfred and Alice. They had a row about money which, Moore said later, was why he took to burglary. It is also well noted that there was another row when Moore allegedly attacked Alice with a chair, which Alice may have referred to in a later statement to the police, although she also was quoted as saying that he had never been violent to her (however, he did admit hitting her when he found she had run up some debt, this was again the financial mire that led to his career in crime). On one occasion an altercation noted by neighbours involved a gentleman called 'George' in some capacity, but exactly how isn't clear.

Their neighbour on the other side was a thirty-one-year-old schoolmaster, Mr Welsby, who lived with his wife and children. Mr Welsby said that after they had lived in the house for about a fortnight they heard what he described as a 'disturbance' but, apparently, 'George' was involved. Mr Welsby described 'several' occasions when there were '… violent quarrels between him and his wife…' — presumably with Alfred and not George. He also describes visitors at night '… several times'.

They bought Whinney Close Farm at auction in May 1951. It needed a lot of work doing but it seemed that, finally, Moore had the idyllic venue in which to bring up his kids and build-up his farming business. Although there is a report of an attempted break-in at the offices of the brickworks to the south of the farm, it was never strongly linked to Moore. Perhaps because the police felt that if they could get him for murder, then it would probably solve the burglary side of things.

CHAPTER 2

The Burglar

It might seem strange to the casual observer that even though Moore burgled premises and stole property, there is little evidence in the surviving records to show that he was anything other than honest, in what he said and what he did, once he knew the game was up. In fact, the only time that he lied throughout the entire episode was when he said he went to bed at about midnight '... and didn't get up again ...' on the night of the shooting. And this only came to light because the police had seen smoke coming from the chimney. So, there may have been a time of 'honour among thieves', when there was the 'Raffles' type of character—in those days, villains carrying guns was not a commonplace occurrence. But, nonetheless, Moore was a member of the criminal world, a twilight world where 'records' were not kept, receipts for 'purchases' were not issued, any plans were a closely-guarded secret, and, above all else, it was a capital offence to 'help the police with their enquiries'. The concept of crime prevention wasn't something the average member of the public had in their mind; the necessity for every house to have a burglar alarm was decades away. In 1951, things were still bleak after the war, there were still shortages and rationing and, as for the black market, if you didn't use it, then you went hungry. It was also a world of weekly cash wages, the average Joe Public didn't have a bank account. Money was a visible commodity one held in one's hand, invisible money transfers of salaries into the bank and then direct debits out were not that common. The so-called cashless society of credit cards and pin numbers, of ATMs and cashback, just didn't exist. Your bank manager was skilled in looking after your money, not as he is today, just another salesman intent on selling you some of the bank's money.

It was against this backdrop that Moore embarked on his criminal career. It is possible that one or more raids were not reported to the police and there is only one instance of housebreaking. This doesn't mean there were any more than recorded, it just highlights the possibility. There was an incident where Alice Moore was said to be cashing postal orders, which had been stolen some time previously, but the charge was dropped when the police could offer no evidence and Alfred claimed he had bought the postal orders from a sailor—he was in the Merchant Navy at the time.

At first, his forays into the criminal world were spasmodic, with only two events recorded in 1946, and they were several months apart. Between 26th and 28th January, £120 7s 1d in cash was stolen from the premises of John Crowther & Sons along with a fairly large collection of other items, mainly crockery and glassware, with a value just short of £17. Between 27th and 28th November, the same firm was raided but this time the value of the haul was much less, only some £13 8s 10d in cash, a tape measure, and interestingly a 'Kaye' grand master key. Amy Firth Shaw, who was a private secretary at the firm, identified the items when they were later recovered from Whinney Close Farm, but it is unclear as to whether this included the key. It is also not noted as to whether the premises were forcibly entered or not.

Things went quiet again for a long time until James Sykes & Sons Ltd was raided. Like John Crowther & Sons, they were based in the Milnsbridge area of Huddersfield. The offices of James Sykes of Stafford Mills were broken into between 2nd and 3rd April 1949, and £27 was stolen. A gold watch to the value of £40 was also stolen, which was later recovered at Whinney Close Farm; this was positively identified by a Mr Beaumont, a director of the firm. Again, there is no record of how Moore got into the premises.

It wasn't until nearly a year later that the Colne Valley Spinning Company in Linthwaite was raided. At just after 6.30 am on 9th February 1950, the manager of the company, Fred Bamford, arrived at his office. He found the office in some disarray; it had been ransacked and the safe was lying open. The police attended, and the rough estimation of what was stolen—£19 1s 1d in cash and a brown leather bag—was noted. A brown leather bag was later recovered from Whinney Close Farm and Mr Bamford was fairly sure this was the bag which had been stolen from his office back in February 1950. It was also found that one of the keys recovered from the farm also fitted and opened all the locks at the Colne Valley Spinning Company premises. This key had originally been supplied by Joseph Kaye & Sons, which was a firm of Locksmiths in Leeds, but Sam Cooper, their technical sales manager, could not say anything about the history of this key. It certainly had the company name stamped on it, but the shoulder of the key had been '... badly mutilated by filing'. There was some speculation that Moore's criminal associates included the son of a locksmith, but nothing is certain. A grand master key, manufactured by Joseph Kaye & Sons, had been stolen from John Crowther & Sons of Huddersfield during a break-in in November 1946, but whether this was the key or not was never established. Again, there is no record of how entry to the premises was effected.

Between 25th and 27th February 1950, the offices of The Grove Engineering Company of Longwood in Huddersfield were raided. The haul here was £8 in cash, but tools and some small equipment was also stolen. The premises had been secured by a Yale droplock which had been forced off and was found on the floor. One of the partners in the firm, Charles Lacey, was able to identify the stolen equipment from what was later found at Whinney Close Farm. But it is interesting that here the premises were forcibly entered.

The following week, another burglary occurred at the premises of B & J Whitman of Milnsbridge in Huddersfield. This time a larger sum of money was stolen: some £405 17s 2d. This was in a leather cash bag, which was later identified by Peel Bamford; it was also recorded in one of Mr Bamford's statements that the offices were forcibly entered.

Three months later, between 8th and 9th June 1950, offices on the premises of Josiah France Ltd of Honley were burgled and £126 6s 3d was stolen, together with a cigarette box and, just as significant, three keys. In his statement, Mr Pollack, the managing director, said the entry to the premises had been forced. The cashier was able to say that one safe on the premises had not been opened, but another director, Mr Sanderson, said the safe in his office had been opened.

Just about five weeks later, on the night of 13th/14th July 1950, a factory was burgled on the premises of Huddersfield Fine Worsteds at Brockholes, near Huddersfield when £192 10s 5½d was stolen, together with a safe key. Again, the premises were forcibly entered. Gilbert Crossland, who was a conscientious secretary, had noted some of the serial numbers of pound notes (which were new and had never been in circulation) and there was also a batch of ten shilling notes, the numbers from these he hadn't noted, though he could say they ran in number order.

An extremely large haul was awaiting Moore on his next foray because the total amount stolen from Bruck & Engleman Ltd. of Huddersfield was £2,500. This robbery took place on 13th July 1950. Richard Hanak made a statement but, for some reason, it was altered. In the first draft he says: 'At about 3.00am on Thursday 13th of July, 1950, I was aroused from bed and, as a result of what was said to me, I went to the mills.' But this was changed to, 'About 3.00am on Thursday 13th of July, 1950, as a result of a message, I went to the mills.' It is not known who 'edited' this statement but there is a scribble in the margin '… no signs of forcible entry', though the handwriting is poor. The safe and the safe drawers were forcibly opened however.

Again, after a break of five weeks, between 24th and 25th August 1950, John Brooke & Sons Ltd was raided. This time the haul was less, but still a substantial £526 12s 6d, of which only the metal cash box valued at £6 was recovered. Harold Crossland, the cashier, described this by saying, 'The side of my safe had been ripped open…' In another office, a safe had been opened but with a key which had been found in Mr Crossland's office. Mr Crossland could later say that entry to the building had been effected by means of a duplicate key.

By mid-October, Moore was ready to go to work again and paid a clandestine visit to the Co-operative Society Store, Westgate, in Honley. This time the value wasn't that large at £60 0s 2d, of which goods to the value of £11 18s 10d were recovered from Whinney Close Farm after Moore's arrest. The recovered property consisted of cigarettes, a cigarette box and a butter knife. There is no note as to whether the premises were forcibly entered or not.

The offices of John Woodhead Ltd of Thongsbridge were turned over on the night of 25th/26th November 1950. A total of £299 11s 0½d was lifted, of which goods to the value of £19 5s 0d were later recovered. The premises were 'forcibly entered and the safes ripped from their stands and both had their backs… ripped off.' Ten keys were also stolen.

Then, just three days before Christmas, £13 18s 8d and a safe key were stolen from the offices of Ben Hall & Son Ltd of Milnsbridge. John Wilson, cashier with the firm, later identified the key as one recovered at the farm. Mr Wilson explained in his statement that the keys to the safe were kept in a small drawer in a roll-top desk in his office. It is unclear whether the premises were forcibly entered or not.

Come the New Year, Moore was active again between 20th and 22nd January.

The offices at the premises of Alan Thornton and Sons of Honley were broken into and as well as a key, valued at 2s, £5 in cash seems to have been taken. On this occasion the office door had been forced, as had been the safe.

Out of a total value of £18 originally reported stolen from the offices of Sykes & Tunnacliffe Ltd of Almondbury, goods to the value of £12 15s 6d were later recovered at the farm. So, out of the two raids in January 1951—Sykes and Thorntons were burgled between 26th and 27th January—a total cash haul of approximately £10 4s 6d was achieved. Godfrey Sykes, managing director, was to later refer to this as a 'break-in', which suggests a forcible entry.

On the night of 4th/5th February 1951, Moore committed his only burglary at a private residence; the home of John and Constance Hirst of Northgate Mount, in Honley. This time £475 in notes together with numerous items of jewellery and other valuable items were stolen. Some alcoholic drink was also taken. Significantly, in one of his drawers, Mr Hirst had kept some .303 and 9 mm ammunition (he had been a Home Guard Officer during the war—a Sten Gun which takes 9 mm ammunition was the weapon generally issued to the Home Guard). Mrs Hirst, in a much later statement (29th July 1951), said:

> 'I showed Chief Inspector Jenkins a drawer in the sideboard, at the back of which there was one .303 cartridge. This is the same drawer in which prior to 4th February 1951, I had seen six or seven rounds of 9 mm ammunition and a number of .303 cartridges, with some golf balls, in a tin. The contents of the tin were stolen when our house was broken into on the night of 4th-5th February 1951. I took Chief Inspector Jenkins to my husband's dressing-room and from one drawer he took possession of one round of 9 mm ammunition and one round of .303 ammunition, and from another drawer he took a box containing 13 rounds of 9 mm ammunition.'

Just why this suddenly became topical at the end of July, especially when Mrs Hirst had given a further statement only four days before this one, is not made clear. It would, however, have been topical as the murder weapon hadn't been found. But it demonstrates how sometimes large amounts of ammunition were just lying about the country in people's houses, so soon after the war. It is not noted whether the 9 mm rounds of ammunition matched any of the spent cartridges later recovered from Whinney Close Farm. When asked, Mr Hirst said he did not own a gun, but why he had this ammunition is unclear. And it seems Mrs Hirst had some knowledge of ammunition but this was not uncommon for women so soon after the war.

That was not the last of a connection with Mr and Mrs Hirst. On 13th April their son, also John, reported the theft of his bicycle from the garage of the premises. It may well be that his bicycle was stolen on or about 13th April. But it is curious that if the bicycle was taken at the time of the main break-in, Mrs Hirst didn't know about it, when she seemed to know a good bit about the cache of ammunition her husband had, knew when she had seen it and knew where else he kept similar things.

Finally, Moore hit his biggest haul between 1st and 2nd March when he burgled the offices of Martin, Sons & Co Ltd and lifted property to the value of £3,135 13s 0d, of which only a key valued at ten shillings was recovered from the farm. These premises were forcibly entered, and also with the haul were four safe keys stolen from the safe in John Senior's office (he was the company secretary). As part of the police enquiry, the keys recovered from the farm were investigated and it was found that the four safe keys stolen from Martin, Sons & Co. Ltd were among them.

It was heavily hinted during the research for this book that one of Moore's closest associates was the son of a local locksmith. With this in mind, it is worth re-considering the raids. There are seventeen accounted for above, of which nine were definitely by a forced entry but, in the case of six of the raids, there is no record. In only two there was either no sign of forced entry, or a duplicate key was used. But another twist to this tale comes from an Arnold Crowther, who lived in the Golcar area. One of the keys recovered from the farm fitted Mr Crowther's house—his front door, back door, garage door and the greenhouse; Mr Crowther had never had any intruders though. Two questions here are, firstly, how did Moore get this key, but also how did the police know to visit this gentleman and try it? Another strange and similar tale, a Dorothy Amphett, who was a 'personal help and companion' to a Miss Christina Ditchbourne, was visited by the police and a key recovered from the farm also fitted all the locks in this house. Unless, for some reason, Moore was given keys by either, or both, Mr Crowther or Miss Amphett then the reason is unclear. But the police seemed to think the keys might fit. This is a piece of the jigsaw that will remain a mystery.

There was not a great deal of distance between Moore's home, which was then in Gynn Lane, Honley, and the various venues of the burglaries. The longest journey he made was about three and a half miles to Longwood to raid the Grove Engineering Co. If a man walks about eighty yards per minute (which is a deliberate under-estimation) then he would cover the distance in about an hour. So, an hour to get in, commit the crime and then an hour home. Some of the distances were considerably less, such as about a mile and a half to Armitage Bridge (John Brooke & Son) or even under a mile (Mr and Mrs Hirst lived in Honley). To commit the burglary in Almondbury, it was about the same distance from Honley as it would have been from Kirkheaton where the farm was.

There is a discussion later about how Mr Hinchcliffe misled the jury, perhaps inadvertently, because he quite simply didn't get his facts right. The burglaries stopped when Moore and his family moved to Whinney Close Farm; they moved to the farm in May — the last burglary was in March. Mr Hinchclife claimed Moore had been involved in burglary until May. Perhaps this is based on something DCI Jenkins said in an early statement: 'Within six weeks of Moore's arrival at Kirkheaton, an office was broken into and a safe attacked'. This didn't become evidence in court as it simply couldn't be proved. But it indicates the police and the prosecutor, even with Moore's admission of guilt about the burglaries, still wanted more.

Would Moore have returned to burglary — a thought, not a question. Considering Moore and his family had a good deal of money at their disposal and certainly enough to set themselves up on the farm, it might not have been worth the risk. The money went on the house, furniture, children's education. Moore didn't gamble and he didn't drink.

So, how much money in actual cash — pounds, shillings and pence — did he pull in? It is difficult to arrive at a definitive figure because some of his haul was of value, but that value couldn't be realised, for example, a gold and platinum ring belonging to Mrs Hirst. The police did try and itemise the burglaries and calculate just how much of the haul was in cash. Excluding any non-English sterling and other overseas currencies, a figure of £5,300 plus wouldn't be much of an underestimate. That seems a small amount by modern standards but, to consider Whinney Close Farm with just over eight acres cost £1,530 and, in one of the employer's statements, it is noted Moore's wage a couple of years before this was on average £7 10s 0d per week—his haul was the equivalent of over thirteen years earnings. Mr Hinchcliffe, for the prosecution was paid a fee of 162 guineas (about £171) for his three days of work, plus the preparation. It is almost impossible to calculate the buying power because, in 1951, there was still some rationing and VAT was referred to by some other name at some other rate; and the black market was rife. There were no tea-bags, frozen oven chips, beef burgers or takeaways. There were no supermarkets. Beer didn't come in cans and whiskey was the equivalent of about £1.60 a bottle.

CHAPTER 3

Police

A case reported in 1943 which was put down to Moore finally came to court in June 1947. This was Moore's only court appearance but, as it was a crime that couldn't be attributed to him, the case against him collapsed. The police said there was a lack of evidence, which meant, in truth, that there was no evidence. Alice Moore had been cashing postal orders that were known to be stolen, so Moore was thought to be associated with this crime. His defence was that he had bought them from another seaman in the Merchant Navy. It is unclear whether the charge was one of theft or receiving. It was at this point, in June 1947, that he was arrested by the Military Police and his Merchant Navy days came to an end. He had actually burgled the premises where the postal orders had originated but it is unclear why no evidence was offered.

In February 1946, a police officer, who seemed to know what he was doing, appeared on the scene. Having recently been promoted to Detective Inspector, Duncan Alexander Fraser now headed the CID in the Huddersfield area. DI Fraser was originally from Inverness in Scotland and had joined the police after he left the Army. He had been in the Cameron Highlanders for fifteen years; and latterly a policeman for twenty-two years. He was married to Catherine and they had a teenage daughter, Patricia.

When DI Fraser took charge of the CID in Huddersfield there was an unsolved burglary on the books. This had been the case of burglary on the premises of John Crowther & Sons of Milnsbridge in January 1946. The trail had gone cold, so there was little that could be done, save for putting the case on file. But DI Fraser was to get a spate of burglaries on his patch before the matter came to a head—at the point of his murder.

In fact, there were eighteen further burglaries (if the garage-breaking at the home of John Hirst actually occurred on a different date to the house-breaking) by Moore prior to DI Fraser's death. It is noted from the statements and depositions that they became suspicious of Moore after a spate of burglaries in the Honley area; elsewhere in the surviving documentation the word 'hint' is used, which suggests an informant. In a statement at the time, DCI Jenkins said:

> '…two young men, walking home early in the morning, saw a man carrying a black box and an iron bar. This was about ten minutes' walk from Moore's home, and the man's description as given by the young men was very like that of Moore. Consequently, discreet enquiries were made and, because of Moore's expensive mode of life and his unemployment, his secretiveness and the fact that he lived almost in the middle of the area which was being attacked, night observations were made by policemen on his home in Honley. By the time that discreet enquiry revealed that Moore was a strong suspect, it was felt that too much time had elapsed to justify application for a search warrant. Therefore, observations by pairs of policemen were kept for many weeks in mill premises which were considered likely for attack.'

So, if DCI Jenkins can actually say that the description given by the young man was '…very like that of Moore' then the identity and appearance of Moore was known to the CID, so almost certainly known by DI Fraser. But, just before he was shot, DI Fraser asked The Man if he was Moore Moore. It might seem strange that the question was asked, but Moore's identity was a source of much controversy, and just what DI Fraser knew of Moore's identity is not known. It is recorded that DI Fraser had used the sitting-room of a local, Mr Stafford, to observe a bus stop Moore was known to use, as the police wanted an up-to-date description of him.

In the spring of 1951, Moore and his family moved to Whinney Close Farm and the raids around the Honley area stopped. It must be acknowledged that Moore did commit the crimes the police thought he had committed, so there is little point in considering the overall investigation; for one thing there is precious little documentation covering it. Available documentation that is, the West Yorkshire Police, as they now are, say that they still have a file.

One document that is useful to this case, however, describes the creation of the cordon and is taken from the statements by the householder of The Bungalow in Cockley Hill, where ultimately DCI Jenkins was to be posted. The rest of the officers were on land owned by either the Stancliffe brothers, whose business owned the land adjacent to and around Whinney Close Farm or was within the boundary of the farm itself. It was land with common footpaths with public rights of way, so the police did not need to seek permission to post officers there. The particular bungalow where DCI Jenkins was posted was owned and occupied by Arthur Woodhead and his wife Lucy. DI Fraser had seen and discussed the plan with Mrs Woodhead in early June 1951, and so thorough was his description of the cordon and where he would be, Mrs Woodhead could actually describe it as the locals did — 'The Mountain', as the land rose in that area. He had let her know a good deal about the operation, specifically that there would be other officers around the locale. It is also recorded that Mrs Woodhead 'observed' the farm for the police and noted details of comings and goings. By the time of the cordons, the police had built up a good knowledge base through the likes of Mrs Woodhead.

This came about because DI Fraser had known Mrs Woodhead for a number of years. He needed to know she was reliable. During the Second World War they had met whilst he was on air raid warden liaison duties. Another link was with a gentleman mentioned earlier, Ben Stafford (DI Fraser had actually borrowed a watch from him on the night of the ill-fated cordon — a pocket watch, which if he had worn it in his breast pocket might have stopped the bullet that probably killed him). As mentioned earlier, DI Fraser had used the position of Mr Stafford's house, which overlooked the bus stop, to obtain an up-to-date description of Moore prior to the cordon team being briefed. And, as the police had adequate notice that Moore was to move to the farm, they could spend a good amount of time in the area familiarising themselves on the lie of the land.

For the first two nights of the first weekend of the cordon, Friday and Saturday, 6th/7th July 1951, DCI Jenkins took up his post as noted by Mrs Woodhead. The following Friday and Saturday night he was there again. Mrs Woodhead reported that DCI Jenkins was usually at the bungalow by about 11.30 pm. There is no evidence that either the police misled the court in the dates and times the cordon was in place around the farm, or what personnel were posted where. However, it is likely that the other officers making up the cordon would be occupying the same positions for each night it would be formed, as DI Fraser had informed Mrs Woodhead about who was to be on her veranda.

All planning and groundwork was undertaken by DI Fraser, such as considering where the senior officers would be and how they could communicate with each other. As to the posting of who and where, this doesn't seem to be anything other than a straight allocation of manpower. There is no reason to doubt that the cordon was in place by 11.40 pm on the night of Saturday 14th July and that it was complete and operational by 11.45 pm, at any rate, well before Moore said he was back at the farm.

But it does look as though at least three people got through the cordon on the night of 14th/15th July 1951: Moore; a local lad of 15, Rex Hallis; and The Man. It is Moore and The Man that are the subject of the present study, but we shall briefly look at Rex Hallis. The night of 14th/15th July 1951 had stuck in his memory because of the events that occurred, but also because 14th July was his 16th birthday. He'd just returned to live with his father after a stay in a children's home following the death of his mother some six or seven years earlier. On the night he had walked with his friend across the fields towards Shroggs Bridge—his friend lived in the Houses Hill area. Rex timed his return journey, through the observed cordoned fields, to arrive at his home quite close, on a north-easterly aspect, to Whinney Close Farm at about 12.45 am; a good hour following the completion of the cordon. On the route he said he took, he would have crossed Shroggs Bridge where DS Butler was posted; passed about fifty yards north of Police Constable Wilfred Sellick's position and would have gone up 'the drive' which leads down to the farm from Cockley Hill Lane, where Police Constable James Hopping said he had a clear view of the drive. So, at least two of the officers would have been expected to have seen him. Rex told his story in 2008. He didn't come forward at the time as two policemen had come to his house (there is no reason recorded for this visit although, in his deposition, DS Lee makes more than a brief reference to this) and threatened him that if he didn't '… keep his trap shut' he'd '… end up in borstal.' Rex said he was timid as his experiences in the children's home had affected his confidence and he was too terrified to come forward at the time. Rex never made any sort of statement or deposition so nothing was recorded in 1951.

It also looks as though The Man did get past PC Jagger and passed approximately sixty yards to the north-west of DI Fraser's position. A map clearly indicates this. The actual murder scene was inside what could be considered as the cordon boundary by sixty-six yards (recorded by DS Butler); it was to the north-east of the position of PC Jagger. There is a photograph which shows the scene and it confirms the shooting took place well within the cordon's boundary. So the question becomes clear: how did The Man get approximately sixty-six yards inside the cordon, along a path on which PC Jagger was posted? And the measurements do not account for the fact that the path goes along the southern and then the eastern aspect of the ash-tip, so the overall distance may be greater. One clue could be in what PC Jagger later said to DCI Jenkins, 'We saw a man ...' and he is probably referring to himself and DI Fraser, so exactly where PC Jagger was when 'we' saw The Man is not known. He goes on to say '... going up a field ...', which suggests the movement was away from PC Jagger's position and towards the direction of the farm. It is impossible to get to this point without passing where PC Jagger was posted, unless The Man came from the east along the path that PC Sellick and DS Butler, as well as DI Fraser, were posted on; even then, The Man would have had to turn right when he got to the junction of paths adjacent to where PC Jagger was posted. In short, he would pass three officers this way.

So, PC Jagger didn't see him come, didn't see him pass, but only saw him go. Of course, what was not asked of any police officer from the cordon by either the prosecution or the defence (or Mr Justice Pearson for that matter) was: 'Did you at any time leave the position in which you were placed in the cordon?' Mr Hylton-Foster for the defence argued that, for the first few minutes, the officer would be likely to be just scouting round his territory to get his bearings. What was kept from Mr Hylton-Foster was the fact that the night of the shooting was the fourth night that the same ten officers had been on cordon duty, so not only does this clearly indicate some documents which could have helped the defence were withheld, it also demonstrates that the officers should have been quite conversant with their 'patch'. There is the 'call of nature' but, as this is a normal function, it would almost certainly have been mentioned by PC Jagger: 'I went to relieve myself and as soon as I got back to my position. I (we) saw a man ... go up a field.' All perfectly acceptable, but this *wasn't* said.

Figure 1 below shows the murder scene in relation to the postings of the individual officers together with their names—this is crudely to scale and representative; the lines joining the officers' locations form the invisible boundary of the cordon. It also shows the approximate plotting of the footpath leading from roughly the point of the cemetery through the farm and out of the northern boundary. It would have been along this pathway that Moore walked home that night (this was just one of the pathways across the farm).

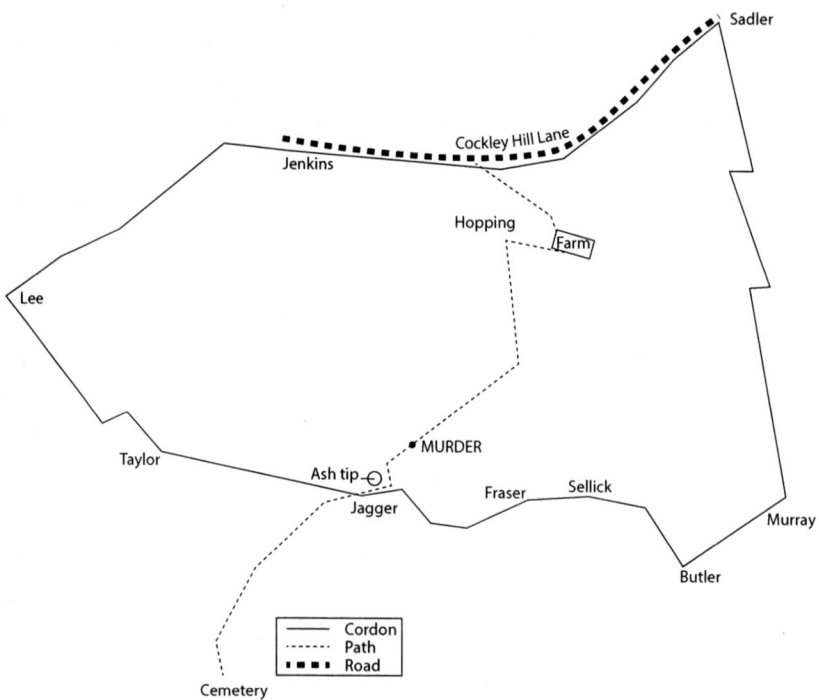

Figure 1: Simplified map of the area of the police cordon.

So, if the cordon 'brief' had been to 'intercept' anyone heading in the direction of the farm, the question has to be addressed: why is the scene of the shooting so far inside the cordon boundary?

When the shooting occurred, the police activity turned from an observation into an investigation.

Chapter 4

Shooting

One thing that is ever shrouded in mystery is the level of knowledge the police had about Moore's identity. On the 30th September 1951 a number of the officers who had been on the cordon that night in July made statements in which they said they could not have made a positive identification of Moore based on what they had been told at DI Fraser's briefing. In that briefing the officers were given a description of Moore; some officers actually knew what he looked like. However, it is what was known of Moore's identity by DI Fraser, the CID officer in charge of the Huddersfield Division, and therefore the pivot of police activity throughout the investigation prior to the shooting, that is well worth assessing.

If it is true that DI Fraser made observations of Moore at the bus stop opposite Ben Stafford's house, then he would have had to have known him first in order to recognise who he was observing, either through his own knowledge or by having another officer with him at some stage. According to five of the officers in the cordon on the night of the shooting, PC Jagger stated quite categorically that the man who shot him and DI Fraser was Moore, but it is claimed PC Jagger did not know Moore nor had he seen his photograph. It could only have been what was said between DI Fraser and The Man that prompted PC Jagger to this conclusion.

What was not asked in court was how much about the identity of Moore was known by DI Fraser. It can be noted that PC Jagger's level of knowledge of Moore's identity was a key feature, and was an issue, but DI Fraser's level of knowledge of Moore's identity wasn't mentioned in court at all. One reason for this was that the prosecution knew about other activities, including the observation of Moore at the bus stop. However, it is possible that they didn't want the jury to know this—they wanted to bolster PC Jagger's credibility as an independent witness. (The question of how reliable PC Jagger's purported identification was is dealt with later and is a central theme of this book).

There is also the assumption that everything The Man said to DI Fraser and PC Jagger was accurate and true. However, it is unlikely that he was pursuing a legal activity as he was armed with a gun, and so the certainty around the accuracy of what he said has to be questioned. Is it possible that he just said 'Yes', that he was Moore, to give a false clue? What truth would issue forth from an armed man walking on a lonely farm footpath at 2 am is anybody's guess. If he was up to no good would his answer to a surprise police enquiry be truthful, or at any rate, reliable?

On to Moore's identity. A man who had been burgling regularly. The police, aware of this, particularly the head of Huddersfield CID, had observed his home in Gynn Lane in Honley, and had 'staked-out' likely targets he might have contemplated burgling, observed him from Ben Stafford's lounge, had another witness observe his day-to-day activities and had them recorded, and had observed his new home at the farm. Was DI Fraser, the officer leading these inquiries, unsure of Moore's identity? It seems unlikely but, if he was, then it makes sense as to why, on the night of the shooting, he had to ask The Man if he was Alfred, or Alf or Albert Moore. It is possible that DI Fraser only got a brief glance of him on that night, too brief to be sure, but that doesn't seem to tally with the idea that The Man stood stock still while the light was shone or flashed on him. Of course, The Man was standing stock still with a light flashing or shining on his face for a full fifteen, or more, seconds under the supervision of PC Jagger, something I shall discuss later. For police operational activities it seems very strange that the head of the investigation of Moore did not know, or was unsure of, his identity. So, it is reasonable that DI Fraser, in all likelihood, knew the identity of Moore, and the idea that DI Fraser didn't know Moore's identity is not something easily reconcilable with DI Fraser's activity prior to the cordon, or his position in the enquiry. Consequently, the claim that the conversation was as PC Jagger described it at the point of the shooting has to be treated with caution.

As DI Fraser was in charge of the CID in Huddersfield it could be expected that his knowledge of the local crime scene was high. Even when police know who has committed a particular crime, they will not be able to act until they have proof. But, as the police observed Moore's home in Gynn Lane in Honley, 'staked out' likely targets, observed his behaviour and his new home, then the inquiry into his criminal activity would have been several months, if not over a year old. Considering he made a court appearance in 1943 (seven or eight years previously) then it would suggest that the inquiry was in place for even longer. DI Fraser also spoke to people about Moore, which would be expected if the inquiry was ongoing. The jury was then asked to believe that DI Fraser actually asked him who he was, rather than knowing full-well who he was.

No matter which way the question is addressed, DI Fraser's knowledge of Moore's identity is a central issue. But the problem is that there is only PC Jagger's word on what actually happened on that hillside that night. He had just been shot and had seen his colleague murdered — enough shock for his mind to switch off. This could explain why there are five similar but not exact same verbal reports and two similar but not exact same written statements, or dying declarations or court depositions.

So, as DI Fraser asked The Man who he was, then the suggestion is he didn't know who The Man was. Otherwise why ask? Therefore, the suggestion emerges that if The Man wasn't Moore and DI Fraser knew this, hence the lack of recognition, then who was The Man?

It would also seem that the description given to the other officers making up the cordon was up-to-date. It had been DI Fraser who had noted and created the description of Moore — the whole point being it was someone who had seen Moore recently. It was a police description, created by a policeman. Was the head of the local CID a well-placed officer to create this description, especially as he had been observing him?

There is doubt that The Man would give his true identity if stopped on a hill in a field at 2 am but there might also be some doubt as to whether he was actually asked any of what he was said to have been asked. If DI Fraser knew who The Man was then it would have been superfluous to ask, and probably wouldn't have happened, but that doesn't explain why PC Jagger's verbal reports and written statements are not more readily reconcilable with each other. So, to move on to the inevitable question: what happened at the point of the shooting?

The simple answer to this is, it'll never be known for sure. But what is clear is that it was someone who knew something of the pathways around the farm. It was possibly a member of the local criminal fraternity, which would explain the gun. But what is more important is the question of identity, and for the answer to this it might help to actually consider what can be gleaned from the facts that are known, or that are fair to assume:

(a) The Man was walking towards Whinney Close Farm at 2 am in the morning.

(b) Two police officers were shot whilst trying to apprehend him.

(c) He was carrying a gun, which was never found.

(d) In all the mayhem it might not have been possible to repeat PC Jagger's flashing or shining of his torch on this man, at any rate, for any useful amount of time.

(e) If The Man *was* a member of the local criminal fraternity he may very well have known he was dealing with the head of the local CID by recognising DI Fraser's distinctive accent — he was a Scotsman.

(f) He was prepared to do anything to avoid being apprehended, and possibly to avoid his true identity being known by the one officer who he knew might recognise him, because that officer was head of the local CID.

(g) When asked, The Man said 'Yes', that he was Alfred Moore, and this fact locks into PC Jagger's mind. He might not have known him previously, might not have had more than a fleeting glimpse of The Man under the beam of the torchlight flash or shining, but the answer 'Yes' to the question 'Are you Alfred Moore?' becomes crucial.

(h) PC Jagger is shot once. DI Fraser is shot four times (one round mis-fired). So rather than being shot to stop identification of Moore, PC Jagger and DI Fraser may have been shot to avoid discovering it was *not* Moore. The Man knew that it probably was police officers he'd shot and, if he is approached by one and another arrives a short while later, then he could rightly assume there would be others not too far away. As he has not seen anyone else on his approach to the farm he can simply go back the way he has come.

It is highly likely, but not completely conclusive, that The Man knew Moore. But, moving on, a highly likely scenario he is about 300 yards from the farm at 2 am in the morning. Was he going to the farm to see Moore? One suggestion was that he was a 'fence'—a person who traded in stolen goods. But no premises had been broken into for which Moore came under suspicion for over four months and, by his own testimony, he hadn't left the farm for three weeks.

There are some other points to also bear in mind. The police officers on the cordon were given a description of Moore thus: '…about 35 years, 5' 6", stocky build, dark hair (bald at the crown), usually without a hat'. These attributes would have been impossible to ascertain in the time PC Jagger and DI Fraser had, unless The Man stood stock still for long enough to get any more than the briefest of glimpses. The Man would have winced when the torch was shone in his face, making his age difficult to determine. His height would be difficult to assess also, as the ground was uneven. Stocky build would have been okay to see, but it is doubtful if the police officers would have had time to examine his hair. For DI Fraser it wouldn't have been a question of *identification*, it would have been more likely a question of *recognition*.

To take an amalgam of what this suggests is that, in preparation for the cordon duty, PC Jagger is given a description of Moore. Then take DI Fraser asking The Man '…are you Moore?' Then the identity parade. It has been locked into his mind that The Man was Moore. In the identity parade he picks out Moore, but whether he picked out the killer or not is another question.

What is certain is that three men, two police officers and an armed villain came into contact with each other at 1.55 am on Sunday 15th July 1951. First PC Jagger and The Man, and then DI Fraser joined them.

An important factor with any crime is where it actually took place, but there are problems with this too. Firstly, in PC Jagger's deposition he stated, 'I first saw the accused at two am on the 15th of July. He was walking towards his home. As I got nearer to him…'. When PC Jagger stated, 'As I got nearer to him…' it indicates that PC Jagger had left his position and was moving towards The Man. The statement clearly says PC Jagger was moving towards The Man and does not give the indication that The Man was walking up the path and past PC Jagger's position. Is it more likely then, that PC Jagger had to move off his position to intercept The Man?

Unless The Man knew of the police activity around the farm that night and thought he should go across fields to get to the farm, which is possible but doubtful, he would have used the recognised paths. They are the most direct route. So the actual scene of the shooting and how close it was to PC Jagger's position becomes a relevant question. If PC Jagger was posted on a path, which he was, then the confrontation would have taken place there, he would be in position, see The Man and intercept him. But this is not what happened. He states that he '… saw a man go up a hill' and then '… as I got near to him', which suggests a time-lapse between seeing The Man and getting near him. Regardless, the scene of the shooting was a considerable distance from PC Jagger's position, some sixty-six yards to the north-west.

The exact location was not an issue in the trial, which is surprising; with further probing it looks likely that counsel for the prosecution took steps to blur this piece of evidence. Firstly, he prevented the jury from clearly seeing where on the map of the area PC Sellick marked the location of the shooting—he expected the jury to see the mark across the distance of the courtroom. The map had been shown at once to them when it first appeared, but—crucially—was only held up from the witness box after having the mark added. Secondly, he casually told DCI Jenkins, who had made a sketch of the scene of the shootings, to just leave the sketch '… in case it should be needed.' However, if DCI Jenkins' sketch is considered, and the individual evidence of the officers present is, together with photographs taken at the scene (photographs taken by the police photographer), and various landmarks, it places the actual scene of the shooting sixty-odd yards from PC Jagger's position—something like fifty-five yards inside the 'invisible wall' of the cordon. This is confirmed by measurements taken at the scene by Sgt Butler.

This begs the question, how did the shooting happen so far away from PC Jagger's position?

In evidence in court the first three police officers, PC Sellick, DS Butler and PC Taylor were not specific about the exact location of the shooting. It is Sgt Lee who offers the first hint by discussing going to a point where PC Jagger's '… original' position was. DCI Jenkins was the next officer to give evidence, and Mr Hinchcliffe for the prosecution asked:

Mr Hinchcliffe: Did you go to the tip?
DCI Jenkins: Yes.
Mr Hinchcliffe: And then turn to where Police Constable Jagger had been posted?
DCI Jenkins: Near there; just above.

DCI Jenkins was, as discussed, able to make a sketch of the positions of the two officers, and it shows them in relation to the ash-tip; they were actually to the east of the tip; on the farm side of it. The point is that PC Jagger's position of observation was not where he was shot; it was a considerable distance away.

As for the sketch by DCI Jenkins, it became an exhibit, but when he produced it Mr Hinchcliffe for the prosecution was rather flippant, telling him to leave it '… in case it is needed.' One wonders if the jury would have liked to have seen the sketch; it was relevant. If they did and had asked, it would have demonstrated that the indication of where the shooting took place was in a different place to what he (Mr Hinchcliffe) had said in the opening speech.

PC Jagger was actually posted to the south-west of the tip, as evidenced by other officers and the map DCI King produced. The shooting took place to the east of the tip as evidenced by the sketch by DCI Jenkins and indicated in the photographs. But, in his final speech, Mr Hinchcliffe for the prosecution says the following: 'Again, I remind you that PC Jagger was posted in this position a little *to the east of the tip* at a few minutes before 11.40.'

Counsel for the prosecution, having asked PC Sellick in examination-in-chief where PC Jagger was posted and received the answer '… 20 yards to the south-west' (of the ash-tip) now changes this testimony and places PC Jagger's posting position to the east of the tip. If it wasn't Mr Justice Pearson's place to correct him, it would be the obligation of counsel for the defence to do so, yet he wasn't corrected. We might wonder just how many members of the jury would think they had misheard the witness?

In summary, the posting of PC Jagger was to the south-west of the tip, the shooting sixty-six yards to the east of that point. Counsel for the prosecution established this in evidence but then had the dilemma that the shooting took place so far from PC Jagger's posting and to the east of the ash-tip, so prosecuting counsel changed the evidence: 'Again, I remind you that PC

Jagger was posted in this position … to the east of the tip …' This is wrong, and it is a point to return to later.

CHAPTER 5

Police Constable Jagger

Throughout the reading of all the witness statements, used and unused, and the depositions, and after sifting through the trial transcript, one is struck by the rigid adherence to detail practised by all the police officers who were members of the cordon that night. But that, in itself, would not prove guilt; the eight surviving officers could only relate what they had seen and heard. Therefore, it is essential that what PC Jagger said is assessed, because his dying declaration and court deposition have some discrepancies. It is necessary to consider possible reasons for those discrepancies. It is almost certain that the identity of The Man was not in question after Moore was taken into custody and there is no mention in any of the documentation that any other individual was at any time under suspicion.

After the shooting, PC Jagger spoke to the other members of the cordon as they came to help. The inevitable question asked was who had committed the crime and, fortunately, there was an abundance of officers whose memories for detail, when the court depositions are analysed, were apparent. So, because PC Jagger gave two related, but different, versions of events in his dying declaration and court deposition, it is important to consider anything else he said to any other officer. Or anything else he was supposed to have said.

What is not known and can only be guessed at is any conversation between PC Jagger and DI Fraser after the shooting. With the injuries sustained by the latter, it is probable that DI Fraser was either completely incapacitated and unable to talk before he died or died very soon after he was shot.

It is documented in the trial transcript that Mr Hinchcliffe prevented at least one officer saying in court what PC Jagger had said to him, when he got to him after the shooting. However, considering DCS Metcalfe arrested Moore and had none other under suspicion, it suggests that the police must have taken anything PC Jagger said as accurate and acted on it. Anything PC Jagger said to another officer would not be admissible in court as it was hearsay. What would be plain was that if PC Jagger's story varied, which can be demonstrated, then it would be expected that anything he said to colleagues would vary too. In short, was what he said reliable or not? It is clear that some of what he said was later suppressed, ignored, or blocked. Of course, the police officers, as well as investigating, made up the bulk of the prosecution witnesses. It is, therefore, only fair to Moore that this evidence is now aired.

However, being fair to Moore does not give any reason or consent to be unfair to anyone else. If any other witness' story varies, then one has to look at possible reasons for that variation.

The first person to arrive at the scene of the shooting was PC Sellick. He said he could see that DI Fraser was dead, so concentrated on PC Jagger. He spoke to him and asked, 'Whose [sic] done it?' In reply, PC Jagger said, 'Alfred Moore'. This is significant because, before the cordon duty and the shooting, PC Jagger was quoted to have said he didn't know Moore. So what PC Jagger said to PC Sellick was almost entirely based on what The Man had said in response to questions asked by DI Fraser and PC Jagger, whether The Man gave the correct information is quite another question.

The next officer to arrive at the scene of the shooting was DS Butler. He asked, 'Who was it Gordon?' This time PC Jagger gives a little more detail: 'The Inspector said to him, "Is your name Moore?" and he said "Yes, Alfred Moore." Inspector Fraser told him, "We are police officers", and Moore shot me in the guts.' In neither the dying declaration nor the court deposition does The Man offer his name but, according to DS Butler, PC Jagger said he did. And nowhere else does it record that the question asked was 'Is your name Moore?' So that raises the possibility that PC Jagger remembered one thing when talking to DS Butler, another thing in his dying declaration and a third version in the court deposition. It is doubtful that PC Jagger would have served twenty-two years in the police force unless he could get his facts straight, so the question then emerges as to whether the injury and the trauma of the shooting blanked his mind to certain aspects of the incident. This would be perfectly in keeping with the way the mind functions where the conscious mind is said to suppress painful experiences, or even that the mind might seal up the information completely and not allow recognition of the traumatic experience and the events surrounding it—this is called 'denial', and largely it is out of voluntary control.

DCI Jenkins makes a tacit reference to DI Fraser or PC Jagger, or both, being away from the position in which they were posted. In a statement he made, but which was never used, he asked PC Jagger at the scene of the crime, 'What happened?' to which PC Jagger replied, 'We saw a man. Mister Fraser said to him "Are you Alfred Moore?" The man said "Yes" then he shot us and ran up the fields.' As well as recording a different question from DI Fraser, this version uses the word 'we'. The problem here is that DI Fraser and PC Jagger were posted, and should have been eighty-four yards apart, and they could not have been in verbal communication at this distance. So, if the word 'we' is accurate, then either PC Jagger was at DI Fraser's position with him, or vice versa. Or they were both out of their position. PC Hopping also spoke to PC Jagger. He said,

> 'I asked him how it had happened and PC Jagger replied, "He came up to me and when I got up" he said "Christ, I thought it was a cow". I said to him, "Who are you? Do they call you Alf Moore?" He replied, "Yes, what for?" Mr Fraser arrived, saying, "We're police." He then whipped out a revolver and let us have it.'

As well as PC Jagger now asking the name instead of DI Fraser, PC Jagger is also quoted to have said, 'He came up to me...' suggesting Moore arrived at a point PC Jagger was occupying. Yet, in his dying declaration, PC Jagger says, '...saw a man going up a field. I went after him' which suggests PC Jagger went towards the point The Man was occupying. Further, on no occasion, in any of his other recorded evidence, does PC Jagger refer to a revolver.

PC Murray said he discussed the weapon with PC Jagger in the ambulance on the way to Huddersfield Royal Infirmary. He quotes PC Jagger as saying, 'I saw a small gun in his hand, it looked like a small, black automatic.'

The five statements from the five officers differ from what PC Jagger put in both his dying declaration and his court deposition. Not a huge difference, but a difference nevertheless. The fact that the statements were almost certainly not seen by counsel for the defence and were not admitted as evidence does not alter the fact that the officers all said what they said, what it means is that the jury didn't hear it. That leaves a dilemma, because the question emerges: were the five officers unreliable in the facts they recalled or was PC Jagger? But is the answer to this essential to the argument? Simply because it presents itself the case against Moore has started to show cracks.

Once PC Sellick had been stopped, before he could give the hearsay evidence in court, then it meant that any cross-examination, although possible, could have been objected to as revealing mere hearsay evidence. The other four officers did not find the subject broached in their evidence in court. And because Mr Hinchcliffe stopped PC Sellick from offering the court any hearsay evidence from PC Jagger, he could be said to have abided by the rule of law. This rule of law does not alter a fact; it just highlights the mechanism by which it can be concealed.

The whole case hinged on PC Jagger, and what PC Jagger had said.

Mr Hinchcliffe, for the prosecution: 'One is tempted to ask: If the man who shot those two police officers, as is described in PC Jagger's evidence, was not the prisoner, do you really think that such a man would have answered to the name of Moore?'

To expect a villain, in the dead of night, on an isolated pathway and carrying a gun, to be completely honest, seems the epitome of naïvety — or manipulation. Mr Hinchcliffe would not be so naïve as to believe this himself, but he would want the jury to believe it.

Mr Hylton-Foster, for the defence: 'The prosecution, having been given the opportunity in law now of proving that some place was broken into that night, so that he should have been in possession of stolen goods, have not done so …' and therefore '… this is a case of suspicion of guilt of murder on my client's behalf.'

CHAPTER 6

Arrest

There doesn't seem to be any dispute that DCS Metcalfe together with Police Constable Sydney Cleaver approached the farm from the south at about 4.40 am on the morning of Sunday 15th July. DCS Metcalfe was in plain clothes and was unarmed; PC Cleaver, who walked a few feet behind him, was in uniform and was armed with a revolver in his right trousers pocket. Some time earlier that morning DCS Metcalfe had spoken to DCI Jenkins who had spoken to PC Jagger before he was taken to hospital. In an early undated statement, DCI Jenkins relates the conversation he had with PC Jagger thus: 'Police Constable Jagger said: "We saw a man, Mr Fraser said to him, 'Are you Alfred Moore?' The man said 'Yes.' Then he shot us and ran up the fields."' In his statement, Sgt Sadler says he actually saw DCI Jenkins write down in his pocket book what PC Jagger had said to him, so it was this that in all probability sent DCS Metcalfe together with PC Cleaver to the farm at 4.40 am.

However, the question again comes up as to the reliability of what The Man said when asked by DI Fraser and PC Jagger: 'Are you Alfred Moore?' The five recorded versions of what PC Jagger said after he had been wounded and before he was taken to hospital all agree on the point that the question came from DI Fraser or PC Jagger, but they asked The Man for confirmation of his identity rather than asking who he was. Asking for confirmation of someone's identity and asking them who they are, although related questions, are not seeking the same information, but, more to the point, it gives the opportunity to mislead. It is possible The Man wished to mislead the two officers, but this might depend on the crime he had committed or was intent on committing. As he had a gun in his pocket, the seriousness of the crime was likely to be high. The real possibility then is that The Man had either committed or was intent on committing some kind of crime—but this neither confirms nor denies that it was Moore. If The Man had crime in mind, would he be expected to be truthful about his identity?

It is also worth considering two possible scenarios and the issues they raise, when DCS Metcalfe together with PC Cleaver arrested Moore that morning. They are presumptive, but there are a number of issues around the point of arrest that are worth discussing, and the first issue actually considers that Moore was The Man.

It was the early hours of the morning on a day in mid-July and both Mr and Mrs Moore and their four children were sleeping in one bedroom. It is likely the window would be open to allow a breeze into the room. There had been some commotion going on a few hundred yards from the bedroom window. Moore was later to explain that his wife had been bobbing up and down out of bed to the window to look out and was giving, what he described as, a 'running commentary'. This probably explains why Mrs Moore was observed by PC Cleaver as standing in the window, a point which he drew to the attention of DCS Metcalfe as the two officers approached the farm. There followed a short exchange of conversation between Mrs Moore at the bedroom window and the police officers below.

With this scene in mind, the first consideration is that Moore had been out until nearly 2 am that morning and, when climbing up the fields to the farm, he was accosted by two men claiming to be police officers. They ask for confirmation that he is Moore, whereupon he whips out a gun, shoots them and then makes good his escape up the hill to the farm. With all the ensuing confusion he would have a few minutes to dispose of the gun in the most ingenious way (so ingenious it hasn't been found since) before going into his home. Leaving aside for the moment how unlikely it would be that he would have admitted to being Moore if he was Moore, consider what might be the likely response to the question allegedly put to him by DCS Metcalfe, at the point of arrest: 'Where is the firearm?' The likely response by a villain having just shot two police officers would be along the lines of:

'What firearm?'

'I know nothing!'

'I don't know what you mean!'

'I am not saying anything!'

'I want a solicitor!', etc.

Secondly, if The Man wasn't Moore, and he had returned to the farm at about midnight and therefore was without the knowledge, at the point of his arrest, that two police officers had been shot, it is more likely that a response from him to the question of 'Where is the firearm?' would be something along the lines of bewilderment. Most people when asked a question they don't understand will await further information, or ask for some explanation or clarification as to the meaning of the question. But DCS Metcalfe announced Moore was '... being arrested for the shooting of... police officers at two o'clock that morning...' and DCS Metcalfe followed this with the question: 'Where is the firearm?' The response is likely to be a blank expression, shrugging shoulders and shaking the head, possibly all three, possibly something else. But, add to this that, according to Moore, DCS Metcalfe said only that, 'There has been an accident... Someone has been hurt... Have you a gun?...' then it is small wonder that his behaviour at the point of arrest might be misunderstood, but it was assumed that Moore's lack of response was a refusal to answer.

Crucially then, DCS Metcalfe claims to have said Moore was '... being arrested for the shooting of police officers at 2 am that morning. Where is the firearm?' Short and to the point. However, what Moore says differs from what DCS Metcalfe said. Moore said he arrived home at about midnight and he was not out by the ash-tip at 2 am and he did not shoot the two police officers. To take what Moore says happened at the point of arrest: Moore said a conversation started with DCS Metcalfe asking him 'Are these your poultry?' to which Moore confirmed they were. There were further questions from DCS Metcalfe; this is from the court transcript, Mr Hinchcliffe relaying Metcalfe's questions:

Mr Hinchliffe: 'Are these your pullets?'
Alfred Moore: 'Yes.'
Mr Hinchliffe: 'Have you had any foxes?' or 'Do you have any trouble with foxes?'

The answer to this comes a little while after counsel had asked, and the judge repeated the question:

Alfred Moore: 'Yes'.
Mr Hinchliffe: 'Have you been shooting foxes lately?'

This might have been linked to the next question — or the two questions were asked without giving Moore time to answer.

Mr Hinchliffe: 'Were you shooting them last night?'
Alfred Moore: 'No.'
Mr Hinchliffe: 'Did you go out last night?'
Alfred Moore: '… I went with my brother out [sic] last night.'
Mr Hinchliffe: 'What clothes had you on?'
Alfred Moore: 'Sports coat, flannels, raincoat.'

At this point in his evidence in court Moore remembered that 'time was also mentioned'.

Mr Hinchliffe: 'What time was it you went out last night?'
Alfred Moore: 'About 12.' (He added 'They also asked was I Mr Moore').
Mr Hinchliffe: 'Have you a gun?'
Alfred Moore: 'Yes.'

This was followed by DCS Metcalfe informing him that

Mr Hinchliffe: 'There has been an accident. Someone has been hurt.'
Alfred Moore: 'Oh yes. Where?'
Mr Hinchliffe: 'In your field. Have you a gun?'
Alfred Moore: 'Yes.'

As described in a later chapter as Moore was saying 'Yes' Mrs Moore said: 'We have a gun upstairs'. At which point Moore describes PC Cleaver 'fumbling' with a pair of handcuffs and DCS Metcalfe saying 'I shall have to take you with me.' Moore was handcuffed as soon as he confirmed he had a gun. Every response though seems a reasonable and logical progression from the previous point.

There are two quite different versions of what happened at the point of arrest. Because there are discrepancies it is worth giving thought to what the other police officer present, PC Cleaver, said.

The police and the prosecution wished to emphasise the point that Moore was a dangerous criminal who was likely to be in possession of the gun, which he had used less than three hours previously to shoot two police officers, with little apparent regard as to whether he killed them or not. It is an assumption, but a logical one, that both DCS Metcalfe and PC Cleaver would have been vigilant for any behaviour displayed by Moore (which may indicate a gun was in his possession or immediately at his disposal.)

Both DCS Metcalfe and PC Cleaver relate how when Moore comes down the stairs he is behind, or partly behind, a door, and the door is shielding his body—he is peeping around the door, suggestive that only a part of his face and head was visible to the two officers. If the door is shielding his body and the police wish to make a point about this in relation to his behaviour to portray him as a sinister crook, then his arms and hands would also be shielded behind the door. These are the hands, they said, that just about three hours before held a gun with which they said Moore, without warning, suddenly produced and shot two police officers indiscriminately. Yet DCS Metcalfe and PC Cleaver both describe, almost word-for-word, the exchange that took place between them, Moore and Mrs Moore with a seeming emphasis on Moore concealing the greater part of his body behind a door. Even the most amateur writer of crime stories would not let this go by without inserting the phrase either into DCS Metcalfe's or PC Cleaver's mouth: 'Get your hands up!'

The jury is given accounts of incidents in a trial and it is for them to decide which is the most plausible, logical and so on, based on the information they have been given and after cross-examination has tested what they have been told. So, if the above is reconsidered then the question is: which is more likely to be the truth; or which is more likely to be nearer the truth, Moore's or DCS Metcalfe's account? It does not make sense that Moore was partly hidden by the door, and that DCS Metcalfe and PC Cleaver just stood by. Unless they knew that it hadn't been Moore and he probably wasn't armed.

There is another quite astonishing twist to this scene. In his deposition, PC Cleaver times the approach of himself and DCS Metcalfe and the start of this exchange at 4.40 am. By the time the exchange has concluded and

PC Cleaver has entered the house with Mrs Moore to take possession of the gun (the shotgun) which he later hands to Sgt Sadler, he notes the time as being 5 am. So a twenty minute period in which the level of danger to the two officers could be described as high—according to the evidence they gave. In court, Mr Justice Pearson interrupts PC Cleaver's evidence where he is describing this scene taking place between 4.40 am and 5 am. 'Are they notes you took at the time?' asked Mr Justice Pearson, 'Yes,' replies PC Cleaver. So the police are now saying Moore shot two police officers without warning and returned to his house; three hours later two police officers go to the house, one armed, and allowed this dangerous individual to shield the greater part of his body behind a door—where he could have been holding almost any weapon; meantime PC Cleaver, the armed officer who has a revolver in his right trousers pocket, is making notes. It is likely he wrote up the notes a little later, but he didn't say that in his evidence.

It is all written down for future historians to pore over. The way the scene is described here is only one person's interpretation of it, but it seems that all sense of danger and security, reason and logic of what situation the two police officers were about had vanished. Unless, of course, Moore's version of events is nearer the truth, which would imply that DCS Metcalfe and PC Cleaver were not being truthful.

A close consideration of what Moore said on oath does not reveal any anomalies for analysis, like the incident at the point of arrest where what is said by Moore differs from what is said by both DCS Metcalfe and PC Cleaver. It is doubtful whether any of what PC Cleaver says is unreliable because he admits to making notes '… at the time'—the time being when a dangerous individual was mostly hidden behind a door. But DCS Metcalfe's relationship with the truth seems more distant. In his statement and deposition, PC Cleaver's evidence tallies with Moore's as to what DCS Metcalfe says at the actual point of arrest, that Moore was being arrested for shooting a police officer; whereas DCS Metcalfe, even under specific cross-examination on that point, insists he said it was two officers. When this point is pursued by counsel for the defence DCS Metcalfe insists he said it was two officers and not one: 'I wouldn't make that mistake'.

But he did make that mistake, or at any rate he said two officers and PC Cleaver said that he said 'a' officer, which does not confirm DCS Metcalfe's evidence. This is a crucial factor which brings doubt into where the truth lay. Later, on this point, Mr Justice Pearson gets his facts horribly wrong in his summing-up.

On balance it would be reasonable to suggest that both DCS Metcalfe's and PC Cleaver's recollection of the scenario at the point of arrest with a dangerous man, partly hiding behind a door, lacks credibility. So, if what the police said here was unreliable, it prompts the question: what else was unreliable? But why would DCS Metcalfe and PC Cleaver invent this story? The story is not a complete fabrication; it just doesn't seem credible the way they said they behaved with such a dangerous man.

The idea perhaps of the conversation about fowls, foxes and shooting them, followed by a denial that this took place does tend to undermine what Moore said happened at the point of arrest, which might be the key to it. The whole idea of what is portrayed in front of a jury though is for the immediate impact on the jury, not for the assessment of credibility years later, it is for the jury at the time to believe. It doesn't seem to matter what is fact, it does seem to matter though what the jury believe.

CHAPTER 7

Hospital

Ward Four in the old Huddersfield Royal Infirmary was known as a 'Nightingale'-type ward where there is one, long main dormitory-like room with about twenty or so beds—arranged down each side. There was usually a sister's office and a 'nurses' station'; which was often just a desk, but from which an overall view of the ward could be had. As well as the main ward area there was usually a side room for any patient requiring non-routine nursing attention, a clean utility room, a treatment room where patients' dressings might be changed, a 'dirty' utility room where soiled dressings were disposed of, a sluice and some form of linen or bedding store. Nursing in those days was an experience-based as well as an academic-based discipline. That experience was hard-earned and senior nurses especially were looked up to. Nurses generally were single and often lived in the hospital grounds in hostels. Work was hard and the hours long; the pay was notoriously poor. Nurses were seen as 'handmaidens' to the doctors. Things have changed through the years, but this was the situation in 1951.

Mr James Hall Wrigley qualified in medicine in 1945 in Manchester, and was the resident surgical officer on duty on the night of the shootings. Dr Jessie Muriel Beard was the junior doctor to whom the two police officers were first brought. She quickly ascertained that DI Fraser was dead, so, although she made a more detailed examination later, concentrated on PC Jagger. He was seriously injured and had lost a lot of blood. She commenced a saline infusion and called for Mr Wrigley. He was obviously a skilled surgeon, as at only twenty-nine-years-old he had received the accolade of Fellow of the Royal College of Surgeons.

But just as Ward Four was a hive of medical and nursing activity, it quickly became the focus of the police and soon had the presence of at least two senior police officers. Police Superintendent Sydney Foster and Police Inspector George Knapton, both of the West Riding of Yorkshire Constabulary, arrived to see PC Jagger at 3.50 am. PC Jagger recognised them and could talk about the shooting, and he spoke of DI Fraser's death. Supt Foster asked PC Jagger if he knew what a dying declaration was, which he did, and asked if he thought he should make one: PC Jagger said he thought he should. PC Jagger dictated and then signed the document. Although the contents of a dying declaration cannot be tested by the usual process of cross-examination, the belief is that a dying person will not lie. In the event, PC Jagger's declaration was not necessary as he lived long enough to give his evidence under oath before the magistrate in court.

Responding to Dr Beard's summons, Mr Wrigley arrived to see the patient at about 4.40 am. PC Jagger's pulse was then 80 per minute and his temperature 98C, his blood pressure was 120/80 and his respirations were 20 per minute: all within the normal limits. PC Jagger remained fully conscious, and was able to answer questions about what had happened. There was a wound in his abdomen of about half-an-inch in diameter which was the gunshot wound, but no corresponding 'exit' wound either in his abdomen or on his back was found. The muscles of the anterior (front) wall of the abdomen were stiff and his loins were tender, and percussion showed lack of liver dullness (indicative of gas in the abdominal cavity — the peritoneum; it indicates some kind of puncture as the gas could only have come from the stomach or the intestines). This suggested to Mr Wrigley that either the stomach or the large intestine (gut) had been perforated by the bullet. In either instance there was a real danger of leakage of faecal matter into the abdominal cavity from the intestines, which could endanger the patient's life because an infection from the faecal matter would be inevitable — and likely fatal. Mr Wrigley felt that surgery was needed, quickly. A tube was passed into PC Jagger's stomach and when some of his stomach contents were examined, surprisingly no blood staining was apparent. Similarly, a tube was passed into his bladder where again, no obvious blood staining was in evidence which lessened the likelihood of bladder or kidney damage.

An X-ray gave the location of the bullet. PC Jagger was given a quarter of a grain of morphia (pain-killer) and one hundredth of a grain of atropine (pre-med to ensure the secretions in the mouth, gullet and wind-pipe were more manageable) both very likely given by injection into a muscle. At 5.10 am he was taken to the operating theatre were Dr Crispian Ward administered Pentathol (an anaesthetic drug given by injection into the vein — a barbiturate which will act quickly to render the patient unconscious and give the anaesthetist time to pass a tube into his trachea (windpipe), which connects his mouth and nose to his lungs) and cyclopropane, a gas which induces anaesthesia. He was later given ether onto oxygen and, finally, pure oxygen, which returns consciousness. Mr Wrigley found about two pints of blood and clotting in the peritoneal cavity (the lining of the abdomen) which was removed, and a small tear was found in the small intestine adjacent to the lower end of the stomach. The intestines were examined for any other injury but none was found. However, a hole was discovered in the anterior (front) wall of the stomach with a corresponding hole in the rear (posterior) wall. This was where the bullet went through the stomach and this was repaired with suture. The operation lasted for an hour and twenty minutes; Mr Wrigley was assisted by Dr Beard and a Mr Thompson, a surgeon was also present.

All of this was standard practice for the time and the understanding of anaesthetics and the drugs used would have been complete. PC Jagger was given three pints of blood during the operation and afterwards was started on a cocktail (a concurrent course of more than one) of antibiotics, and also had a fourth pint of blood during the morning. At noon he was seen by Mr Wrigley, but his pulse had increased to 140. Shortly after this he was given a quarter grain of morphia for any pain. Mr Wrigley returned to see him at about 2 pm when his pulse remained at 140 but he believed his patient's general condition to be good. PC Jagger was said to be alert and he did not seem unduly stressed.

There is no evidence that PC Jagger received any blood, by transfusion, until the time of his operation at 5.20 am. It was noted that on admission to Ward Four he had an intravenous solution of saline being infused, and although this was never said to be discontinued it was noted to be continuing by Mr Wrigley when he first examined the patient.

Giving blood by transfusion carries a risk; its need will depend on the haemoglobin level (oxygen carrying capacity) of the patient's blood and on his blood pressure, which was within normal limits. Blood is generally not given on the need to replace pint for pint; if a patient's haemoglobin is of a satisfactory level then the patient will continue to carry oxygen around without the 'top-up'. But with any injury or trauma, the loss of body fluid can result in an urgent need for replacement, which is why PC Jagger had the saline infusion.

As Mr Wrigley concluded his initial examination he noted that Dr Beard had commenced the intravenous infusion of saline on, or shortly after, admission. It is highly unlikely that PC Jagger had any blood transfused prior to surgery, and almost certainly had the saline infusion continued. In those days infusions or transfusions came in clear glass bottles, and saline is a clear colourless fluid; blood is red and appears red in the transfusion bottle, and is opaque.

As PC Jagger didn't have any blood until after 5.20 am (the time of the operation), it is strange that Insp Knapton, present when PC Jagger made his dying declaration to Supt Foster between 4.10 am and 4.25 am, should note that he had a transfusion of blood at that time, when the medical records, such as are available, record a saline solution. With the available information of PC Jagger's medical condition and needs, it would seem unlikely he would have had a blood transfusion before surgery, and it was before the surgery that the dying declaration was said to have been made. But if Insp Knapton did see blood being transfused, this would put the dying declaration of PC Jagger after about 6.30 am, at the very earliest: when he was recovering from the immediate effects of the anaesthetic and surgery.

One possibility is that Insp Knapton was colour-blind or had difficulty in distinguishing some colours — the relevant colour would obviously be red (a sub-group of colour-blindness is one affecting red and green hues). The prevalence of this is about eight per cent of the (Caucasian) population and is far more prevalent in men than women. But usually with any disability or deficit, the human can learn to compensate — and it is a difficulty distinguishing between the red and the green hue, not between opaque red and clear colourless. Therefore, the most important factor would be the clear and colourless appearance of saline, which would still appear clear and colourless to a colour-blind individual. So, if colour-blindness was a difficulty for Insp Knapton he would still be able to distinguish between blood and saline.

Another possibility is that he simply didn't notice the bottle but only saw it fleetingly so assumed it was a blood transfusion. There are a number of facts which undermine this idea. He was an experienced police inspector and he would know to say what he saw and not what he thought he may have seen. He knew it was a murder inquiry so the facts needed to be facts; and statements needed to be accurate. He may have been keen to know of PC Jagger's injuries and treatments — policemen are curious by necessity and therefore curious habitually. But, ultimately, saline and blood in infusion/transfusion form, even in 1951, were instantly and easily distinguishable.

One would expect the dying declaration and the deposition PC Jagger was to make about twelve hours later to be broadly the same. But because PC Jagger lived long enough to give evidence in court verbally, and make his deposition, which rendered the dying declaration superfluous, the defence seemed unaware of its existence.

Nowadays, after an anaesthetic is given the patient is advised to avoid making major life decisions, operating machinery and so on, as their judgment may be impaired. It is interesting to note, however, that the dying declaration held information which was absent or of a differing emphasis from the later deposition PC Jagger made in court. Both documents are short enough to be quoted in full.

Dying declaration timed at 4.25am, 15th July 1951.

'I make this statement with the fear of death before me and with no hope of recovery.

Saw a man going up a field. I went after him. As I get near him he must have heard me and dashed into the other hedge. I says, "Hello." He must have heard me and shouted. He says, "I thought it was a cow. Who are you?" I flashed my torch on him. Inspector Fraser came up. The man had both hands in his mac coat pocket. I took hold of his left arm. Inspector Fraser shone his light on him and said, "Are you Moore?" He said, "Yes." "Albert Moore?" He said, "Yes." Mr Fraser said, "We're police, you're coming with us." Moore said, "No sir. Oh no sir." Mr Fraser said, "Yes." Moore pulled what appeared to be an automatic pistol out of his pocket and shot at me. I staggered and fell to the ground. He shot at Inspector Fraser, who staggered and shot him a second time. While Mr Fraser was on the ground he shot at him again. I think I heard another shot. That is all I know.

It would be about two o'clock. He was going towards his home.

Was wearing what I call a wool gabardine coat, like the Inspector's (here indicated Knapton). Think it had a belt. Collar and tie. No hat. I think he had a white silk scarf.'

The following document doesn't carry a record of the time it was made, but it would be after the 4.50 pm identity parade and before the 6.00 pm medical examination of the patient by Mr Wrigley. In the transcript of the Assize Court proceedings PC Owen Earnshaw said he was present at the Huddersfield Royal Infirmary at 5.40 pm on 15th July when PC Jagger was examined by the magistrate, and on oath, made the deposition.

Deposition sworn before Magistrate.

'I am Police Constable 1117 in the West Riding Police Force.

In the small hours of this morning the 15th July 1951 I received a wound. It was inflicted by the prisoner Moore with what appeared to be an automatic pistol. At the time I received the wound I was on duty with Detective Inspector Duncan Alexander Fraser. The prisoner shot at Mr Fraser with the automatic pistol. Mr Fraser staggered a few yards and the prisoner shot him again. At the time of the second shot Mr Fraser was stumbling and fell to the ground and whilst he was on the ground the prisoner fired a third shot at him. I believe there was another shot fired but I can't be sure. At the time I saw this happened to Mr Fraser I was on the ground as a result of the shot fired at me. I had been on duty with Mr Fraser near the accused home at Cockley Hill, Kirkheaton.

I first saw the accused at 2 am on the 15th July. He was walking towards his home. As I got near to him he must have heard my feet in the grass and he dashed under the hedge. I said, "Hello" and I shouted. He said, "I thought it was a cow." I shone my torch on his face and took hold of his left arm. I saw his face clearly in the light of the torch. As I took hold of the accused's left arm Mr Fraser approached and shone his torch in the accused's face. Mr Fraser said, "Are you Moore, Albert Moore?" He replied "Yes." Mr Fraser said, "We are police officers and you are coming with us." He said "No sir. Oh no sir." As soon as the accused said that he whipped his hand, his right hand, out of his overcoat pocket and shot me and Mr Fraser. The accused was at the time wearing the coat he is now wearing (produced and marked Exhibit 1).'

There followed comment on the subsequent hospitalisation and Moore's cross-examination. PC Jagger's dying declaration lacks detail, but the detail comes back into his mind after 12 hours, a general anaesthetic and fairly major surgery when he says, 'I shone my torch on his face and … I saw his face clearly in the light of the torch.' PC Jagger's dying declaration says, 'I flashed my torch on him,' which suggests his torch was not concentrated on The Man for more than an instant; and '… my torch on him' suggests a lack of focus on any one part of The Man, such as his face. On the deposition read out in court, of this part of the incident PC Jagger says: 'I shone my torch on his face and … I saw his face clearly in the light of the torch.' Here the word shone has substituted flash, and the different word changes the complexion of the first part of the statement and suggests a longer look at The Man. And there is the further embroidery of, 'I saw his face clearly in the light of the torch.' It may be that PC Jagger did see The Man's face clearly in the light of the torch which makes it a mystery as to why he didn't say so in his dying declaration.

Further, he says in the court deposition that he shouted just as he approached The Man, which would alert DI Fraser. When he heard it, DI Fraser would need a second or two to consider from where the shout had come. After a short exchange between The Man and PC Jagger about a cow, PC Jagger either flashed or shone his torch and took hold of The Man's left arm. And just as he took hold of his left arm, DI Fraser approached. But this doesn't take into account any possible time-lapse. Inferred by the deposition and the accepted facts about distance between the two officers (DI Fraser and PC Jagger), a rough estimate as to how long after PC Jagger took hold of 'The Man's' arm and the arrival of DI Fraser can be made.

DI Fraser could accurately assess from where the shout of PC Jagger originated, and possibly PC Jagger flashing or shining his torch would pinpoint the location, so he could go directly there, if he wasn't already on his way. He probably didn't see The Man as he would have been about eighty-odd yards away, with visibility being up to about sixty yards. And The Man would have blended into the hedgerow to his left. But, when PC Jagger shouts, DI

Fraser could have moved directly down the slight incline and across the field. He would cover the eighty-odd yards in about fifteen to twenty seconds.

So, PC Jagger is flashing or shining a torch for a minimum approximation of fifteen seconds on The Man's face who, it would appear, neither winces at the sudden light on his face nor attempts to move out of the beam of the light, or struggle from PC Jagger's grip. For a minimum of fifteen seconds! On the contrary PC Jagger may only have got a fleeting glance and The Man may have been grimacing because of the light in his face. This man was armed and very dangerous (not an inference, because he was about to shoot them both), so one might assume his reluctance to be properly seen would be almost automatic.

In short, the information contained in the original dying declaration taken with or without the information in the court deposition makes it hard to be certain what happened at the point of the shooting. The wording of the two documents, and the behaviour of The Man immediately prior to the shooting, together with the distance covered by DI Fraser in the time-frame, demonstrate significant inconsistencies in the evidence. And the information contained in DI Knapton's account of the taking of the dying declaration also when held up to scrutiny raises questions about just *when* it was taken.

CHAPTER 8

Identification

As far as can be gathered, this was the first time that a police identity parade took place in a hospital ward, and I could not find any further examples. Whether or not it was done with the blessing, consent, cajoling, or bullying of the hospital staff is not known. It is also unclear as to who decided that the identity parade should happen. Supt Foster was at the infirmary from early morning on 15th July together with Insp Knapton, but Insp Knapton left. It was said that Detective Inspector David Bradley of the Huddersfield Borough Police arranged the men for the identity parade out of '…sheer neutrality'. There is a distinction to be made from the West Riding Police who had already been investigating Moore and subsequently the murders, and the Huddersfield Borough Police. DI Bradley was in the latter. They are now amalgamated.

As for the identity parade itself, it is not known how many of the other men matched the description that had been given to the police, including PC Jagger, at the briefing. There is a clear record kept of what they were all wearing, but Moore was below average height and no record is available as to the height of the other men Similarly their ages are all recorded but not the style of their hair or even if they had a full head of hair. Although there was a photograph of Moore in the possession of the police, it was said to be of a poor likeness. All of this aside, if PC Jagger picked out Moore in the way DI Bradley, who was present at the identity parade, said he did, then so far as the police were concerned they had got the right man.

However, it is worth considering the dynamics apparent to any independent observer at the time, or that might occur to an historian later. The two issues for discussion are the non-verbal and possible unconscious communication between Supt Foster, DI Bradley and PC Jagger — so, even though the officers may have conducted the identity parade with integrity and fairness, they might have inadvertently communicated to PC Jagger who the suspect was.

Unfortunately, all of the men on that identity parade as well as the two police officers, Supt Foster and DI Bradley, are now dead. The newspapers around Huddersfield ran a feature in 1991 on the 40th anniversary of the Whinney Close Farm murders, and a member of that identity parade, Herbert Woodhouse, contacted the paper. There was no suggestion of a discrepancy in the identity parade proceedings, but Mr Woodhouse thought PC Jagger was a great deal more infirm than the documents in the archives would suggest. He also said it was not a case of PC Jagger pointing straight at Moore without hesitation. Mr Woodhouse stood next to Moore on the identity parade. He was quoted to have said of PC Jagger:

> 'He looked like a man who had been hit by a car. He was being given blood and must have been in a state of shock. Constable Jagger could not keep his hand steady as he was asked to point to his attacker, and his finger kept wavering between myself and Moore. This was why he was asked to count first from one side of the line, and then from the other.'

The journalist concluded that,

> '…Jagger did identify Moore and Mr Woodhouse's temporary anxiety was soon over. But he has often wondered about the case since, and asked himself whether the Constable was really in a fit state to make a positive identification.'

What cannot be escaped from is this: at that time Mr Woodhouse was twenty-three-years-old. If PC Jagger knew, and he almost certainly did, that Moore was in his mid-thirties then was it that difficult to distinguish between the two men? What about the ages of the other men on the identity parade? Excluding Moore:

- Hubert Thornton was forty-five
- Sam Milnes was thirty-one
- Tom Moore was forty-eight
- Herbert Woodhouse was twenty-three
- George Gil was thirty-six
- George Mitchell was twenty-nine
- Frederick Sallinger was thirty-eight

- Frank Webster was twenty-seven
- They all wore raincoats.

Generally they all wore similar clothes, but it was only George Gil who wore a fawn sports coat and flannels similar to Moore. Moore was only 5' 6" tall and of stocky build—below the average height. What height was George Gil, the man nearest to Moore in age? In the identity parade all the men were stood on the flat, when Moore's shortness of height would be apparent. So, how many of the men in the identity parade were 5' 6" tall? How many had dark hair, swept back? How many had a bald patch on the crown?

In a briefing prior to the cordon duty, DI Fraser gave a description of Moore to the men engaged on the cordon. It is not known exactly what DI Fraser knew about Moore's appearance, but it is known that he had observed him from Ben Stafford's home shortly before the cordon duties. The investigation, under the command of DI Fraser, had been going on for a period of at least several months. In statements, however, the other officers said that with what they had been told in the briefings about Moore's identity, they were unsure about making a formal identification of him. But it is possible that Moore was identified at the parade because of the two separate experiences which locked, and then blended into one in PC Jagger's mind. Firstly, the description of Moore as given in the cordon briefing and, secondly, the responses given by The Man to him and DI Fraser on the hillside. It is possible Moore and The Man were actually different people and that, because of the questionable admission by The Man to being Alfred Moore, all PC Jagger had to do was pick out who he thought was *Moore*—not necessarily who he thought was *The Man*.

To consider what dynamics and non-verbal communication went on in that side ward can only be conjecture, but nevertheless most people would be able to picture the following. The room itself, as a side ward to a main ward in a hospital of the time, would be a smallish room, just enough for a bed and locker, an oxygen cylinder, perhaps a trolley for dressings and probably a couple of chairs. There must have been hardly enough room for nine men on an identity parade and two police officers officiating.

The dynamics: Arthur Gordon Jagger had been a police constable for over twenty years and would well know the hierarchy of the police, and be highly disciplined. There were two senior officers in the room with him, one from his own constabulary, and also one from the Huddersfield Borough Police. One might assume a closer bond between PC Jagger and Supt Foster as the two colleagues, but equally they might both have wished to show DI Bradley their professionalism. So, there is a likelihood that eye-contact between Supt Foster and PC Jagger would have been maintained—and the senior is superior and the junior subservient. But as the junior officer had the key role, the possibility is that PC Jagger would look to Supt Foster for guidance, and Supt Foster would be on the lookout for PC Jagger needing guidance. What non-verbal communication this led to cannot be positively defined, but, 'a nod is as good as a wink'.

When the identification process moved away from the 'pointing' part to the 'counting' part, subtle movements could have prompted PC Jagger's choice. PC Jagger was asked to count from one end of the parade to the other and stop at the suspect. Then he was to count from the other end of the parade, and again stop at the suspect. The conducting of an identity parade in this way is certainly unusual and I can find no other case where the counting 'method' was used. This is where the identity parade is at its most vulnerable to mistake. It is not clear how long PC Jagger paused between each member of the identity parade. It is possible he got as far as Moore and then Supt Foster asked him now to count from the other end; and of course, as a consequence of this action by Supt Foster, he knew where to stop.

CHAPTER 9

Police Evidence

The police, as well as being the investigating force, were also the source of the main bulk of witness evidence. So there was a dual role for them, but there didn't seem to be any conflict of interests. When it is acknowledged that the two dead officers would almost certainly have had some social interaction and strong friendships with the other officers, then it becomes clear that the pressure on the officers was high. And that's the internal pressure, or the pressure the officers put themselves under: there was also the external pressure, the public, the media—such as it was in the early-1950s, and the political pressure. But once an arrest had been made—almost before people would have even heard there had been a murder—the pressure shifted.

In the 1950s it was unheard of for a police officer to depart from correctness, now it is simply unheard of for a police officer to admit it. It must also be acknowledged that two people will witness the same event but take differing memories away from it, so, if later they are asked to relate their experiences then the two recollections would be expected to differ. But a distinction should be made where a conflict of recall might actually be expected, and the deliberate attempt to coax an edited memory, or the possibility that if a witness was told often enough that the sequence of events was A, then B, then C, then D; but they recalled them as D, then C, then B and then A, they might start to think they had made a mistake and were pleased to correct it. Not realising they had just had their evidence tampered with. Planting and manufacturing evidence is wrong but so is tampering with evidence when that evidence is what someone's memory tells them happened. So it is worth considering the various statements, but excluded from this are the details PC Jagger gave to his colleagues.

Of the various statements and depositions, some were taken at the time of the shootings or just afterwards; a series of statements was taken at the end of September 1951 and a further set of statements in mid-January 1952.

If taken in the order of appearance in court then the first two statements were of the two police officers, Detective Chief Inspector Jack King who prepared the plan of the area and also of the detailed layouts of Whinney Close Farm and the farmhouse, and Inspector John Little who provided a range of photographs. The evidence of these two officers gave good points of reference and this supported, by visual reference, most, but not all, of what was said in court.

The other eight officers from the cordon all made statements fairly soon after the night's events. Some made follow-up statements as to what action they took in the investigation.

PC Sellick gave an overall impression of the night's events, which, as with most of the others, detailed the other officers engaged on the cordon. He gave details of his own position, the time he arrived there and related that nothing happened until about 1.55 am on the Sunday. All of the statements taken at the time are pretty much standard insofar as they say similar things, so only a consideration of anything else is noted.

The various distances covered by Moore and his brother, as they walked towards his brother's home and the return on the night of the shootings, were noted and timed by PC Sellick with PC Hopping.

DS Butler had explained how he had seen a torchlight as he approached PC Jagger's position—but the shooting occurred sixty-odd yards away from where PC Jagger had been posted. DS Butler also produced a second statement, but, whereas the other statements have pencil marks underling particular points, this second statement of DS Butler's had two pencil scores which seem to 'cross out' all of the points he made. However, the theme of his second statement is various measurements and includes the point that 'PC Jagger's ... posting was ... 66 yards from the scene of the crime.' If the pencil scorings were made by counsel for the prosecution (and notes in margins, etc. seem similar in style to the handwriting of Mr Norman Black, junior counsel for the prosecution) then this is where some evidence concealment can be traced. There was a considerable distance from where PC Jagger's posting on the cordon was and the scene of the shootings, and less this be an issue in court it might be better first to remove it from the evidence.

PC Taylor produced a standard statement which didn't mention anything out of the ordinary. However, there is detail of his work at the Huddersfield Royal Infirmary as he was the officer who received the clothes of DI Fraser and PC Jagger, which he presented to the forensic scientist, Mr Nickolls. Later, PC Taylor was also in the cell with Moore and took his clothes from him, which he also presented to Mr Nickolls.

Sgt Lee's statement was unremarkable.

DCI Jenkins made a statement which gave some background to the investigation and how the cordon came to be formed. He also detailed how communications were to work throughout the cordon and what action was to be taken if Moore was seen to *leave* the farm. He also noted the sketch of the scene of the crime he had made. But DCI Jenkins' statement also detailed when he saw Moore in the cell at the police station and indicates two occasions: once when he took a letter from Moore addressed to Alice (15th) and then when he took Moore's fingerprints (17th). DCI Jenkins made a further statement, which mainly dealt with evidence he had received and to whom he had forwarded it.

PC Hopping made a standard statement, or so it seemed (a closer examination of his behaviour and actions is made later). His follow-up statement gave various details of walking to and between various places, and the time it took.

PC Murray's statement was again quite a standard record of the night.

Sgt Sadler made the standard commentary of the night, punctuated by him receiving Moore's shotgun at 5 am, which he later forwarded to the forensic scientist. He was also instrumental in searching the farm. He made a number of follow-up statements which detailed various things he had found around the farm.

The police officers involved with the aftermath of the shootings were as above but more officers arrived later in the morning.

The two most notable of the statements taken from the police officers who arrived after the shooting were those of DCS Metcalfe and PC Cleaver.

DCS Metcalfe had received a message from Supt Foster and the two of them met at the police station before DCS Metcalfe left for the farm. He got to the farm with other officers, some of whom were armed, at just after 4 am. One of the first things he noticed, as dawn began to break, was that smoke appeared to be coming out of the chimney of the farm. At about 4.40 am, with PC Cleaver, he went to the farm, as previously discussed. It was at this point that some important factors are noted — in each factor the police and later counsel for the prosecution miss a vital point.

An important part of the ensuing conversation between DCS Metcalfe and Moore centred on the question of 'Where's the firearm?', which Moore was either unable or unwilling to answer. When the statements are actually seen by counsel, both DCS Metcalfe's and PC Cleaver's statements are marked: 'Prisoner said nothing' and 'Moore said nothing'. There is an assumption, possibly misplaced, that Moore understood what he was being asked.

Both DCS Metcalfe and PC Cleaver had contradicted each other in an issue the defence made much of later. Mr Hylton-Foster related in a question to DCS Metcalfe that he had not said to Moore that two officers had been shot, but only one. DCS Metcalfe denied this implicitly. But, in his statement, PC Cleaver said 'a... officer'. It might seem a small point but the idea seems to be to discredit what Moore said happened at the point of arrest but inadvertently they seem to be relating different stories. If DCS Metcalfe hadn't been so insistent with what he'd said at this point, then it might have been overlooked, but one is left wondering if he made a mistake, which he denied, or he lied. What also disturbs is that during Mr Justice Pearson's summing-up he says (not merely suggests) that DCS Metcalfe's evidence at this point was supported by PC Cleaver's, when it was not.

The police also managed to convince the jury that Moore was a sinister character even though he could have held almost anything behind that door, and counsel got their conviction even though they missed a clear clash of evidence. But, as this entire set of documents does not seem to have been seen by defence, then this clash of evidence didn't really matter — it was easy to conceal and if the verdict went against the accused then he would probably be hanged.

Police Constable Harold Hudson made a statement that he saw a figure move around in the downstairs of the farm in the latter part of the morning, before DCS Metcalfe went in. This may well have been Moore hiding burglary evidence in the cavity wall.

Police Sergeant Jack Barber made a statement which indicated that he had found a bullet at the scene of the shooting (probably the one that mis-fired at the time of the shooting) and had produced this and it had been catalogued.

PC Earnshaw had been occupied at Huddersfield Royal Infirmary and had identified DI Fraser to the medical staff. He was also present when PC Jagger made his deposition. As he had known the two officers, PC Earnshaw was later present at the *post mortem* examinations. His statement also details exhibits taken from the bodies (bullets, nail scrapings, blood and hair) which he later forwarded to the forensic scientist, Mr Nickolls. He also received a sample of Moore's hair.

Detective Chief Inspector John Edington made a long, complicated statement. He had not been present at the farm but was with DCS Metcalfe when he interviewed Moore over the following few days. He agrees with almost everything that DCS Metcalfe says in his statements, depositions and evidence in court, and is at odds with what Moore said DCS Metcalfe had said. DCI Edington does relate the time when DCS Metcalfe knew Moore wasn't telling the truth. Moore said he went to bed at about midnight but then is supposed to have said '... I never got up again lad.' But, as soon as Moore is confronted with the question of smoke coming out of his chimney at 4 am he seems to then tell the truth. And there is nothing in the surviving documentation to prove otherwise. DCI Edington is later asked about a comment Moore denied making: 'Oh, my head is bad, don't talk about it, it's awful.' It would not make sense to say this, if he had possessed a gun and it was concealed then it just would not make sense to give nonsensical answers. A clear denial would suffice; Moore was not a fool. But it wouldn't make sense at all to answer in the way the police officers described, if he did not have a gun.

However, if a prisoner is in custody then there seems no reason why he shouldn't have a headache and complain about it. For Moore to admit he lied and clear up the doubt was setting the record straight: he knew when he was caught. Then later Moore was said to have exercised his right to remain silent, that he wouldn't talk to the police — the police seem to have complained at this and so did the prosecution in court, so it makes a farce of the prisoner's right to silence: but did this sow seeds of Moore's guilt in the jury's mind? However, DCI Edington and DCS Metcalfe then leave him for a long period until about 3.30 pm on the Sunday afternoon (the 15th) before they see him again.

At that time Moore is told that an identity parade has been planned at the Huddersfield Royal Infirmary to see if the man who shot DI Fraser and PC Jagger could be identified. If Moore was the killer then he would have been aware of the light being shone (or flashed) in his face and would be nervous of identification. But he seems to have displayed no reluctance to cooperate with the police. Moore does ask for a particular solicitor to represent him, but this, it was claimed, was not possible to arrange. According to DCI Edington the officers made an attempt to contact the solicitor and his partner but were unable to do so. When they saw Moore about twenty minutes later, he seemed to accept this and planned to ask for his solicitor the following day, Monday.

Before the identity parade, Moore was informed by the police what he would be wearing and he agreed the items of clothing. After the identification parade, Moore was seen again by DCS Metcalfe and DCI Edington, and he was charged with murder. 'How can it be me. I told you I was in bed.' This could be *disputed*; but it was only the fact that Moore got up again at around 4 am that could be *proved*. Moore then made an interesting point about the comparison of his story with PC Jagger's: 'I have as much right to be believed as he has.' But why would PC Jagger lie? Yet it may not have been a case of lies; it might have been misperceptions, which is discussed in the next chapter.

DCI Edington related how the following morning he was present when Moore was told that PC Jagger had died and was charged with his murder.

Supt Foster also made a statement which is divided into two parts, the earlier part sees him at the Huddersfield Royal Infirmary at around about 4 am, and then the later part continues with the identity parade at the hospital, just before 5 pm. The first half has two thick pencil lines scoring-out everything. As PC Jagger made a deposition later in the day, it is understandable that the information contained in the first part of the statement which relates to the dying declaration is scored out. But there is a problem with the officer accompanying Supt Foster, Detective Inspector George Knapton. The latter said that at the time Supt Foster took a statement from PC Jagger (which would have been a dying declaration) he was having a blood transfusion — it is unlikely he would have mistaken this — but Supt Foster timed the dying declaration as being *before* surgery when PC Jagger was having a different infusion — visibly not blood. This could have led to a problem for the prosecution, but as PC Jagger lived long enough to make a deposition to a magistrate then it rendered the dying declaration superfluous. However, that does not account for DI Knapton's observations, so it is no surprise that his statement was never disclosed.

CHAPTER 10

Consistency

A thorough enough examination has been made into how PC Jagger gave five verbal and two written reports, which differed. Had he lived and entered the witness box, and the five verbal statements as well as the two written reports (i.e. the dying declaration and the court deposition) had been known to counsel for the defence, then it is likely some heavy lines of questioning would have been pursued to reconcile or ridicule them. As that didn't happen, it raises an intriguing question: why did an experienced police officer, who would be trained in giving concise, accurate reports, give such differing reports of the crime against him? The answer may be that is was the way his mind worked at the time and immediately afterwards, that left the situation confused.

This discussion is straightforward and simplistic, as this is about a murder case and not about the intricate workings of the mind.

There is a difference between psychology and psychiatry, but both involve the normal day-to-day functioning of the mind. And it is the functioning of the mind that is the core. Severe mental illnesses fall into two main categories: organic and functional. Organic illnesses usually involve some kind of physical deterioration of the brain, of which dementias, including Alzheimer's disease, are good examples. But functional illnesses affect thoughts and behaviour and are not caused by a physical impairment *per se*. Functional mental illness is a misnomer as the illnesses in this group generally involve a malfunction. Functional mental illnesses don't generally affect conscious recall and recognition but they do usually affect how that recall and recognition is processed and understood, or how an event is perceived. For instance, when a mentally healthy person sees a man standing on a corner, they take this for simply what it is—a man standing on a corner. However, for someone in an acute phase of paranoid schizophrenia the thought patterns can take on all sorts of unhealthy and alarming overtones, such as the man is 'spying' or is 'affecting people's thoughts' or is about to 'poison through the electricity system, by X-ray' etc. The point is this unfortunate individual could tell a thousand people and make a dozen written reports and they would probably be very similar, if not exactly the same. This is because his powers of recall and recognition are unaffected; it is how he *perceives* the information which causes the problem. Recognition is unaffected because he sees a man standing on the corner; recall is unaffected as he knows what a man is and what a corner is.

It is in that process of recall and recognition, and where their smooth running falls down, that a possible explanation for PC Jagger's list of statements and their anomalies can be found. It is not because of a mental illness, but more his mental functioning that is involved. So the answer is not likely to be found in an abnormality, but in the normal day-to-day functioning of the mind. There is then a further explanation necessary as to why the mind of a person who is not suffering from a mental illness can be impaired.

Unfortunately, much blurring has happened in recent years about the relationship between the aspects and inter-relations of the various parts of the mind. To simplify things, the mind can be seen to work on several different plains: conscious, sub-conscious, unconscious (not as in comatose) and so on. For present purposes, it would be convenient to focus on two areas — conscious and impeded conscious, or 'awareness' and 'impeded awareness'. But it would be far too simplistic to call this model, 'what we are aware of and what we are not'. To use a domiciliary simile, the body is a house but the mind controls the front door. Hunger knocks on the door, it is recalled and recognised and is sent to the kitchen. Sleep knocks on the door, it is recalled and recognised and is sent to the bedroom.

The difficulty is when hunger knocks on the door and for some reason the information surrounding the need doesn't get processed, because something happens to impede this process in its recognition. So something happens, usually unpleasant, but a mechanism in the mind acts as a kind of editor; instead of the usual path of recognition and recall, the mind can go blank for a part or all of the event, and generally one doesn't decide this as a course of action. It is the more advanced parts of the mind that make the decision automatically and usually without any awareness of the decision either. But part of the experience or event can be, and often is, processed properly. And this is the centre of the discussion, because if one breaks down the most simple daily function then there are a whole host of different things happening. Take hunger as an example. The experiences are, hunger, stomach pangs, recognition of the signs, recalling the description, recalling the needed course of action, recall of what is needed, recall of where to find it, recognition of it, recognition of impairments—the smell of rotten eggs, the sight of mould on bread, the knowledge of salmonella in chicken. What we prefer to do: have a sandwich, toast, boiled egg, fried egg. How much is needed. Washing hands. The list is always long, but for a simple thing like lunch there are many processes going on in the mind simultaneously.

Let's consider the mind of PC Arthur Gordon Jagger.

He is on cordon duty and is not expecting immediate danger. He is possibly bored. He might have been thinking all sorts of things, about his wife, daughters, the mortgage, overdraft, bills, the front guttering needing repairing, whether a recent cold or upset stomach has passed, etc. Then, to his amazement, he actually sees someone, he has to think for a minute to recognise and recall what it is all about. He approaches The Man, he calls for help. At this point his mind has disengaged automatic pilot.

What he is expecting, and what actually happens are two vastly different things. He is expecting to approach The Man, and follow his briefing that if he thinks it is Moore, he is to intercept him and see if he is carrying any spoils of a burglary or any tools he might use in a burglary. Intercepting a suspect is something he has done countless times in his twenty-two years as a police officer. DI Fraser's help is quickly at hand when, all of a sudden, very grave danger—a gun, shots, knocked to floor, pain, threat. Where will danger or threat end? The latter points may not have registered in his conscious mind but his higher levels of brain functioning would be dealing or have even have dealt with them already. Then shots.

PC Jagger is shot. In a job where he might routinely have been obliged to face unpleasant hazards, he finds himself lying on the floor and probably in pain, and quite likely in sheer disbelief at what has happened. Let's stop here for a moment. A man has been shot but is still alive and conscious, as the horror starts to sink in then, as discussed above, his mind will possibly, and to a greater or lesser degree, rescue him from the trauma. It won't be a question of suppressing it, because suppression is within the power of the conscious mind; what happens to PC Jagger is more like denial. It hasn't happened: something has happened but not that, I can't die. The trauma is denied and his mind will effectively edit and, therefore, alter the processing of information. Recall and recognition or other day-to-day functions of the mind are impeded.

If this isn't bad enough, he then sees a colleague shot four times. This again is hugely traumatic and an experience that would be a prime candidate for the denial mechanism. That is two experiences in the space of less than a minute. But it isn't as simple as this because there might be partial recall and recognition. But he will not be able to accurately describe what has happened; it might come back quickly, might come back slowly and might even fail to come back to his mind at all.

Also, he is vulnerable to what is now described as post-traumatic stress disorder. But vulnerability doesn't mean one will get a full-blown episode, and it is unclear when it might manifest itself. And his mind is aware that there is a severe physical injury to deal with, so will want that danger to pass before the 'stress disorder' can be dealt with. But what is characteristic of the disorder are what are known as 'flashbacks' or 're-experiences' which might mean little bits of information start spilling out in his mind/memory as the flashbacks occur. Those phenomena might be inadvertently set off by colleagues asking questions; talking about the experience is difficult and yet there are two written documents and five verbal reports of PC Jagger being asked to record the events.

Is the statement actually what the witness says, or is it just what the police officer asks and, more importantly, how he asks it? Or is it an amalgam of the two?

The level of stress is not always increased if the sufferer of a 'stress disorder' comes into contact with an agent causing the stress, but it is likely. It is difficult to accept they will just 'take it in their stride'. PC Jagger's pulse went up from 140 (high anyway, especially as the drugs with the side-effect of increased heartbeat had worn off) before he saw Moore on the Sunday afternoon in Huddersfield Royal Infirmary, for the identity parade. His pulse went up from 140 per minute to 146, but as discussed elsewhere this could have been the onset of a medical emergency. But PC Jagger was also described as being '… very mentally alert' which may have been an unrecognised hypervigilance (fear of the danger experienced).

It would be unfair to criticise the doctors for not recognising these symptoms because they were decades away from being recognised, let alone defined. In short, PC Jagger was so badly injured physically and so traumatised mentally that it might have taken him weeks to clarify in his own mind what had actually happened—if clarification happened at all. These days he would be offered counselling too. So, bearing this argument in mind, the question to consider is this—how reliable was the identification of Moore Moore by PC Jagger during the identity parade?

The short answer to this would be, it is unknown. But somehow that identity parade took place with a desperately ill man whose mind was unsettled and traumatised. A surgeon's assertion that he was '… mentally alert' has to be treated with caution. It is highly unlikely PC Jagger was probed by the surgeon to see what sort of shape he was in mentally, and the surgeon wouldn't have known, nor would have the professional skills and knowledge to know what to look for. Neither would he have had the skills, knowledge or experience to judge.

But going back to the dying declaration and court deposition, there is a possibility that PC Jagger was 'helped' to make them and taking a simple approach, here are a couple of questions that occur:

In the court deposition: 'I first saw the accused at 2 am on 15th July. He was walking towards his home.' But in the dying declaration: 'Saw a man going up a field. I went after him.' If you saw a man 'going up a field', was he going away from you? Where then, was PC Jagger? If he was on the path, at his posting position, PC Jagger would have seen The Man there. The little change makes the statement run smoother and avoids the question about where PC Jagger was. 'I flashed my torch in his face' became 'I shone my torch in his face', but that doesn't alter the seeds of doubt about the identity parade when he purported to recognise The Man again. In the dying declaration: 'Inspector Fraser shone his light on him and said: "Are you Moore…"' It seems very strange that the head of the local CID, trying to apprehend a persistent burglar, needed him to say who he was—and more so as DI Fraser had given Moore's description to PC Jagger *et al* in the earlier briefing. So why did he ask The Man what he asked him? All most unsatisfactory. But, of course, good police procedure should have been adhered to, and some form of identification would have been desirable. But it would have been more likely would it not that DI Fraser would have announced to The Man that he was known to be Alfred Moore? So was the dying declaration later edited for impact and to avoid questions: and to become the court deposition?

It became imperative, therefore, that if PC Jagger flashed or shone his torch into The Man's face and saw it clearly as he said he did, that he identified Alfred Moore in the identity parade. That is possibly why the identity parade had to happen, and be conclusive. So a solicitor for Moore was undesirable, and he didn't have one.

All of this took place years, or even decades, from any helpful description of the way the mind works, so the individuals concerned can't be criticised for their lack of awareness. Today the whole thing would have been handled quite differently, but identification evidence, which this case relied upon, is notoriously unreliable.

Chapter 11

Family

The eldest of Moore's four daughters was just over ten-years-old at the time of his arrest. On the night of the shooting the children had stayed up late to see their Uncle Charles off home with their father, and then stayed at the farm with their mother. The police felt that the daughter was an important prosecution witness and so she appeared at the magistrates' court by subpoena. In a book compiled in the early-1970s by the writer and barrister Fenton Bressler, the evidence of the girl was described thus: 'on balance, inconclusive'. Legally, it probably was, but that might not be an adequate description, because one thing that *is* conclusive is witness coercion. The daughter's court deposition, which is quoted first here, was taken after the statement which is quoted second. The reason these two have been switched around is so that these particular phrases can be discussed:

1. 'I don't know what time it was.'
2. 'I think I heard something — it might have been a train.'
3. 'It was a whistle.'
4. 'I have never heard a police whistle before in my life.'
5. 'I did not look out of the window.'

With these phrases to refer back to, it can be argued that the evidence in the magistrates' court was conclusive, if one takes conclusive to mean: 'putting an end to doubt, decisive and final'. It was made plain that some of the things she was supposed to have said in the statement taken on 15th July 1951 were just not true.

The court deposition is quoted here in full, errors and omissions included.

> 'I live at Whinney Close Farm with my sisters, three girls. My Mother lives there as well. Alfred Moore is my father. I remember a Sunday when my father went away with some policemen. I have got an Uncle Charles. He had been at

the farm on the Saturday before the Sunday. When my Uncle Charles left to go home my daddy went with him. I don't know what time it was. It was just coming dark. After they had gone my Mummy and I stopped and read. We had to wait a short time. I think I heard something—it might have been a train. It was not the puffing noise. It was a whistle. I have never heard a police whistle before in my life. I was in bed. My mother was in bed. I did not look out of the window. My Daddy came in through the french windows and came straight upstairs and was cross because I was not asleep. I don't know what he was wearing. When he came in he got straight into bed. I don't think he put the light on at all. He didn't do anything else after he had got into bed.'

It is possible that she was falling in and out of sleep, because Moore did do something after he had got into bed: he got up again to conceal some of his cache of stolen goods and keys in the cavity wall, and burn the stamps and the foreign currency. It is also said that Moore went straight in and up the stairs when he came home from walking with Charles. He had to take off his wet shoes, which he did downstairs, and he had a wash. So there was a time lapse from when he came in, to when he went upstairs. It might have only been a short time lapse of a few minutes, say three to five minutes, but that is not 'coming straight upstairs'. However, this might possibly be the second time that night that Moore had returned to the house. The first time was at around midnight when he had returned from walking with his brother and had taken off and dealt with his wet shoes and had a wash; and the second time was after hearing the whistles and the commotion outside, he went out to check his poultry in case they were being stolen. Moore himself said that he went straight upstairs after returning from this brief second excursion. So it could be here that his story about coming home earlier, at midnight, can be tested. If she was asleep at that time then she wouldn't have heard him come in or notice the short time-lapse—when he was dealing with his wet shoes and having a wash—before he went up to the bedroom. But if this was a second return, that is *after* he had gone out to check his poultry at the time of the commotion outside, then it does suggest she heard what Moore later described in evidence. But what is not known is exactly when she was awake.

There does appear to be a logical sequence in how she describes the events, and also the gaps when something has happened, such as the return and the pause to take off his shoes, lay them out to dry and have a wash downstairs, all of which can be accounted for by her falling in and out of sleep. As for the train—the police visited the British Railways staff to check the movements of trains that night (steam engines had a very shrill whistle) but nothing could be discovered which could explain what was thought to have been heard. On the other hand, in summer, in a rural location, with bedroom windows open and being half asleep, there is every reason to believe it was an animal or a bird making a noise that was mistaken for a whistle. And it was only said she *thought* she heard a whistle. The child was making the statement at the police station for six hours—if a policeman was asking if she had heard a whistle of any description during that length of questioning, then she might begin to think she had, or that 'something' she heard was actually a whistle. But, in the court deposition quoted above, made before a magistrate, it is quite clear she could not have identified a police whistle if one was heard.

It might be useful to consider at this point what was claimed to have been said to the policeman in her earlier statement. The best way to make this consideration is to study the statement in full (errors and omissions included).

'I know what it means to be truthful and I promise to tell all the truth to the policeman who is writing this statement.

My father [is] Alfred Moore and my mother is Alice Moore and I live with them and my three sisters at the above address.

There is only one bedroom in the house and we all sleep there. There are three beds in which we sleep in two's. My father and mother are in one, me and [the youngest] in one and [the other two girls] are in the other. I am the oldest of the four children.

Last night, Saturday, 14th July 1951, I was in the kitchen when my Uncle Charles and my father went out. My dad was taking my uncle home. I don't know what time it was but it was late. My Uncle Charles had been at our home all day helping to build a pigsty.

I stopped up with my mother after my father and Uncle had gone out.

My father did not come home for a long time and I got worried about it. Then after a long time I heard a police whistle being blown outside. It sounded a fair way off. When I heard the police whistle I was scared because I thought my dad was in trouble and I went and hugged my mother. My mother and I then went upstairs. I switched the electric light off, but my mother switched a reading lamp on which we have in the kitchen. I don't know whether my mother left the reading lamp on because I went upstairs first, then mummy followed.

I got undressed upstairs but didn't switch the upstairs light on. When I got my pyjama's on I went and stood by the window and my mother who had undressed, sat on the edge of her bed looking out of the window. After a little while my mother said something like, "daddy's coming now". I then heard a rattle downstairs as though someone had come in through the french window.

My father came straight upstairs shining his torch, I mean flashlight. He was wearing a jacket I believe, and trousers, but I don't know what colour. He didn't have a cap or hat on. He took his jacket and trousers off, putting the trousers under the bed. I don't know where he put his jacket.

I don't think my dad got into bed, I think he went to his wardrobe and got something out which I think was paper. He took the paper downstairs and after a short time my mother went down to him. I heard them talking downstairs but don't know what they said.

My mother came back upstairs and sat on the edge of the bed looking out of the window, and my father came upstairs got some more stuff which I think was paper, out of his wardrobe. He took it downstairs.

I forgot to say that when mummy and I were waiting upstairs for daddy to come home, and when mummy said "Daddy's coming now" I saw some lights being flashed in the fields in front of our farm.

When my father came upstairs after taking the last lot of paper down, he said to mummy, "I'm going to hide." I don't know whether my mother said anything in answer. He put his trousers on and went downstairs again, but just as he was going down I remember mother said, "Don't go Alf."

I heard my dad open the kitchen door and go outside. My mother went to the top of the stairs and shouted to him, but he did not answer.

After a short while I heard my father come back into the house and straight upstairs. He took his trousers off again and got into bed. I didn't hear my father or mother say anything.

I think I went to sleep then because the next I remember is my mother and a policeman coming upstairs. I then go up and went downstairs and saw my father go away with some policemen.

I have never seen my father with a revolver or a small gun.'

Alice Moore added:

'I was present when my [daughter] made the above statement and believe it to be a perfectly true statement.'

The statement was taken by DCI Edington.

The statement dated 15th July 1951, above, differs from the court deposition. Firstly, she said in the court deposition that she had never heard a police whistle in her life, yet in two different places in the statement it is said that she heard a police whistle, and actually described it as a 'police whistle'. Secondly, in the court deposition she said she did not look out of the window, yet in the statement she says there were 'lights being flashed in the field in front of our farm'; it is difficult to imagine how this could have been seen if she did not look out of the window.

For a ten-year-old to make a statement she would have a parent with her, even in those days, and it is difficult to understand why Alice Moore let her child say what was quoted to have been said. The girl (by subpoena) and her deposition was thought vital at the lower court. There are a number of possibilities for this, but the most striking is the fact that the girl said in the deposition: 'I have never heard a police whistle before in my life.' There is no room for doubt—not 'I don't think…' or 'I can't remember ever hearing…' or 'There may have been a time when perhaps I heard…' No, it is a straight, 'I have never heard a police whistle before in my life.'

So why was a statement that said, '… I heard a police whistle being blown outside' and 'When I heard the police whistle…' made in the first place? The answer to this seems to be as discussed, that something was heard, some noise of the night—but she wasn't sure what, so thought it might have been a train. So if a policeman is taking a statement he will continually ask if such-and-such happened—he shouldn't, but he does. If one is not careful then one tends to doubt the accuracy of one's own memory. But she did not doubt her memory and said quite categorically that she had '… never heard a police whistle in my life.' That does suggest a final and decisive end to doubt, so is, on balance, conclusive.

It does seem clear that she said she '… saw some lights being flashed in the field in front of our farm' because it had been 'fed', so in her court deposition doubt is removed with the categoric, 'I did not look out of the window.'

So, because of one small conflict her evidence was described as inconclusive. Compare that with PC Jagger who made five different statements to five different people and a written statement and a dying declaration all saying slightly different things—it is surprising therefore that his evidence was not also considered inconclusive. But it was inconclusive—what got to court was only what it was thought the jury should hear.

When taking the statement on 15th July there is no proof that DCI Edington did put words into her mouth, but it seems inexplicable that two things (what she thought might have been a whistle and that she did not look out of the window so could not have seen the flashing lights) are described. The evidence of Moore's daughter did not help the prosecution but neither did it strongly support Moore's alibi. But what it does do is suggest that the earlier statement had been 'fed', and thus the possibility of witness coercion.

Alice Moore made two statements, the first on 15th July and the second unfortunately undated, though it seems likely, considering its contents, it was within a day or two of the first.

Her first statement is fairly bland with nothing of real substance. The middle and the latter part of the statement is quoted below, with the rest shortened. Paragraph one introduces the statement, who she is and so forth; paragraph two describes ownership and the price of the farm; paragraph three was moving in, as in relocation details, etc. Paragraphs four and five describe the stock of pigs, how they needed a third sty and how Moore's brother was involved in its construction, which was why he was at the farm on the Saturday. Paragraph six introduces the Saturday, details the afternoon and evening up to when Moore and his brother Charles left to walk towards Charles' house. This excerpt therefore starts from paragraph seven (errors and omissions included):

'At about 10.45 p.m. my husband changed his clothing and said he would walk down to Waterloo, Huddersfield, with Charles who was ready for going home. My husband said he had a headache and thought the walk would clear him a bit. I also gave him a letter address to the Director, Post Office Savings Dept., London W.14. to put in the post box for me.

They went out together at about 11 p.m., my husband being dressed in grey flannel trousers, brown sports coat and fawn macintosh coat. He had no headgear. So far as I know he had no firearm with him at that time. They left the house by way of a french window which I left open for my husband's return, the only door was locked.

I went to bed about midnight and switched the electric lights off, leaving all in darkness. I was not concerned about my husband being out so late because it's a thing he often does.

There is no clock in the bedroom, but I had not been to sleep and think it would be about 12.30 a.m. when I heard my husband come into the house. I heard him lock the French window and he then came straight upstairs to bed. He muttered something about being tired and then got straight into bed. He didn't speak any more but then went straight to sleep. I didn't disturb him.

I didn't go to sleep and was dozing when, about half an hour after Alfred came to bed, I heard police whistles being blown not very far away and saw lights being flashed in the field of the valley below our farm. I sleep by the side of the window, which looks right out over the valley, and could see the lights quite clearly.

Shortly afterwards I saw what I took to be an ambulance driven into the yard of the brickworks at the bottom of our fields. I didn't see the ambulance driven away.

I think it would be about quarter past to half past two in the morning by now, and because of the police whistles and lights flashing I wakened up my husband and said, "Have a look outside. I wonder what's happened." He replied, "I don't know", but a few minutes later he said, "I have my suspicions I'm being watched." He then got up, put his trousers on and went downstairs.

I heard my husband switch the electric light on in the kitchen and then a minute or two later I heard him switch the light off and he came upstairs again, showing a light from an electric torch.

He went to his wardrobe and got out some sheets of postage stamps and Foreign paper money which I know was there and which I believed my husband had stolen somewhere in Honley months ago.

I didn't say anything to my husband, and he went back downstairs with the paper money. I did not hear him switch on the light downstairs, where he remained about half an hour.

He then came back upstairs and I said, "What have you been doing." He replied "I've burnt them." I took that to mean the stamps and paper money.

My husband then took his trousers off and got back into bed. He did not speak nor did I. I don't know whether he went to sleep or not, but I didn't because I was wondering what was going on outside. I wasn't really worried because I didn't think the commotion outside concerned us.

My husband had been in bed about one hour on the second occasion when, at 4 a.m. Two police officers shouted from the yard outside, "Alfred, Alfred". I opened the bedroom window and shouted "What do you want?" One of the officers said, "We want to see Alfred."

My husband had wakened up and looked over my shoulder, he shouted down to the police, "I will be down in a minute."

I got out of bed, slipped a dress on and went downstairs, my husband followed me immediately after. I opened the door and my husband walked out into the yard to the policemen. I saw one of them handcuff him and they took him away.

I did not know why my husband had been arrested, but learned from police officers who came into the house that a police officer had been shot.

My husband has had a single barrelled shot gun about a month. I think he bought it at the "Model Shop", Queen Street, Huddersfield. He had some cartridges for this gun. He kept this gun upstairs in a corner by his wardrobe.

My husband got this gun to try and kill a fox which had been after the poultry.

Alfred also had an air pistol which fires darts. This he kept in the corner of the kitchen. I have not seen any ammunition for this gun for a long time.

I know he also had a small toy pistol which fired blank ammunition. So far as I know he had no blank ammunition. He kept this latter gun upstairs in his wardrobe.

I have never seen my husband with a revolver or a rifle and have never heard him talk of having one or wanting one.

> I know my husband is a criminal and that he was going out at nights and was getting money, which I thought he may have stolen He never told me where he had been and I never asked him. I do not know whether Alfred had gone out to do a job last night, Saturday 14th July, but I don't think he had, because he went with his brother, just like I've told you.
>
> My husband does not drink intoxicants, but is a very hasty tempered man and gets nasty, but I don't want to say anymore about that side of him. I will say, however, that his parents were always quarrelling and fighting, and when he was younger the home conditions were very bad.
>
> I have never heard my husband say he would shoot a police officer who tackled him, or anyone else.
>
> My husband served in the Merchant Navy for about 3 years, 1942 to 1945 I believe.'

The temper of Moore has never been a secret, but the impression given in all of the available documentation is that The Man did not shoot out of anger or temper or anything remotely like it; he fired the gun calmly and rationally. In the second statement, quoted below, Alice makes some quite extreme comments about Moore and gives the impression that life with him was unpleasant. Neither of Alice's statements got to court.

The second statement in full (errors and omissions included):

> 'Further to my statement of the 15th July, 1951, I want to say I have thought further about it and am more clear about what happened at our farm during the night of the 14th-15th July, 1951.
>
> I said I went to bed about midnight on Saturday, 14th, but am not sure really what time it was, it may have been much later. My daughter was with me and went upstairs to bed with me. My husband had not returned to the house when my daughter and I went to bed.
>
> Immediately before my daughter and I went upstairs to bed we had heard the sound of a police whistle which seemed to be not very far away from our house.

I was worried because my husband was out so late and I also thought the sounding of the police whistle might be connected with my husband's activities.

When my daughter and I went to bed it was my daughter who switched the kitchen light off and I switched a reading lamp on, but switched it off practically straight away and followed my daughter upstairs.

Both my daughter and I got undressed and I went and sat on the edge of the bed and looked out of the window over the valley in front of our house. My daughter stood by me. We had not been there many minutes when I heard the french windows downstairs unlatched and my husband came upstairs to the bedroom. He didn't switch the light on upstairs, but was shining an electric torch.

When he saw us looking out of the window he said, "Fucking well get into bed." We did so, and then he took off his raincoat, jacket and trousers, and put them on the floor and got into bed with me. About five or ten minutes later I looked through the window and saw torches being flashed in the fields in front of our house. I said to my husband, "What's matter, look at all those lights down there, they are all flashlights, I can't understand it."

It was then that he got out of bed and took what I believed to be sheets of Postage Stamps out of his wardrobe and took them downstairs. By the noises at the fireplace downstairs I thought he was burning the stamps. He came upstairs about twice I think to collect more stamps, and took them downstairs. He was dressed in his shirt at this time and hadn't put his trousers on.

When my husband came upstairs to get stamps out of his wardrobe on the second occasion, he said, "I'm going to hide", and started off downstairs with nothing on but his shirt and a pair of short pants and socks on his feet. I shouted to him, "Come back and get into bed." He took no notice and I heard him unlock the door and go outside. He wouldn't be away more than two minutes before he returned back into the house. I heard him re-lock the door and he came straight back upstairs and got into bed. He then appeared to go to sleep.

About ten minutes after my husband had got into bed on the last occasion I saw the blue-green street lighting at the Pre-Fab houses at Almondbury go out.

I didn't go to sleep and think it would be about another hour after my husband got into bed the last time, before the police came and arrested him. I think he was arrested at 4 a.m.

I haven't wanted to say anything before, but I must tell you now that since I married Alfred Moore on the 24th, February, 1940, he has suffered from fits of depression and nerves. When he was depressed he was violent. He would smash anything he laid hands on in the house. He has struck me many times and bruised and marked me. About two and a half years ago, when I was pregnant with my youngest child, my husband, without any provocation, in a fit of temper, broke a leg off a chair and split my head open. I was treated at Huddersfield Royal Infirmary as an out-patient.

My husband has also struck our children unnecessarily.

This past six weeks my husband has seemed queer and depressed. He has been irritable and talked to himself a lot. He has also complained a lot of pains in his head.'

Such was the second statement.

She says: 'I was worried because my husband was out so late and I also thought the sounding of the police whistle might be connected with my husband's activities.' Two issues — did Alice know a police whistle when she heard one? But, more importantly, in her first statement she gave a completely opposite feeling about her husband being out so late.

'I'm going to hide' was something mentioned by both the daughter and Alice, but was it a complete statement of what Moore said at the time? Or was it part of a sentence — such as 'I'm going to hide the keys and other stolen goods'?

Most people would agree that there is some difficulty tracking time if one is dozing or sleeping. What might seem about ten minutes could range from a couple of minutes to a couple of hours. Our body clocks tend to slow down at night and we dip in and out of deep sleep.

In her first statement on 15th July, Alice identifies herself as the wife of Moore. Thereafter she refers to him twenty-nine times as 'my husband.' She refers to him as Alfred on three occasions, as well as a fair sprinkling of 'he' and 'him(s)'. But what is striking about the second statement is how she refers to Alfred, '... since I married Alfred Moore on the 24th, February, 1940...' Now, although she refers to him by name on three occasions in her first statement, then it is only as 'Alfred'. It seems strange that she would refer to him now as 'Alfred Moore'. True, most married couples have a way of habitually referring to their spouse, but Alice seemed to say 'my husband' most of the time and also 'Alfred' very occasionally. It seems strange for someone to say '... since I married Alfred Moore on the 24th, February, 1940.' It would be more usual to say '... since we married' or 'after I married...' And for someone to habitually use the term 'my husband' it is strange that she seems to distance herself to almost a formality of name and date. By using the term 'my husband', it conveys a feeling of possession, not of a stifling possession, more a possession of something she held dear. So does the fact that she describes him as 'Alfred Moore' mean this statement was truly representative of what she said? With the general differences between the two statements, what really is truly representative of what she actually said? Just how much of each statement was actually written *for* her?

What remains is the statement of the daughter and Alice of 15th July, and then Alice's second statement a day or so later, and then the daughter's court deposition, none of which is readily reconcilable with the other. The main question for Alice would revolve around the differences between her first and second statements and more-or-less the same confusion over the daughter's statements.

It looks as though the police left the Moores alone for a bit after the statement scenario described above. Moore was then remanded to the prison hospital to test his mental state. More of this later, but it is interesting that there was an interview between Alice and the prison doctor. It is quoted as fully as the surviving documentation allows.

'Mrs Alice Moore (33), of 11, Birkhead St. Heckmondwike (wife of prisoner) interviewed.

She knew prisoner about 18 months before marrying him on Feb 24th 1940. There are 4 children.

Children have always been healthy. Says her husband has always been a healthy man and has never been subject to fits or mental trouble. She says their marriage has been happy and he has been a good husband and father. She says he has never used any violence to her or the children and has spent most of his time at home with them. There has been no infidelity on either side.

She says she has changed her name to Mrs Hirst to avoid publicity for the sake of her eldest [child], who has already been a witness in this case. They have moved to their present address from Huddersfield.

Witness says her husband has always been quite normal in his behaviour both with his own family and to other people. He has a bad temper but only when provoked and then it passes away very quickly. Witness is as cool as a cucumber and appears quite unconcerned. She tells me she is "not really worried" as she knows her husband is innocent and adds "If I did not think so, then I would be really worried."

This interview appears to concur with Alice's first statement of the 15th July, but contradicts the second statement in three areas. In the second statement she said he had '… seemed queer and depressed … Irritable and talked to himself a lot.' But in this interview she says he has '… never been subject to … mental trouble.' Secondly, in this statement she says he hit her across the head with the leg of a chair but then says he is a good husband. And thirdly, though related to the second point, '… he has never used any violence to her or the children.'

The daughter's evidence was not used and the fact that Alice's statements were found in a file of statements marked 'Not Used' might add to the mystery. Then again, the solution to the mystery of the daughter's and Alice Moore's evidence might be self-evident. But if what the daughter said in her court deposition and what Alice said to the hospital doctor are true, and they can be (semi-)collaborated by each other, then the statements made by both Alice and her daughter on 15th July, and Alice's later undated statement of a day or two later were, at best, what they were *told* happened rather than what they *witnessed* happening; and at worst, further evidence that the police were trying to edit or even manufacture evidence. It would seem that in trying to make the crime fit the movements of Moore that night, or possibly vice-versa, the police overlooked the fact that his daughter only saw and heard what was actually seen and heard, and was only prepared to say this. If she wasn't sure she said so: 'I think I heard something—it might have been a train.' It looks as though the police may have made witnesses unreliable by trying to make them say things that fitted their theory of Moore's guilt, rather than what fitted the facts.

CHAPTER 12

Evidence

Apart from the deposition of PC Jagger, there was no evidence to support the charge that Moore murdered DI Fraser and PC Jagger. He was only associated with the crime by PC Jagger's evidence. The one thing that would have linked him to the crime, or proved he was not linked to the crime, would have been the murder weapon. But this has never been discovered, despite the police making a thorough attempt at finding it. The fire brigade was called in to drain water troughs round about and they also drained ditches on the farm. The police got a local farmer to cut the grass right down. They climbed trees and searched undergrowth; one member of the search party saw a hole in a tree and thought it was odd, so the tree was cut down and cut up. They had two teams of ten policemen each working alternate shifts. They had many voluntary helpers at the weekend. Even a team of ten soldiers, from what was then called the Army Engineering Regiment, was on the farm for ten days with metal detectors. Dry stone walls were 'opened up' and an internal wall was pulled down. If the gun was on the farm, then it would have been found.

However, a number of spent cartridges were found. Some were inside the cavity wall which had been demolished and one was in the tallboy in the bedroom. Moore said he had obtained them some years before and he'd intended to make lipsticks with them—but this didn't happen.

Although the cartridges were 9 mm, the same as the bullets that had killed the two police officers, it couldn't be proved that they were from the bullets recovered from DI Fraser or PC Jagger. The ballistics expert said the bullets had almost certainly been fired by a revolver and not an automatic pistol—an automatic pistol would have ejected the shells or cartridges at the scene. There were also markings on the bullets consistent with a small indent where the bullet leaves the revolving magazine and enters the barrel as it is propelled. Cartridges were found, but no gun. After a murder it seems unlikely that the murderer would take the cartridges out of the gun and hide them around a farm in silly places like a tallboy in the bedroom, but hide the weapon with such cunning that it never came to light. I will return to the cartridges later.

Evidence in the form of witness testimony was plentiful, so it will aid understanding if the various statements are analysed. They fall into three categories: the civilians, the police, and the scientific staff.

Two of the civilian witnesses were Charles and Mahala Moore, Moore's brother and sister-in-law, but they said nothing that he didn't agree with, and might even have told the court himself. The core piece of evidence was the time Moore and his brother parted, after their walk towards Charles' home from the farm, which was at approximately 11.25 pm. There was nothing in court which challenged this and the evidence had been consistent throughout.

Moore said he was traversing the footpaths up to his farm at around midnight. In his summing-up, the judge gave a thorough analysis of the various times Moore and the brother parted and how long it would take him to get back to the farm, and in doing so miss the cordon. The judge pointed out that the two figures didn't tally. A lot of time was spent by the court in considering Charles Moore's evidence of their parting, and how long the walk would take; and how Mahala was so accurate with the timing of when Charles got home; and how conscientious and helpful PC Sellick had been in retracing Moore's steps and noting the times taken to get from one place to another; and just how much more was needed to add to this senseless charade.

The police and the court, didn't need to assess to the nth degree how the timings went—the police cordon was said to have been fully set by 11.45 pm, and Moore said he passed through it at around midnight. The midnight timing would tie in with the evidence of the brother and sister-in-law. There simply was no argument from Moore about the time that he passed, a time at which the cordon would have been fully operational. But the prosecution argued that it would be impossible for Moore to do this, although he insisted this is what he did and got back to the farm at around midnight. But as it can be clearly demonstrated that PC Jagger was off his cordon position when The Man passed, then there is an argument that PC Jagger was off position when Moore passed. A big hole in the prosecution evidence is Moore's whereabouts from midnight until 1.55 am and it seems little, if anything, was done to fill this gap. Moore leaves his brother at around 11.25 pm, and it would take him about 30–35 minutes to walk back to the farm. It raised suspicions when he said it was 'bad luck' to return by the way he came, but if one considers he almost fell into a stream then it is not without some sense. The police traced all manner of people who would have been out and about in Kirkheaton that night, that late, but no evidence was found of anyone resembling Moore or indeed anyone acting suspiciously around the town. But, more to the point, there were no burglaries or attempted burglaries committed that night. Of course, that might mean none were reported to the police.

So Moore leaves his brother at about 11.25 pm, and arrives at the farm at around midnight; or that is his story. *Or* he leaves his brother at about 11.25 pm and appears armed at 1.55 am. But there is a two-and-a-half-hour interval with no apparent clue as to his whereabouts — this interval is not accounted for in any police documents, statements or depositions available. If Moore was going to be out and alone for two and a half hours at night then his destination would have been a mill office and a safe somewhere. And it is more likely he would have been carrying a bag of tools used in a burglary, not a revolver. Yet there was no report or record of a burglary, so it is not possible to account for these two-and-a-half hours.

The only other civilian witness to give evidence in court was Joe Baxter who worked for the removals firm which the Moores engaged for their move to the farm. His evidence said the gun, alleged to be the murder weapon, was in Moore's possession in May when they moved to the farm. Mr Baxter, an ex-Navy man had received small-arms training during the war, so he was thought to be a credible witness. His first statement claimed he had seen an *automatic* pistol in Moore's possession.

Other civilian evidence, involving background information was collected by police but not used in court. For instance, Moore's extended family all gave statements, and many folk who recovered stolen property from the farm were interviewed. Moore's previous employers all spoke fairly well of him, as did tradesmen who had worked at the farm. This included Arthur Hartley, an electrician who thought there might have been holes in a window where projectiles had come through — holes that were consistent with bullet holes. Business associates gave statements, taxi drivers, food wholesalers, neighbours new and old. Folk conjectured on how the Moores couldn't earn enough to support themselves on the production of eggs alone, the list is extensive.

The Met Office gave a statement which nobody read; if they had they would have been able to correct DCI Jenkins in that it did not rain on the night.

The police also analysed the money the Moores had spent during the months leading up to the crime, seemingly to prove that he had secured his income by unconventional and deceptive means. But when he was advised to tell the court of the income details he agreed with most, if not all, of what the police said. It would have been inappropriate for the prosecution to have referred to the robberies whether Moore had been convicted of them or not, due to the law of evidence which until quite recent times prevented this unless for example Moore had tried to rely on his previous good character. There were plenty of details forthcoming about the robberies Moore had committed, and, again, he agreed with most things.

A lot of this evidence was filed in a 'not used' folder and it is doubtful whether the defence saw any of it.

Another peculiar absentee from the civilian statements, used and unused, is a Ben Stafford. During the war years DI Fraser (then a sergeant) took on the role of liaison with the Air Raid Wardens—one of which was Mr Stafford. A friendship between the two men was noted from his being mentioned in various statements; indeed DI Fraser was at Mr Stafford's house prior to reporting for cordon duty. Mr Stafford's lounge was used to observe the bus stop Moore was said to use. After DI Fraser's death, later the same day, Supt Foster attended DI Fraser's home ostensibly to return a watch taken from his body. But in attendance also was Mr Stafford, so the men must have been more than just 'copper and liaison'.

As discussed in the previous chapter, part of what seems the harassment of Moore's daughter to glean information, there is reference to a whistling noise:

> 'Then after a time I heard a police whistle being blown outside. It sounded a fair way off.'

But, in the court evidence, the whistle doesn't seem to belong to the police after all:

'I think I heard something—it might have been a train. It was not the puffing noise. It was a whistle. I have never heard a police whistle before in my life.'

So, as has been asked previously, why did she say two contradictory things? It does suggest some police coercion and an attempt by DCI Edington to manipulate the evidence of the daughter, but what he got fell short of convincing. What it does suggest, however, is that DCI Edington reported back to DCS Metcalfe that the girl might just tell the truth, the whole truth and nothing but the truth—and this wouldn't tally with what he wanted her to say. So DCS Metcalfe sent a detective officer (now a detective constable) to thoroughly investigate the possibility that it was a train she heard.

Detective Officer Yeates was keen to respond to his senior's orders. He took a collection of statements from railwaymen. From the information he gathered he reported that the nearest railway line was about 1,500 yards away. The next nearest, the Huddersfield to Leeds line, where it runs close to the junction with the Kirkburton Branch, was a mile and three quarters away from the farm, and runs in a valley which has a range of hills up to 550 feet on the Kirkheaton side. There were also hills, he went on, between the farm and Bradley Junction, which is about three quarters of a mile roughly north-west of the farm.[1] Heaton Lodge Junction was about a mile and three quarters away with hills stretching up to 550 feet between the railway line and Moore's daughter's ears. It is not necessary to consider the line which ran from Huddersfield to Penistone as this was approximately four miles from the farm, with intervening hills of between 625 and 650 feet. The local ICI Plant had a small internal railway but no traffic was on it that night.

Quite a lot of information for an eminent KC to confront a ten-year-old girl with, as the focus of DO Yeates' investigation seems to have been to disprove that what she heard was a train. It probably wasn't but why couldn't they consider that she fell in and out of sleep between midnight and 2 am? Most people dream, and it is not unusual on a summer's night to hear strange animal noises in a rural area. She only said: 'I think I heard something—it might have been a train.' It is strange that the police made this enquiry when DCI Edington had it clear in the statement: 'Then after a time

---

1. The discrepancy here—three quarters of a mile is less than 1500 yards—seems to come from the way two different railwaymen described things.

I heard a police whistle being blown outside.' But how did that line get into the statement if she had never heard a police whistle? It begs the question as to whether DCI Edington misused his position to achieve this. And if he manipulated this evidence then the question emerges: did he manipulate any other evidence?

A detailed examination of the police statements was made earlier and there is little to add. The inconsistencies of the statements and depositions are also highlighted.

So, to look briefly at the scientific evidence.

Dr Alfred Horace Mayes was a scientist employed by the Home Office and based at Woolwich in London. He had many years' experience in the study of firearms. He had examined the bullets that had been taken from the bodies of DI Fraser and PC Jagger. They were 9 mm in size. Apparently the barrel of the weapon which fired the bullets was slightly too large for them and they had, Dr Mayes explained, 'wobbled' in the barrel on their way out of the weapon. The particular markings on the bullets suggested they had been fired from a revolver rather than an automatic pistol. But it was certain that all of the bullets had been fired from the same weapon.

Dr Mayes also examined the empty cartridge cases, which had been found in the cavity wall and the tallboy in the bedroom. Even though they were from different batches and had not been manufactured at the same time, Dr Mayes thought it likely that all three had been fired by the same weapon, again, probably a revolver. But whether the weapon had been the same one that fired the bullets that killed the police officers and the cartridge cases found in the house, it was impossible to say. Nor could he say when the cartridges had been fired.

However, one thing was certain in Dr Mayes' experience and knowledge, that the bullets and the cartridges had not been fired by a Luger weapon. Luger had not manufactured a revolver. It is true the company produced a weapon that fired 9 mm bullets, but in this case the murder weapon had a bore that was larger than the bullets, which explained why the bullets seemed to have 'wobbled' as they were leaving the chamber and travelling down the barrel. So it probably wasn't a 9 mm gun.

It also emerged that 9 mm ammunition was one of the most common scales of ammunition manufactured. It was made in many parts of the world, in Europe, the USA and Latin America, Australia, and Asia; the Chinese also used a 9 mm service revolver. And just how many spent 9 mm cartridges survived the Second World War is a question nobody will ever be able to answer.

Lewis Charles Nickolls was the director of the forensic laboratories at Wakefield at the time of the investigation but by the time the trial came round he had moved to another post. On the day of the murder he had attended Whinney Close Farm quite early. He outlined that he had found some charred fragments of postage stamps in the hearth. Mr Hinchcliffe in examination-in-chief quickly moved him on to the shoes Moore had been wearing on the night. His shoes were 'wringing wet' and had light shaly soil on their soles. Mr Nickolls compared the seeds he had found on Moore's shoes with seeds he had found at the scene of the murders and they were said to be 'similar in all respects'. Not surprising as Moore said he had earlier walked along the path where the murders were committed. Also an examination was made of the soil traces on the soles of the shoes, which were found to match the subsoil around the farm — but it was in two distinct places, one at the end of the path, the other at the other end of the house. One argument was that Moore would have picked up this shaly soil on his way to concealing a 9 mm round found on the farm. But he could also have picked up the soil on his return when he checked his hen huts.

Mr Nickolls also answered questions about a set of keys and a jack-knife found in a field. This elicited that the implements had only been in the field about twelve to twenty-four hours, which didn't establish much, except that the keys were probably not thrown there as Moore would have had to cross a field from the path leading up to the farm, and would have left a track across the field. But it was established from Insp Little and PC Sellick that the grass was about knee high and anyone walking through it would leave a track. In answer to a direct question DCI Jenkins said 'There was no track visible.' As no track was left showing where he had crossed a field, then he couldn't have crossed it.

The clothing of DI Fraser and PC Jagger had also been examined. The gabardine coat Moore had worn on the night was examined and a number of animal and vegetable fibres were found. The animal fibres consisted of wool and chicken feathers, and the vegetable was cotton. There was also a single human hair found, which might have been DI Fraser's, but even if it was it could also be proved that cross-contamination of evidence could have easily occurred.

Later, Mr Hylton-Foster established that in Mr Nickolls' laboratory, the examination of the gabardine coat Moore had worn for his walk to and from Charles' showed no evidence of gun oil, gun rust, powder residue, or blood. So there was no evidence of a gun anywhere on Moore's farm, and no evidence of a gun ever being in the coat Moore wore on the night of the crime.

This still leaves questions about some of the other cartridges in the enquiry; those found in the cavity wall and the tallboy. Another expert was engaged by the defence to examine the bullets and cartridges. This was Major Pollard.

There is a letter from Moore's solicitor, George Edward Hutchinson (usually known as 'Ted'), advising the chief constable that Messrs Churchill's, Gunsmiths of Leicester Square, London, had been engaged to provide an opinion for the defence on the bullets as recovered from the deceased officers and the cartridge cases recovered from the farm. The bullets and cartridge cases were actually taken to London by DCI Jenkins and he reported back in a letter to the chief constable. He noted that the findings of Major Pollard were essentially in agreement with Mr Nickolls of the forensic laboratories, but there was not complete agreement with the findings of Dr Mayes. Mr Nickolls was more of a generalist, but Dr Mayes was a specialist in ballistics.

Not only is it interesting that Mr Hylton-Foster does not bring this up in his presentation of the case for the defence, but also Major Pollard is said to have told DCI Jenkins that his advice to the defence '… may probably be to leave well alone'. It seems strange that if there was doubt between the two ballistics experts, then it wasn't aired in court; the main difference surrounded their suggestions as to the make of the weapon. Dr Mayes had suggested a .38 Smith and Wesson. However, he said that was '… but only an indication'. Major Pollard was quoted to have said '… that it could be an old English type of revolver … a .38 Trentor or the Old Bulldog or the same calibre'. Major Pollard, according to DCI Jenkins, '… would not express this opinion in court'.

The evidence surrounding a weapon which couldn't be found took an unexpected turn under the assessment of Major Pollard. In his expert opinion, the pressure with which the bullets had been ejected out of the barrel (the bullets recovered from the deceased officers), were fired under '… low pressure'. But the cartridge cases found on the farm had been fired under '… high pressure'. DCI Jenkins then quotes Major Pollard as being '… certain … that the cartridge cases and the bullets could not be related to each other'. So the cartridge cases on the farm could not be tied to the shootings by the evidence.

There was also some comment by Major Pollard on what both Dr Mayes and Mr Nickolls referred to as 'extractor marks'. It is strange that if the bullet was too small for the barrel then there was no apparent consideration of the cartridges fitting into the chamber. Major Pollard took the view that the cartridge cases had been '… packed by some means which it may have been necessary to extract them by digging them out with something like a knife or small screwdriver', leaving the marks which are referred to in the depositions of Dr Mayes and Mr Nickolls as 'extractor marks'. It is possible that the knife found on the farm could have been used to extract the cartridge cases, but there is no other evidence to support this hypothesis.

So, if the cartridge cases and the bullets are not '… related to each other' and the cartridges of the bullets that were fired at the two officers may have been '… packed', then why were the jury not engaged to do their job — to judge the facts regarding this?

CHAPTER 13

The Farm

As discussed in *Chapter 12*, one of the most important items of evidence in a murder trial where a weapon is used is the weapon itself. There are a number of evidential opportunities with a firearm, but mainly these are in the area of ballistics. The bullets that were extracted from the two officers could be irrevocably linked to a particular gun if it could be found.

There has been a case where a gun traced to a murder (again of a policeman) was found many months later and one line of defence was that, at the time of the crime, the gun had been in someone else's possession. On 27th September 1927 Police Constable George Gutteridge was shot dead in Essex. The gun was found a number of months later in a garage owned by one Frederick Guy Browne. He claimed that at the time of the shooting the gun belonged to someone else and he'd only acquired it more recently. But he was found guilty of murder as his partner William Kennedy gave evidence against him. Both were later hanged.[1]

Back to 1951, and it was possible that the spent cartridges of the bullets used were still in the revolving chamber but, whatever the facts were, the prosecution would have taken a different line and the defence would have had less of an uphill battle.

The murder of a police officer always leads to a police and public determination to help catch a murderer. The two murdered officers had served the community well. There were two teams of police officers of twenty men, each working in shifts. There were ten or so members of the Army Engineering Regiment scouring the land around the farm with mine detectors trying to find the gun. There were also X-ray machines brought in to check the remaining internal walls of the farm but no gun was found.

One would be forgiven for thinking that with this amount of personnel available then it would be a thorough search. But no conclusive evidence was found and there is a strong argument that a white hair found on Moore's

---

1. *R v. Browne and Kennedy*, 1928. See murderpedia.org/male.B/b/browne-frederick.htm

coat was a result of contamination. In 1951 it could not be proved as it can today that a particular hair would have come from a particular head, so this evidence wasn't going to be conclusive from the outset. But a short white hair (later classified as human) was found on Moore's coat together with fibre—vegetable (cotton). It may trace back to the ambulance when the preservation of life may have been more important than the consideration of evidence. It is possible that in this activity a hair could have passed from one of the wounded officers to one of the stretcher carriers—or 'lifters' of the two onto the stretchers.

PC Hopping and Sgt Sadler were involved in this. They were both later in the bedroom of the farm and they stripped the bed, searched the wardrobe and the tallboy. So it is possible that the hair passed from DI Fraser to a colleague and into the farm bedroom, where it might well have come to land on Moore's coat.

A set of three keys were found and an analysis of the rust on them suggested they were where they had been found for only a short period. The place they were found being in a large field to the south of the farm where Moore's children were known to play. But the children also played in the kitchen, where Moore kept his keys in a box under the table. Moore said it was possible one of the children took the keys. It isn't inconceivable that one of the children took some of the keys and their absence (among about 150 other keys) wouldn't have been noticed.

Moore hadn't left the farm for a significant period of time, about three weeks. During this time there is no evidence that anywhere was burgled or that an attempt was made to burgle.

A spent cartridge will smell of the heated discharge for a short while after it has been shot. But Detective Officer John Garnett who found a spent cartridge in the farmhouse didn't sniff it to see if it had been recently fired. It might have been quite helpful to the police if he had, as the murder weapon was not to be found anywhere. Though it might have remained elusive for one good reason, and that is that the gun was never in Moore's possession in the first place. Even if the gun was found later it would still pose the question of who had it in their possession and used it in the early hours of Sunday 15th July, 1951.

There was no doubt, and it wasn't denied, that Moore's house held many stolen items which could be traced. And this evidence would probably have resulted in a conviction even if he could have persuaded a court that the goods were received rather than stolen. But nothing was found in and around the farm that could positively link him to the murder.

By far the most damaging of the evidence found on the farm were the spent cartridges discovered after the demolition in the cavity wall. The prosecution maintained they were concealed there; it is possible that they were, but only inadvertently. But as there was no gun to match up the cartridges with, there was nothing to link them to the murder.

So, how can one explain the cartridges in the wall anyway? The bricklayer who built the wall made a statement to say there was nothing of the kind anywhere remotely near the wall when he constructed it. The only workable explanation seems to be that the cartridges were in the box with the keys and Moore just tipped the entire contents into the cavity wall. But, if Moore *did* deliberately hide spent cartridges in the wall then it certainly begs the question, why was a cartridge found in the tallboy in the bedroom? This was not concealed and was in a position in which it was unlikely to land were it, for instance, to have fallen from Moore's coat pocket.

Then there is the issue of a live 9 mm bullet that was found by Police Constable George Barclay, who had been searching a pile of building rubble. This wasn't until the following Thursday and this evidence too has its problems. Firstly the way PC Barclay and Police Sergeant William Brown, who was searching the area with him, were conducting their search was by carefully moving pieces of rubble from the top of the pile of rubble and placing it on a second pile. There was some question as to whether the pile of rubble had previously been raked over, but it was said not to have been. Yet what came out of this evidence was that there was no way of telling whether the bullet had been hidden there deliberately or had found its way there by some other means. How long it had been there was another question. Also, as the piles of rubble may or may not have been raked over, or other searching activity had occurred, the question of where the bullet 'started' in the pile; or where in the pile it was when the search then commenced was not addressed adequately. Whereas with evidence such as the keys because of the lack of rust evident on them it was approximated just how long they had lain where they were found, it is not possible to make any approximation with the live round.

A point raised by counsel for the defence was that the spent cartridges had come from different batches from different times, and even from different countries. But it was an assumption to think that an armed thug would have all his bullets from the same batch. Moore could explain where he had got the spent cartridges and why he had got them—to make lipsticks.

The search of the farm had started as soon as personnel could get there. On the Sunday evening Police Constable Ralph Clanton found an 'Army-type jack-knife' in the large field to the south of the farm where Moore had been re-roofing some of the chicken huts. Some of the huts were new. Roofing felt has to be cut, and an Army-type jack-knife was how he cut it. But it is difficult to see how this evidence helped the court to decide if he had shot two police officers. As I discussed above, the prosecution may have had in its mind that the knife was to be used to extract the bullets from the gun, but this was not mentioned in evidence at all.

All of the property in the cavity wall and a great deal elsewhere in the farm could be traced to the spate of burglaries which had commenced in January 1946 and carried on through to March 1951.

The keys proved very little, save that some had been stolen on the burglaries. Some had not been stolen and any investigation as to their origins would not seem to matter one way or another. But it does suggest that somewhere in Moore's connections, either directly or indirectly, there may have been a locksmith. What was also demonstrated was that Moore had some considerable knowledge of how locks worked and he could convert a key to make it a 'skeleton'. As well as this it is also possible Moore obtained some of his collection of keys from another source.

CHAPTER 14

Mistakes

Much of the prosecution evidence wasn't challenged by the defence which may have been for a number of reasons. All these years later the general public has easier access to the documentation than counsel did at the time. Even to this day there are documents held by what is now called the West Yorkshire Police which are pertinent to the case. This case is a straightforward one of identification, but there is not a lot of evidence to support PC Jagger's identification and, although he identified Alfred Moore as the murderer, it might not have been Alfred Moore who he saw on the hillside. So, let's take a few witnesses' evidence and see if rather than strengthening the prosecution case, they actually weakened it.

The removals man Joe Baxter's evidence was a sham, but it provided a link between Moore and a gun. One would have thought with his naval training, or the training he claimed to have had in the Navy, that Mr Baxter knew what he was talking about. However, this is not supported by the facts. For some reason Mr Baxter swore that he had seen '... what appeared to be...' a Luger revolver in Moore's toolbox when it burst open during the removal. There is no doubt that there was a toolbox and that it burst open, and Mr Baxter claimed he could tell the difference between an automatic pistol and a revolver in a good light. But firstly, there is the evidence of the ballistics expert to say the murder weapon was a revolver. Secondly, Mr Baxter swore on oath he had seen what '... appeared to be a Luger revolver...' a non-existent make in the toolbox. However, was there something left out—something the jury didn't hear? In a statement made on 28th July Mr Baxter said the following:

> 'I can recognize a revolver or an automatic on sight and tell the difference immediately particularly if the light is good.'

And he goes on to say when the toolbox burst open

'...I saw it contained rusty tools and nails and also an automatic pistol like a Luger.'

[An automatic—didn't Mr Baxter say a revolver in court?]

His statement continues: 'It was an automatic pistol like I had seen and used in the Navy.' There doesn't seem to be much room for doubt, Mr Baxter knew the difference between an automatic pistol and a revolver and he said in his statement '... an automatic pistol like a Luger.' But Luger did make an automatic pistol. Leaving that apart then, this was a straightforward piece of recognition of a weapon '... like ...' he says he had seen and used.

A month later, on 24th August 1951, the ballistics expert Dr Alfred Horace Mayes stated that the bullets recovered from the bodies of DI Fraser and PC Jagger had a certain pattern on them which he described thus: 'This condition is more consistent with firing in a revolver than in an automatic pistol.' Two witnesses were giving conflicting evidence. Mr Baxter said he had seen an automatic pistol, and he knew an automatic pistol when he saw one; but Dr Mayes was saying the bullets had probably been fired by a revolver and not an automatic. This created a dilemma as the police needed to link Moore with a gun, and unless they could find the murder weapon then the only possibility of linking Moore with a gun was what the removal man had seen. So, considering what Mr Baxter said in his deposition at the magistrates' court, here he is talking about the toolbox:

> 'When it broke open I saw a lot of rusty old screws, nails and what appeared to be a Luger automatic revolver.

[The evidence has changed.]

> I served in the Navy during the war. I had quite a lot of small arm training while I was in the Navy. I know the difference between a revolver and an automatic. This was a revolver which I saw in the box.'

[So he did say it was a revolver?]

Asked in examination-in-chief by the prosecution what he saw in the box:

'Rusty old nails and saw blades and one thing and another and what appeared to me to be a German automatic Luger revolver.'

Now this is under oath. Counsel for the prosecution, Mr Hinchcliffe, continues:

Mr Hinchcliffe: 'Had you small arms training when you were in that Service?'
Mr Baxter: 'Yes.'
Mr Hinchcliffe: 'Do you know the difference between a revolver and an automatic pistol?'
Mr Baxter: 'Yes.'
Mr Hinchcliffe: 'Which was this?'
Mr Baxter: 'A revolver.'

Not much doubt in Mr Baxter's mind. But why did he say he saw an automatic in his statement of 28th July 1951. Inevitably the considerations fall to what Mr Baxter said in cross-examination by the defence. When examined by Mr Hylton-Foster:

Mr Baxter: 'I said it appeared to be a Luger. I have seen Luger revolvers before and it just appeared to be of the similar type as a German Luger revolver. I have not had practice with German Luger revolvers. I was in the British Navy, not the German Navy.'
Mr Hinchcliffe: 'This is a serious matter, you know.'
Mr Baxter: 'I know.'
Mr Hinchcliffe: 'How did you think that observation helped us? Where have you seen a Luger revolver?'
Mr Baxter: 'Where have I seen one? In Davenport.'
Mr Hinchcliffe: 'When have you seen a Luger revolver?'
Mr Baxter: 'In the Naval Barracks, Davenport, during my time in the Navy, and…'

Mr Baxter seems confused as to what he saw; and what he, the police and the prosecution wanted him to see. His evidence now seems unreliable as he doesn't seem to know the difference between an automatic pistol and a revolver, despite his claims. Mr Hylton-Foster for the defence goes on:

Mr Hinchcliffe: 'I am putting to you that there never was a revolver shaped weapon in the box—never.'
Mr Baxter: 'Well, I said I saw what appeared to be a German automatic revolver in the box.'
Mr Hinchcliffe: 'A Luger —.'
Mr Baxter: 'A Luger revolver.'
Mr Hinchcliffe: '— automatic revolver.'
Mr Baxter: 'Well, Luger automatic revolver.'

So, to recap. He saw an automatic pistol in his statement. This changed into a revolver in the magistrate's court, which then became an automatic revolver in the Assize Court. But he slips up and tries to make both automatic and revolver fit the evidence. This seemed to turn his confidence into arrogance. 'Lugers are heavyweight automatics, a completely different thing' concluded Mr Hylton-Foster.

In his summing-up, Mr Justice Pearson said:

> 'Joe Baxter did say…that it was a Luger revolver, and you have had the evidence of the expert called by the prosecution that there is no such thing as a Luger revolver; the Luger people make automatics, but not revolvers. However, that is the evidence of Mr Baxter. He said he did see a revolver and it was a Luger, that is to say a German make of revolver. Of course, there are several possibilities, members of the jury. He may not have seen anything at all. He may have seen one of the two exhibits 24 and 25 and mistaken it for a revolver. He may have seen a revolver which was not a Luger, or he may have seen a Luger revolver and it has disappeared since.'

Mr Justice Pearson is diplomatic when he suggests Mr Baxter '… may not have seen anything at all'. But what a shame counsel for the defence did not see Joe Baxter's statement of 28th July, because with careful cross-examination it might have emerged that Mr Baxter was lying, but more importantly it might have shown the reason why he was lying.

In fairness to Mr Baxter he could still have been mistaken about the weapon and be one of those people who would swear black was white rather than admit he was wrong. In a statement made a couple of days after his original statement of 28th July, he made a further statement in which the 12 bore shot gun was shown to him and he said categorically that he hadn't seen this weapon before. But he went on to say that on 30th July when he made this further statement, that the police also showed him a .22 air rifle which was similar to the weapon he saw in the toolbox (the toolbox was large — it took two men to lift it) but he couldn't be certain that it was the same. He was also shown a Webley Scott air pistol, but although the shape was similar it was, he said, definitely not the weapon he saw, because the weapon he saw had rust on the barrel.

On Mr Baxter's evidence, Mr Justice Pearson said in summing-up: '... or he may have seen a Luger revolver and it has disappeared since.' One wonders how Mr Justice Pearson could raise this as a possibility because as emphasised, Luger never manufactured a revolver. How could Mr Justice Pearson suggest Mr Baxter saw something that never existed?

There were several mistakes made in the police evidence, but there are two interesting contrasts of mistakes made by the two senior members of the police, DCS Metcalfe and DCI Jenkins. It also demonstrates how a senior police officer may have made an honest mistake but was too arrogant to correct it, or it is possible he was lying.

The first of DCI Jenkins' evidence was in connection with the weather on the night of the observation. In the examination-in-chief, Mr Hinchcliffe for the prosecution was pursuing the circumstances behind the finding of a bunch of three keys which had very little rust on them. The rust was so slight it ruled out the possibility of the keys lying anywhere in grass on the farm for longer than about twenty-four hours. DCI Jenkins was asked: 'On Friday, the 13th of July, had it rained do you know?' DCI Jenkins replied that: 'It had rained while we were on observation that night at the same place.' This was for the night prior to the shootings. In cross-examination Mr Hylton-Foster asked him about the weather again but as he had not referred back to the previous night it is unclear as to whether DCI Jenkins realised he was being asked about the night of Saturday 14th/Sunday 15th July. But the two men (counsel and the DCI) didn't pick up on their crossed wires and that the line of questioning was about the night he and other officers had testified that the weather had been dry and clear: that is the night of Saturday 14th/ Sunday 15th July. Indeed Mr Hylton-Foster picked him up on the timing of the rain which DCI Jenkins had described as being towards the end of the observation, just after midnight. Mr Hylton-Foster reminded him this was closer to the beginning of the observation; neither man realised they were confusing different nights. It is disappointing that Mr Justice Pearson or indeed the prosecution didn't pick up on this point. It seems DCI Jenkins had made a genuine mistake because he had been asked by the prosecution about the rain of the night of Friday 13th/Saturday 14th a good while earlier. It is unlikely such a slip was deliberate as it seems a trivial point and it does not appear to have been done with any apparent intention to mislead the court. Moreover, documentation also shows the DCI realised the slip and had later recorded the correct version.

In the case of DCS Metcalfe, however, there does seem to be a major flaw with what he claims to have said to Moore at the point of arrest. It is covered in detail earlier so there is no need to duplicate, the bare bones should suffice. DCS Metcalfe had approached the farmhouse at just before 5 am with PC Cleaver as his armed escort and arrested Moore. He insisted in cross-examination that Moore's version of what was said to him by DCS Metcalfe was wrong and his (DCS Metcalfe's version) was right. The central point was what Moore was being arrested for—Moore said that he was told a police officer had been hurt—DCS Metcalfe said, and insisted he said, it was two officers. Alice concurs with Moore's recollection in her statements (which never got to court). But, far more importantly, PC Cleaver said DCS Metcalfe had said 'a' (as in the singular) officer and PC Cleaver said this in cross-examination by the defence too. When counsel for the defence, Mr Hylton-Foster asked DCS Metcalfe he insisted that he had said two officers, stating: 'Oh no, I wouldn't make that mistake'. But he did make that mistake, according to the other three people present when he said what he said. It is sad that the opportunity to challenge DCS Metcalfe was not taken and his approach to the truth was not challenged.

Much has been made of PC Jagger's comments, statements, dying declarations and depositions in this book. So it is not something that needs too much discussion here, except for just one issue. His mind would have been trying to protect him from the trauma and associated fear of what he had witnessed — the gunning down of a fellow officer and being shot himself. As a consequence of this he could not be expected to say with any great continuity what actually happened, mistakes would have been inevitable.

As discussed in *Chapter 9* Insp Knapton inadvertently cast doubt on the time that PC Jagger's dying declaration was taken down. Though the time in itself didn't really matter, the inconsistency makes one wonder about Supt Foster and Insp Knapton. In court little was heard of either officer, Supt Foster answered questions about the identity parade. But if Supt Foster lacked accuracy about the timing of the dying declaration, then was his evidence regarding the identity parade also open to question?

It is not disputed that there was something being introduced into PC Jagger's arm from a drip. This means there was tubing going into his arm via a canula (special needle) conveying fluid from a bottle hung over the bed. Nowadays this fluid would be in a clear plastic bottle with clear plastic tubing, where blood, for example, would easily be distinguished from any clear liquid. In 1951, the equipment was slightly different — the fluid would be in a clear glass bottle and infused through thick red, opaque tubing. But it would be quite apparent whether the fluid in the bottle was clear and colourless or red and opaque.

Before surgery a blood transfusion isn't a medical need if the patient's haemoglobin levels (oxygen carrying capacity of the blood) are satisfactory. A patient's blood pressure is a good indicator, and as discussed in *Chapter 7* PC Jagger's was within normal limits. So if Insp Knapton did see blood being transfused it would mean he saw him sign the dying declaration *after* the operation. But Supt Foster timed the declaration as having been made *before* surgery. So, this suggests Supt Foster altered the timing of the dying declaration to record that it was made much earlier than it was — crucially before the operation and, therefore, *before the anaesthetic.*

Supt Foster was later in charge of the identity parade and if there is a strong suggestion that he had already manipulated one piece of evidence, then it would be difficult to resist the thought that he may have been less than exact with other pieces of evidence too.

CHAPTER 15

Misdeeds

It is quite a common idea that defence counsel goes to court in the hope that much of what the accused has to hide will remain hidden. In the case of Alfred Moore though, it was the opposite, it appeared to be the prosecution who wished to conceal evidence.

But what did the jury hear and what didn't they hear but should have? When asking any question a lawyer may think: What do I want to learn by asking this question? Or: By asking this question, what do I want people listening to learn? So when any question is asked there are two things to consider—what the person asking the question learns, and what effect it might have on the active observer or listener.

There are all sorts of rules and regulations to observe in court, but one thing is certain and that is counsel will use everything in his or her power to convince the jury that their argument is the correct one. There are different rules for examination-in-chief, where the witness is usually called to bolster the evidence of whatever side's counsel calls him or her. After this comes cross-examination where there are less restrictions concerning the nature of the questions which are allowed, but they must still be relevant to the issue, i.e. whether or not the accused is guilty.

Leading the witness is where a series of questions are asked in which the answer is prompted, such as, 'Was the cat sat on the mat?', in which the witness is being made to assume that there was a cat, a mat, and that the cat was sitting on it. It may well be that the witness will be *led* into saying what he thinks counsel might wish him or her to say. One can place all kinds of inflections and use all sorts of cues to emphasise the desired answer.

In cross-examination counsel has more latitude and can ask any question relevant to the issue, in effect to challenge what the witness has already said in examination-in-chief. As with members of any other profession, barristers will be skilled in both and can switch from one to the other in the same way a doctor will use a different method to examine various parts of the body, or a mechanic will use a spanner instead of a screwdriver. The big difference is when a barrister uses such skills of examination they are verbal, out loud and he or she can pause for effect. An experienced barrister will wish to make a point—a perfectly true and relevant point—but the point is made in such a way as to leave an impression in the minds of the jurors. Here is Mr Hinchcliffe for the prosecution in cross-examination—he is using a mixture of leading and non-leading questions, and a little rhetoric:

Mr Hinchcliffe: 'It is true, is it not, Moore, that in the Huddersfield Royal Infirmary an identification parade was held?'
Alfred Moore: 'Yes.'
Mr Hinchcliffe: 'Were you given the opportunity of seeing the eight other men paraded with you?'
Alfred Moore: 'Yes.'
Mr Hinchcliffe: 'Was each wearing a mackintosh?'
Alfred Moore: 'Of various types, yes.'
Mr Hinchcliffe: 'Were you given the opportunity of objecting to any one of them?'
Alfred Moore: 'Yes, Sir.'
Mr Hinchcliffe: 'Did you object?'
Alfred Moore: 'No, Sir.'
Mr Hinchcliffe: 'Were you given the opportunity of taking up a position in a parade wherever you wished?'
Alfred Moore: 'Yes.'
Mr Hinchcliffe: 'Which position did you take up?'
Alfred Moore: 'Third man from the left, Sir.'
Mr Hinchcliffe: 'Was PC Jagger then asked to see if he could pick out the man that had shot him and Inspector Fraser?'
Alfred Moore: 'No; we first filed into the ward.'
Mr Hinchcliffe: 'After you have filed in the ward and were paraded before PC Jagger?'
Alfred Moore: 'Yes.'
Mr Hinchcliffe: 'Who did he pick out?'
Alfred Moore: 'Me, Sir.'
Mr Hinchcliffe: 'Were you given an opportunity of cross-examining him?'

Alfred Moore: 'Yes.'
Mr Hinchcliffe: 'Was the question you put, "Are you quite sure?"?'
Alfred Moore: 'It was, Sir.'
Mr Hinchcliffe: 'And was the answer, "I am quite sure"?'
Alfred Moore: 'Yes.'

The barrister can ooze charm as he or she is asking questions or suddenly change the inflection in his or her voice. In short, get the jury to focus on the point. Tactics, but perfectly permissible; fair under the adversarial system but inevitably geared to showing his or her client's case in the best light; whether this serves justice or not is debatable, as opponents of the adversarial system argue. The accused can elect not to give evidence and should not be put in a position where he or she incriminates himself or herself. But what is described above could be viewed as a form of manipulated self-incrimination. Modern-day changes allow inferences to be drawn from the accused's silence at any time from arrest to trial but this was not the case in the 1950s.

This brings up the point not so much of what was said by counsel, but what could have been said by counsel. It would help to compare the skilled cross-examination used above by Mr Hinchcliffe with an equally skilled cross-examination of a prosecution witness. But this did not happen.

It is possible that something could make its mark with the jury even though it was not actually given in evidence during the trial. A couple of important points Mr Hinchcliffe for the prosecution made in his final speech do not appear to be supported by the evidence, or are just simply wrong. The following passage is from the final speech for the prosecution:

> 'Now, whether the prisoner left his brother at 11.20 on the 15th of July, as the prisoner tells you, or whether he left his brother at 11.25, as the brother told you, whether the prisoner got back to his farm at 11.45 or at midnight…

So far in this passage the matters are undisputed — it seems a simple conflict of recollection between Moore and his brother and not disputed by either.

> You may think on the evidence that has been given that he must inevitably, if he used that footpath, as he says he did, have passed through the point covered by PC Jagger and Detective Inspector Fraser.

Moore did not pass the posting position of DI Fraser. Following the agreed footpath Moore would have passed approximately 70 yards to the northwest of DI Fraser's position, on a different path, where the footpath passes the south of the ash-tip and emerges to come away from the ash-tip at its north-eastern extremity (see *Figure 1* in *Chapter 3*). So Mr Hinchcliffe misinformed the jury.

> Again I remind you…

This suggests he has already made the following point when he has not

> …that PC Jagger was posted in this position a little to the east of the tip at a few minutes before 11.40.

PC Jagger was not posted to the east of the tip. He was posted to the south-west of the tip, by about 30 yards.

> How did he get through those two experienced police officers without being seen? I asked the prisoner not so very long ago, I asked him I think more than once, whether he had seen anything of the police officers, and his answer was "No, I never saw a police officer"; but you may think those police officers in the course of their duty, alert to deal with anyone who came along that footpath either going to the farm or coming from the farm, could not possibly have missed a person who was walking either way upon that footpath.'

Assuming, of course, that the police officers were where they had been posted; but the evidence suggests that at least one, PC Jagger, was not.

So, three evidential inaccuracies in the closing speech are noted above. One of these inaccuracies was blatantly untrue, the others misleading. But the prosecution had a problem here, and there were two things they did not want the jury to realise: the shootings took place a good distance from PC

Jagger's position; and it was well inside the invisible boundary of the cordon. Mr Hinchcliffe got around the problem by changing the evidence; also, of course, some of the evidence was withheld. It was a mixture.

So how could it be done? All counsel for the prosecution needed to do was consider the arguments in the case—the individual positions of the police officers on cordon duty and how those positions inter-related to each other to form the invisible barrier of the cordon. If Mr Hinchcliffe could play with compass points and include both PC Jagger and DI Fraser in the equation, he could set up the illusion that the murderer was skirting around the boundary of, rather than going straight through the cordon. This would place the two officers on a continuum rather than at two points of a triangle—the apex of the triangle being the murder scene well inside the cordon boundary. Of course, the prosecution would soon realise two things: firstly what the defence arguments were; and secondly, as I demonstrate elsewhere, counsel for the defence probably didn't have his mind completely on the job.

One has to question the ethics, of placing PC Jagger out of his true position. If a witness had offered this to counsel then it would have been rejected as unreliable. Yet counsel for the prosecution did it. How many of the jury members would then have a conflict of recall and think they had got it wrong the first time? When, in fact, based on what Mr Hinchcliffe had said in his final speech, the illusion created that PC Jagger's posting position and the scene of his shooting were one and the same place was quite wrong. Nevertheless, that is what was established in the jury's minds, at any rate from leaned counsel for the prosecution.

Of course, in those days the police knew that the general public would believe pretty much everything they were fed, and on occasion they have been shown to have exploited this. Counsel for the prosecution could use this to their benefit. If one of the police officers had said that PC Jagger was posted to the south-west of the ash-tip, then the answer was simple, at any rate in the mind of the juror: he must have misheard that particular officer if it didn't fit with the overall police account.

CHAPTER 16

Doubt

It is difficult to understand how a system that allows the suppression or the changing of evidence can be seen as fair, but on the surface it seems that the legal system of England and Wales in the 1950s lent itself to such suppression (I discuss modern day developments later). Inevitably the question emerges, just how much truth was concealed? In the 1950s almost anything a policeman said was believed, but by the turn of the century a series of well-publicised cases had changed this. Since the 1980s there has been a trail of historical miscarriages of justice including cases from this era.

The right to silence does now seem redundant in its original form: when the rule was first introduced it was mainly to help the uneducated avoid incriminating themselves. Nowadays, due in part to manipulation by professional criminals inferences can be drawn from silence in certain instances. So the right still exists but the judge may well comment if it is exercised and direct the jury concerning the implications. In Moore's case, he did speak, even though he need not have as the law stood at that time. Because he did so this gives us the opportunity to see whether there is any evidence at all of him telling anything except the truth.

There is a way to go yet before the UK can say that miscarriages of justice are a thing of the past, but there have been many reforms. Two of these reforms are relevant here. One was a change in policy and the other, government legislation.

The first deals with identification evidence. In July 1976, two men were convicted of burglary and appealed, including a Mr Turnbull. In the Court of Appeal it was acknowledged that there had been miscarriages of justice in the past as a result of identification evidence. It was also acknowledged that such evidence could be considered sound and had led to proper convictions, but it was generally desired that the risk of erroneous convictions due to identification evidence should be reduced if possible. The Court of Appeal laid down guidelines[1] as to how a judge should sum up when identification evidence was relevant:

> 'If wholly or substantially on identification, the correctness of which is questioned by the defence, a special need for caution, and why a need for caution, should be given.
>
> A consideration of circumstances should be taken into account:
> 1. Length of time accused under observation by the witness.
> 2. Over what distance?
> 3. In what light?
> 4. Any viewing impediment—passing traffic or a crowd of people.
> 5. Had the witness seen the accused before?
> 6. How often?
> 7. Reason for the identification standing out in memory.
> 8. Length of time from observation to identification.
> 9. Material discrepancy of any description by witness.'

If the prosecution felt there was a discrepancy then any description taken by the police should be given to the accused or his lawyer—and here is part of the tightening up of the rules of disclosure discussed a little later. Also it was noted that when a witness was giving identification evidence about a person that he knew (i.e. recognised) there is still the possibility of error.

All of the above goes some way to measure the 'quality' of the evidence. If the quality is good throughout then the risk of a mistake in identification is lessened, but if it is poor then the greater the risk of a mistake.

Their Lordships concluded by pointing out that if

> '…an adequate warning is given then if the quality of the identification evidence is good, even if it is the only evidence, then the jury can be left to assess it. But if the quality of the identification evidence is poor (they instanced a "fleeting glance" or a longer observation made in difficult circumstances), the situation is different and the judge should withdraw the case from the jury and direct an acquittal, unless there is other evidence to support the identification evidence. But

---

1. *R v. Turnbull*, 1976, 63 Cr App R 132.

the judge should identify what evidence he adjudges supports the identification evidence. And the question of what supports the identification evidence can only be addressed by the judge. If the accused has not given evidence then his silence cannot constitute support; but the judge can say that identification evidence was not contradicted by the evidence from the accused. And the jury should take care if they reject an alibi.'

This was a change of practice, not a change of law. But coming as it did, it made any warnings formal and the judge was compelled to give a 'Turnbull direction'. The appeal court judges cited a report made by a committee headed by Lord Devlin. Lord Devlin had headed a committee set up in 1974 by Roy Jenkins, Home Secretary:

'To review, in the light of the wrongful convictions of Mr Luke Dougherty and Mr Laszlo Virag, and of other relevant cases, all aspects of the law and procedure relating to evidence of identification in criminal cases; and to make recommendations.'

The committee reported in April 1976. But some recommendations were watered down, Lord Devlin said later:

'The essential difficulty in identification evidence was that there was no way of testing it. The ordinary process of cross-examination and testing the story aren't available, simply because there isn't a story, there's just a bald statement: "I say that is the man". In the end it becomes you either accept her word or you don't; or his word or you don't.'

What the committee recommended was:

'Our recommendation put in to formal language would run as follows: A Judge shall direct a Jury that experience has shown that as a general rule, the chance of an eye witness, even when he himself is quite certain, making a mistake about identification is high enough to induce a reasonable doubt.'

A jury cannot convict if it has a reasonable doubt. Lord Devlin concluded:

'So that reasonable doubt has to be surmounted before there can be a conviction.'

The Turnbull Rules would therefore, if applied to Moore's case, induce a reasonable doubt, but it is also doubtful whether the case would have even gone to court.

The second major reform worthy of note was the Police and Criminal Evidence Act 1984 (PACE). PACE was an attempt to get a balance between the 'power' of the police and the individual and his or her rights. How it is relevant to Moore's case is twofold. Firstly it created a statutory obligation to record interviews. Secondly, it imposed a requirement for a solicitor to be present when a suspect is interviewed. Although identification parades have changed almost completely with advances in technology, there is now a need for a solicitor to be present unless the suspect chooses for that not to happen.

Over and above this, guidelines for identification parades were not what they might have been and problems date back to a miscarriage of justice during the reign of Queen Victoria when Adolph Beck was erroneously convicted on identification evidence after being mistaken for the true culprit.[2]

Considering PACE and post-1984, it is very doubtful whether Moore would have been charged let alone convicted. Forty-five years after his case the Criminal Procedures and Investigations Act 1996 made it obligatory for the police and the prosecution to disclose anything to the defence which may support their case.

The death penalty was suspended in 1965, abolished in 1969 and is now prevented by European law. The pro-hanging lobby would probably go cold at the thought of a miscarriage of justice, but when given a term of life imprisonment, the substitute for capital punishment, at least a wrongly convicted person can be offered an apology, compensation and be released. However, this doesn't begin to address the wider social, economic and other problems caused to both the wrongly convicted person and his or her family, the victim's family, and the public in general.

---

2. Beck was wrongly convicted of theft and fraud in 1896, solely on the basis of identification evidence which turned out to be mistaken.

CHAPTER 17

Saturday Night

There was a second strange occurrence on the Saturday night/Sunday morning concerning a firearm, but it was thought to be a shotgun. It occurred at about 11.30 pm and it was Frank Stancliffe who heard the gunshots. He said the shots sounded as though they came from the direction of the farm and although it does not say so in the records it is assumed he was at his own farm, which is about a hundred yards or so to the north of Whinney Close Farm. At this time Moore would have been close to his brother Charles' house having just walked him home, and some distance from the farm. This left Alice and the children at the farm. With the temperatures in July, it is likely that neighbouring properties would have windows open but there is no evidence that anyone else heard the shots.

The posting position of DCI Jenkins, at the bungalow occupied by Mr and Mrs Woodhead was over 400 yards from the farm. Mrs Woodhead would have been ready to receive DCI Jenkins at about 11.45 pm. But she didn't make any report of hearing shots and she was being vigilant about occurrences on her neighbour's farm as she was a confidant of DI Fraser. It's true that she heard the five shots at 1.55 am, but there may be reasons why she didn't hear any shots ring out at about 11.30 pm. DCI Jenkins arrived at her home at about 11.30 pm (all times relating to the arrival of the police at various places were recorded as 'about'; and similarly Mr Stancliffe's timing of the gunshot he said he heard). DCI Jenkins and Mrs Woodhead talked for a few minutes before Mrs Woodhead retired. The door from the house to the veranda, where DCI Jenkins was to position himself, was open. The night was still with no wind. However, the bungalow is to the west of the farm, whereas Mr Stancliffe's farm is to the north. The distance from the bungalow to Mr Stancliffe's farm is about the same as the distance from the bungalow to the scene of DI Fraser's and PC Jagger's shooting. But Mr Stancliffe said it '… only sounded as though …' the shots had come from Whinney Close Farm.

Retained in the National Archives are four photographs which show holes in a south-facing window of the farm. They show where small projectiles passed through the window. From the photographs it cannot be determined if the gun was fired inside the house and the bullets travelled outwards, or if the gun was fired outside of the house and the bullets travelled in. The police would have been able to examine the glass had they wanted to and answer that question.

Related to this, there was a peculiar statement in the collection of statements 'not used'. It was made by an Arthur Hartley, who was an electrician sub-contracted to do some work on the farm prior to Moore and the family moving in. He worked at the farm until the end of the first week in May 1951. During the period he had worked at the farm he had smashed a pane of glass in the French doors, which had been replaced by Jack Swallow. As far as Mr Hartley knew, the rest of the glass throughout the house was intact at the time of his completion of work. But, on the Wednesday after the shootings, July 18th, he was taken to the farm by a police officer who showed him an upstairs window at the front of the house. Mr Hartley said:

> 'I saw that the glass of the window was broken in three places as if it had been struck by some kind of missile. I am quite sure that this damage had not been done when I left the house on 8th May 1951.'

His apprentice, Michael Lodge confirmed in a statement that no other windows in the house were broken.

There is no record except that in Mr Stancliffe's and in Mr Hartley's (the electrician's) statements (but there is a mention of the bullet holes in a letter Moore wrote on the eve of his execution '… that there were bullet holes through top bedroom window in unfinished part of house when we first bought it' [sic]). However, what Mr Stancliffe and Mr Hartley say is not supported by further evidence, and there is no evidence to suggest the shooting of DI Fraser and PC Jagger and the holes in the window are linked in any way whatsoever.

So there is no evidence that the shots Mr Stancliffe heard and the holes in the window are connected to the shooting of the two police officers and nothing to tie them up with any cartridge cases found around the house.

In fact there is no evidence surrounding them at all. But it is strange that in a murder enquiry, where bullets and guns were central, there is no record of the police investigating the holes, if only to eliminate them. The police definitely knew about them as they were pointed out to Mr Hartley by a policeman — but it is not known which officer did this.

So it is possible someone fired a gun at the farm that night or on a previous night or at some other time. If there were shots fired at the farm, then who fired them and for what reason? If the nature of the holes could even remotely suggest a pistol, then it seems incredible that this line of enquiry wasn't followed up. But there is still a file on the case held by West Yorkshire Police which is unavailable.

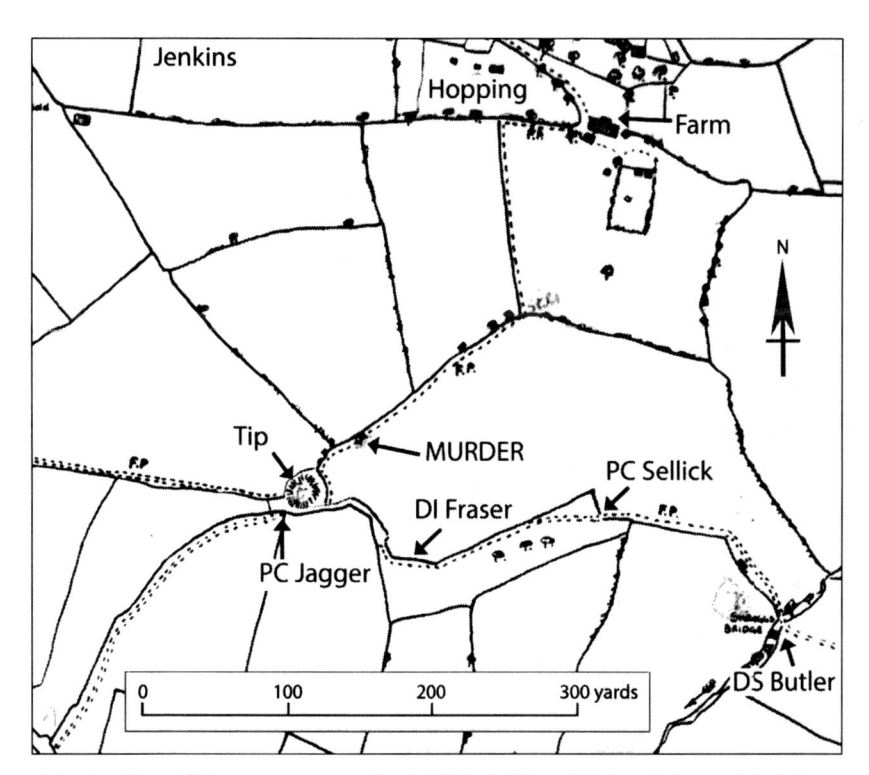

☙

Figure 2: Part of the map prepared by DCI Jack King (his hand drawn labels have been replaced with more legible ones for the purposes of this book).

In DCI King's map, the scene of the shooting is indicated by the label 'MURDER'. The dotted lines are footpaths. It is plain to see that by following the footpath from their respective positions, neither PC Sellick nor Detective Sergeant Herbert Butler would go anywhere near PC Jagger's posting position, but at just past DI Fraser's position and down the slight incline they would see the torchlight at the scene of the shooting, and would head for this. But both officers said that they went to PC Jagger's posting position, which doesn't make sense.

Similarly, the two officers posted to the extreme west of the cordon, PC Taylor and DS Lee would have been able to identify the area of concern as they arrived from their postings—on DCI King's map they would have entered the scene from the more northerly of the two paths on the left-hand (western) side of the map.

DCI Jenkins arrived from his posting to the north of the scene of the shooting together with PC Hopping; they had come straight down the field. DCI Jenkins took charge, and handed this over to DCS Metcalfe when he arrived. The other two members of the cordon party, PC Murray and Sgt Sadler also attended the scene.

Although there are details about the 'southern' team, and how they arrived at the brickworks and made their way north to the dispersal point at PC Jagger's position, there are no details available for the 'northern' team—that is DCI Jenkins, PC Hopping, Sgt Sadler and PC Murray—and how they arrived at their respective positions. This is a slight problem as information about PC Hopping and how he had arrived at his posting position would have been useful.

PC James Hopping was fifty-years-old and had been a policeman for a number of years. He knew Moore. This is significant because there are a few issues with PC Hopping that are worth discussing.

He had been the officer closest to the farm for the cordon observations—some seventy-five or so yards away—in a hen hut. DCI Jenkins was posted in the bungalow 180 yards or so to the west of PC Hopping. From his position, PC Hopping had a clear view of the driveway that led from Cockley Hill Lane down towards the farm, though he couldn't actually see the farm as there were trees in the way.

If Moore had committed the crime and went straight up to the farm then he would have passed within fifty-five yards of PC Hopping's posting position. As it was, when PC Hopping heard the gunshots, he got out of his hen hut and stood still to listen for '…about three minutes'. Some while later PC Hopping actually worked out how long it would take to get from the scene of the shooting to the farm — he timed it at four and a half minutes.

So what was the quickest and easiest way for PC Hopping to get from his position to the scene of the shooting, after he heard the shots? The simple answer to this is the pathway, due south down the field and then southwest — an approximate distance of 355 yards and all downhill. If Moore had shot the two officers then the quickest and easiest way for him to get to the farm would be the diametric opposite, north-east up the field and then due north up the other field. He would have passed PC Hopping who would have recognised him. However, it is recorded that PC Hopping did not take this route from his posting position to the scene of the shooting; from his position he went west and met DCI Jenkins in a field between their two respective posting positions. Then the two officers went down the fields together, not by footpaths at all — total distance about 420 yards. So not the quickest or the easiest route, but it would mean anyone who was negotiating the path from the scene of the shooting, in a north-west direction and then north up the next field would not be seen.

The instruction to the cordon members of what to do if the alarm (whistle) was sounded was to proceed to the point where the alarm seemed to come from. In a statement PC Hopping made on 30th September 1951 he says: 'If the alarm was given from any point during the observation I was instructed to proceed immediately to that point'. But he didn't, he paused for '…about three minutes' and then went the long way around. It is also noted that the seven other surviving officers from the cordon had the same briefing (the eighth was DCI Jenkins) and all would have been instructed to proceed to the point of alarm (where the whistle sounded). It is ironic that only PC Hopping describes how he didn't do this, and backtracking still further, it is just as ironic that his is the only statement that relates the instruction of what to do if the alarm was sounded. What strikes home is that an experienced policeman, who in those days would more likely than not follow his orders, didn't follow his orders. So why did he pause and then take a longer more complicated journey to the scene of the shooting? This would seem to be a crucial question, but was not put to him in court.

In a statement dated 16th July 1951, PC Hopping says:

> 'I then made towards Chief Inspector Jenkins' post and met him in the field between our two posts. ...together we made our way...'.

But in a deposition given 28th August 1951, he says he heard the shots:

> 'At five minutes to two...[and that]...[I] then made my way to the place where the two injured men were lying.'

In court, counsel for the prosecution seems to have controlled PC Hopping's evidence. Quite cleverly too as he questioned the witness previous to him, DCI Jenkins. This is what DCI Jenkins said as the shots rang out:

DCI Jenkins: 'I immediately put my things on, went into the fields, where I was joined by PC Hopping, and made my way down towards the direction from which the shots had come.'
Mr Hinchcliffe: 'Where was Hopping posted?'
DCI Jenkins: 'Hopping was posted in a hen house about 90 yards from Whinney Close Farm, in a field next to it.'
Mr Hinchcliffe: 'Would he be the nearest police officer to you?'
DCI Jenkins: 'Yes, he would.'
Mr Hinchcliffe: 'Is that hen house shown on the plan?'
DCI Jenkins: 'Yes.'
Mr Hinchcliffe: 'Whereabouts is it shown?'
DCI Jenkins: 'If you take the word "Lane" which is part of the expression "Cockley Hill Lane", and go straight down to the bottom of the plan across the road down through the building, there are three huts in a field. It is the first one of those three on the left of the plan.'
Mr Hinchcliffe: 'Is that what appears to be the bigger of the three huts?'
DCI Jenkins: 'No—the one on the left.'
Mr Hinchcliffe: 'The one on the left?'
DCI Jenkins: 'Yes.'
Mr Hinchcliffe: 'Where did you join up with Hopping?'

DCI Jenkins: 'Again looking at the words "Cockley Hill Lane", immediately below the word "Hill" on the opposite side of the road there are three trees, I think. It was in the field below those trees.'
Mr Hinchcliffe: 'That is where you met him?'
DCI Jenkins: 'Where I met Hopping.'
Mr Hinchcliffe: 'Which route did you take? Did you take the footpath?'
DCI Jenkins: 'No.'
Mr Hinchcliffe: 'Did you go straight across the fields?'
DCI Jenkins: 'We went down through the fields.'

Since DCI Jenkins said all of this on oath, what could PC Hopping possibly say after? When PC Hopping gave his evidence it had already been established what he did, so Mr Black could easily control what he said:

Mr Black: 'Did you, as we have been told, meet Chief Detective Inspector Jenkins in the field to the south of Cockley Hill Lane?'
PC Hopping: 'Yes.'
Mr Black: 'Did the two of you together go to the place with the two injured men were lying?'
PC Hopping: 'Yes.'

This is permitted because he was using facts already related. But what would have happened without Mr Black controlling the evidence is another question. And is Mr Black's behaviour intended to get to the truth, or was he simply making sure that Hopping's evidence agreed with that of DCI Jenkins? It does seem strange that PC Hopping would cross a field to meet up with DCI Jenkins, when the footpath south and then south-west to the scene of the shooting was only about fifty yards away.

But to take an amalgam of evidence (some from statements, depositions and sworn in court); and from various officers, it leads to other questions where the answers are not apparent.

Sgt Lee arrived at the scene of the shooting from the west, and took on the role of guiding DCI Jenkins to the scene. He said he made contact with DCI Jenkins from a '… nearby cornfield'. He saw the two officers and shouted to them. He said he '… directed Chief Inspector Jenkins and Police Constable

Hopping through the cornfield to the scene.'

In his statement, DCI Jenkins said: '…whilst we [i.e. he and PC Hopping] were in the middle of the field a light was flashed some 30 to 40 yards in front of me. I flashed in return. I said "Whose [sic] there?" I got the reply "Sergeant Lee" … Police Constable Hopping and I joined Sergeant Lee …'. So when DCI Jenkins and PC Hopping were '… in the middle of the field …' they pick up visually on Sergeant Lee's torchlight and could go directly from the '… middle of the field …' to the scene of the shooting. But this is contradicted by DCI Jenkins during his evidence-in-chief:

Mr Hinchcliffe: 'Did you go straight across the fields?'
DCI Jenkins: 'We went down through the fields.'
Mr Hinchcliffe: 'Did you go to the tip?'
DCI Jenkins: 'Yes.'
Mr Hinchcliffe: And then turn to where Police Constable Jagger had been posted?'
DCI Jenkins: 'Near there. Just above.'

So two officers and two stories but only one teller. One story takes them to the '… middle …' of the field before Sgt Lee guides them in, and the second story sees them go to the ash-tip and then '… turn to …' (not to where PC Jagger had been posted) where he lay injured. Which is the right one? In court the subject is again played down with the only directed questions about how DCI Jenkins and PC Hopping got to the scene of the shooting confined to DCI Jenkins. But if he was saying one thing in his statement and quite another in court then, again, a huge question mark must hang over the accuracy of his evidence.

Photographs taken later that morning show the corn in the field immediately north of the scene of the shooting reached about 2' 6". If two men had run through the corn then they would have left a track. The photograph may not be conclusive but it does not appear to show any track through the field where the men would have run. With all the commotion and the flashing of torches then it seems likely they would have crossed the field directly to the scene. When DCI Jenkins said he and PC Hopping were in the 'middle' of the field, then this might have been figurative, but, regardless, it might be expected that there would have been some trampling of a path on a photograph taken as soon as six or seven hours afterwards. Even at the point where DCI Jenkins, PC Hopping and Sgt Lee would have met there is no marking where men in police footwear had walked, run or stood.

Therefore, does this suggest an alternative explanation, i.e. the court explanation that DCI Jenkins and PC Hopping went to the ash-tip and then east to the scene? It would certainly explain why none of the corn in the field appears to have been trampled. But this leaves the question as to why DCI Jenkins and PC Hopping and DS Lee described in an earlier statement the activities in the cornfield.

Very little of DCI Jenkins' and PC Hopping's movements were an issue in court. They could have been cross-examined. Sgt Lee's evidence does not mention DCI Jenkins and PC Hopping arriving at the scene of the shooting. It is possible that someone might also have noticed the detail on the photograph that showed the cornfield the officers went through still had boldly standing wheat. But the question presents itself as to why DCI Jenkins and PC Hopping had taken two routes to the scene of the shooting; and again it has to be said that PC Hopping did not take the easiest and most direct route. And the question also presents itself as to why three experienced police officers made statements that must have been incorrect. If DCI Jenkins and PC Hopping arrived at the ash-tip rather than the 'middle' of the cornfield then three officers colluded to perpetrate an untruth.

If DCI Jenkins and PC Hopping arrived in the 'middle' of the cornfield and not the ash-tip then it is difficult to think other than that DCI Jenkins lied under oath. But do these two scenarios matter one way or another, unless this story is taken with PC Hopping's story that he made a journey across a couple of fields to meet DCI Jenkins and then a further journey down the fields to either the cornfield or the ash-tip. For then it is necessary to consider what might have happened if PC Hopping had taken the simple and quickest route to the scene of the shooting—he would have bumped straight into Alfred Moore making his way from the scene of the shooting to Whinney Close Farm—or he would not have seen Alfred Moore because he was not there.

If PC Hopping did meet Moore, not only would his orders say to 'intercept' him, but a shooting had just occurred, so his experience would have told him to hold on to Moore. But supposing, just for a moment, that PC Hopping did go down that path: the easiest most direct route to the scene of the shooting, and he did not see Moore coming up it. Then the case against Moore would have collapsed.

All of this: the knowledge that PC Hopping would have had of the farm; his longer circuitous journey to the scene of the shooting, whatever journey that was; the differing stories of DCI Jenkins and PC Hopping and where their journey took them; the evidential straitjacket put around PC Hopping in particular by the prosecution—all converge to place enormous question marks over this key aspect of the prosecution evidence.

CHAPTER 18

On Remand

From 17th July 1951 until the conclusion of the trial on 12th December that same year, Moore was on remand in the hospital wing of the prison and was assessed for any sign of mental illness or other abnormality. The outcome of the assessment was that he was well. However, the record of his time on remand is an interesting document, and although there are lines to 'read between' it does give some idea of his character.

Initially, Moore was admitted to the hospital and was interviewed. Interviews throughout were recorded by the interviewer, but the day-to-day observations were often taken from staff, so were second-hand. It is not clear what training the staff in the hospital wing would have had, or if they were just prison officers who were merely allocated there. In any secure environment it is likely that an individual will present themselves quite differently to how they would in other environments. Records were broadly speaking presented week by week.

Moore was seen and examined by the doctor on arrival:

> '[H]eart and lungs okay. Slight scratch noted on shoulder—probably the bed in the police cell. Non-eventful family history, no TB, epilepsy, mental illness. No past operations. Married, four kids, all healthy.
>
> No previous convictions and Alfred's career was largely uneventful until he took up the poultry farming. Served in the Merchant Navy during the war years.
>
> Not a big drinker, he liked the occasional drop of rum, and smoked. Hobbies, woodwork mainly but is an able cobbler and can sew and cook.'

The doctor's initial impression of Moore was that he was in a perfectly calm and matter-of-fact state, he added that, according to Moore, the charge was a 'misunderstanding'. The doctor noted that, 'If guilty, he is a very cool customer'.

Moore seemed to settle quite well during the first week; he was noted to be restless, but more often than not his sleep was described as 'slept well'. He was described in some relatively positive ways: 'quiet', 'respectful'; and also in some negative ways — twice being described as 'lazy' and 'fussy'. It was also noted that he appeared a little upset when the news came over the radio of PC Jagger's funeral. And he was described as 'worried' on a couple of occasions. But Moore was said to be reading a good bit on several of the days, so his level of concentration seemed quite good, but he was also described as a 'showman' and 'can put on an act'. In context, the comments about him putting on an act seem to be linked more to his level of worry, probably about the case; so he was possibly concealing his feelings rather than concealing anything the 'staff' may have enquired or asked him about. There were also reports of him talking 'sensibly on most subjects' or he was reported to be 'cheerful' and 'talks rationally about what he'll do when he gets out'. As for his social skills, he was equally described as mixing well, and not mixing.

His second week started with the statement: 'Appears to be an unfathomable prisoner. Converses well but does not mention his case.' It is possible he could suppress the thoughts of the case, but the suggestion that he was 'acting' does not play any part in the reports in the second week. There are a number of comments about 'being rational' in his conversation and he was recorded as appearing 'normal'. His excitable nature was noted but not in any detail; yet he was also described as a 'quiet sort of fellow'. His social skills are noted, that he mixed well, far more than not. Sleeping appears satisfactory-to-good and he was reading well, but twice was reported to be 'worried'. On 31st July he was in court for a further remand. 'Seen after return from court. Says no weapon has been found "as there isn't one". Goes on to say: "The police have a very thin case — if they dig anything up it will probably be something of Julius Ceasers [sic]."' The last comment for the week is 'Nothing to report'.

The hospital notes were all reports from what had happened the previous day, and the staff who had the major interactions with Moore didn't appear to keep any records of their own. There are also no records of who said what or the level of their experience or knowledge, or any indication of their place in the hierarchy. Neither were there any records available of what continuity of staff Moore was interacting with, though at that time people tended to stay in employment for longer so it is possible he conversed with the same people.

With regards to any medications he was receiving, there is again no complete record, so his sleeping might have been aided by sleeping tablets, though one comment does refer to an instance of sleeping medication. It is unlikely he was taking tranquillisers as they were so unreliable at that stage in their history (1952 actually saw a major breakthrough in psychiatric medication with the introduction of a new drug: chlorpromazine). But it is not possible to assess someone's mental state if they are taking medication which may calm that state, so it is unlikely Moore was on medication.

The following week he is described as 'quiet' and 'he reads a lot'. But on four occasions he is described as 'lazy', and 'not so fond of work' is added, but there are no details of what the work actually was. However, is it not a contradiction to say a person is 'rather a good actor' and soon after, in the same report, describe his behaviour as 'normal', 'talks normally'? Moore's sleep was okay but only an assumption can be made that he was eating normally, as it is not mentioned. After his appearance again in court for a further remand he is not described as 'worried' and was mixing with other prisoners normally.

As the term 'lazy' is used again, and quite liberally, it might suggest a shift rota by the staff, of one week when they liaise with the doctor and one when they do not, or another group of staff are on duty when the doctor 'does his rounds'.

It will be interesting to compare weeks 1–3 with 4–6. In week four Moore continued to read and smoke, and there does seem a shortage of things to stimulate him apart from this. The label of 'lazy' is used more often than pleasant comments: 'Not so fond of work' and 'Does not like work', but still nothing to say what this 'work' was. Despite his predicament he is said to be rational with 'nothing abnormal displayed' and is quite 'cheerful'.

He was reported to be '… more cheerful than of late' and also to be mixing a lot better and playing chess and reading, occupying himself the best way he could. Again he is said to put on a 'good act', but this seems to be a judgment rather than a statement supported by reason; but, of course, the information is second-hand. The comments about his level of industriousness are not quite so blunt, although the word 'lazy' is used. Towards the end of this week, his fifth in the hospital wing, he was visited by his solicitor and it was observed he '… seems a little worried at times'.

Moore continued with his routine of reading and smoking in an unremarkable sixth week. No sign of worry and he was mixing well; was said to be acting quite normally but also '… rather a showman'. The term 'no change' was used, but there is no mention of 'lazy' or 'lounging about'.

In early-September he saw his solicitor, which initially was said to 'cheer him up', but later he was observed to be 'pensive'. The next day he was 'cheerful' and acting normally and described on more than one occasion as 'well behaved'. He is still smoking and reading, but now he is described as 'studious'. The comments Moore was attracting now seem generally less negative.

The positive comments also persisted about how he talked sensibly and intelligently. Cheerful, but did appear worried at times, and who wouldn't be in that situation? But, out of the blue: 'A lazy type of fellow. Likes to be lazing about reading and smoking'. It is possible the latter comment said more about the person who made it than Moore, and in the type of institution a prison is, sometimes the staff (or a minority of them) might see in a prisoner what they want to see.

He is variously described as 'working well', 'cheerful and mixing', and 'shows above average intelligence on some subjects.' Intelligence is mentioned as often as laziness was in the earlier stages and a noticeable phrase 'seems a lazy sort of fellow' was replaced by 'seems an intelligent sort of fellow'. It is a shame that it is not possible to discover if the two phrases were used by the same staff member—although, on reflection, that is doubtful; certainly when Moore was reading he did not attract the 'lazy' judgment. The tables were turning.

By mid-September he had been in the hospital wing for over eight weeks. His sleep was reported as very good, occasionally restless but at this time appeared to have had a bit of a tummy bug. He was reading still and writing his defence, which suggests his mood was okay. Certainly the word 'normal' is used to describe Moore. One comment made, which may have been unflattering, was that he was '… very sure of himself' but overall the comments remained positive: 'shows above average intelligence on some subjects' and 'enters freely into discussion and shows intelligence'.

But he continued to be cheerful with reports of being intelligent and sensible. However, there are several comments about him seeming worried and although that seemed to pass quite quickly, he was facing a murder trial for which, if the verdict went against him, he knew the penalty would be death. But he mixed well and was observed to pick up in his mood quite well. It is interesting that anyone in Moore's situation, even if they knew they were innocent, would act in the way he did. So it is in keeping with this that he is said to have 'normal reactions to most things'.

The following weeks' reports had no apparent derogatory remarks. Moore was still reading quite avidly, which says a good bit about his concentration and this, together with the fact he was sleeping well, supports the accuracy of the statements that he is quite normal and cheerful. He was also said to be well behaved and mixing well, so there were no signs of him being withdrawn or isolated. He was talking about the future too, which is a good indicator to his mental health.

During his twelfth week on remand, he had a long meeting with his solicitor which didn't have any adverse effect on his mood. So the worry he was said to have had over the previous week or so seems to have passed, but it could possibly be that the staff of the previous week had changed, and the latest observations were made by different people. Even so, the general comments continued to be positive about him.

On 11th October Alice Moore was interviewed by the doctor looking after Moore. By now she had sold Whinney Close Farm and had moved to Heckmondwicke and had adopted the name of Mrs Hirst to try and protect their children. She said their marriage was good—Moore had a bad temper but only when provoked and he calmed down again quite quickly. Alice was said to be '… as cool as a cucumber'. The doctor wrote:

> 'She tells me she is "not really worried" as she knows her husband is innocent and adds "If I did not think so then I would be really worried."'

Moore was also interviewed, but it is not clear if this was a joint interview or both were interviewed separately. The doctor noted:

'Says he is not worrying as "it will not be long before my name is cleared." Says his wife and he are both quite confident of the outcome—"after all we know where we were."'

The following day Moore was interviewed again, and this covered his early years and looked at the reasons he had left home and went to live with his aunt. He was away for over two years and when he returned things were calm at first, but they didn't stay that way for long. Moore said his father came up to his room in a rage, having worked himself up, but there is no mention of why his father seemed so upset. A fight was imminent, but to stop it Moore said he kicked a window in; it was either this or he would kick his father. It stopped the fight but things were not good for Moore at home:

'I met Alice shortly afterwards and that helped me a lot. She hadn't a father and lived with her mother so we decided to get married.'

This courtship was possibly a little more romantic than described.

Moore was interviewed again a few days later, but in the meantime was reported as 'quite cheerful' and 'well behaved', 'an intelligent mixer who also enjoys reading'. Not apparently worried and said to be confident of the outcome.

On 17th October 1951, the doctor interviewed Moore's mother. She broadly agreed with the life history he gave and that he left home aged 18. She is said to have 'reluctantly agreed' that Moore's father was jealous of him and nasty at times. She did report that the father was violent to the son, particularly when he was much younger. As for Alfred's quick temper, she said this would pass off very quickly and he would be remorseful. She described him as always busy, giving the examples of gardening and the keeping of poultry. Overall the way she described Alfred did not categorise him as out of the ordinary—he had a quick temper and he had to be pulled up sometimes, but was always said to be 'good' to his mother and it sounds as though he was a generous boy. After he married and left home, his mother had visited him and Alice and she knew some quite private information about their financial status. Moore's wife was said to have run up some quite heavy debts, which had made him very angry and he was reportedly violent to her at this time, but this is the only time violence was used so far as she knew. Both of Moore's parents were shocked when he was charged with the murder of the two officers and they hoped things would work out. 'He is a decent boy.'

His reports from the staff in the hospital wing continued to be satisfactory. He was again interviewed at length on 18th October 1951. The doctor questioned him about his upbringing and education, as well as his job record up until the time he got married and moved to the farm. Then they discussed the charges and other witness depositions.

The deposition of PC Jagger said that Moore walked the path at 2 am, which he denied, it was midnight, or thereabouts, on his way back from walking home with Charles. Moore suggested that when PC Jagger pointed him out at the identity parade, it was a case of mistaken identity.

Moore's daughter made a deposition, and he said she had been questioned for over six hours. He added that the police were 'feeding the child's mind'. This can be supported because in the magistrates' court a lot of what was in the deposition was actually contradicted (this has already been described in *Chapter 11*).

The deposition of Moore's brother, Charles, he largely agreed with, but said in the walk back towards Charles' house, they didn't go near a sewage works. A small point perhaps, but Charles may have had a better knowledge of that part of Huddersfield.

PC Sellick's deposition was something Moore largely agreed with. He certainly switched a light on as he went out to see if his poultry were alright, but found things were okay and went back into the house; he was out for only about ten minutes.

DCI Jenkins mentioned the smoke issuing from the chimney, but by this time Moore had admitted he got up to burn some things.

PC Hopping noted the wetness of Moore's shoes, but he did come up a path through fields and he had stepped in a stream inadvertently on the way out with Charles.

Moore said that DCS Metcalfe only said one man had been hurt. He denied saying, 'I never got up again, lad'. And Moore further denied saying, 'Oh, my head is bad' or 'I want time to think. I'm in an awful spot'. He said it had been DCS Metcalfe who had told him he was on the spot after the identity parade. Moore said he had repeatedly asked for a solicitor but was not provided with one until the Monday afternoon, 16th July. And he added that the police did their utmost to stop him finding a solicitor until they had finished their questioning. It is difficult to dispute this.

Moore did appear to be very cooperative with the police. However, the description the police gave as to Moore's behaviour, or what can be picked up as the events unfolded, doesn't quite fit the character he showed in court where he was very particular and precise. When Mr Hylton-Foster asked him about the identity parade, he didn't want Moore to give any detail about the procedure:

Mr Hylton-Foster: 'Had you wanted to have a solicitor, had it been possible, to be with you then?'
Alfred Moore: 'I was asked if I did.'
Mr Hylton-Foster: 'Did you want one?'
Alfred Moore: 'I did want one.'
Mr Hylton-Foster: 'In fact, it was not possible for you to have one either there or on the examination of PC Jagger when they took his evidence?'
Alfred Moore: 'Well, I shall have to just go into a little detail, Sir.'
Mr Hylton-Foster: 'No, you will not.'
Alfred Moore: 'It may have been possible.'
Mr Hylton-Foster: 'You did not want, I gather, a strange one?'
Alfred Moore: 'That is right.'
Mr Hylton-Foster: 'But as it turned out you had to deal with the matter yourself?'
Alfred Moore: 'Yes.'
Mr Hylton-Foster: 'Had you any fear that there was any risk of PC Jagger picking you out?'
Alfred Moore: 'None whatsoever, Sir.'
Mr Hylton-Foster: 'Was it a dire shock to you when he did?'
Alfred Moore: 'Yes.'
Mr Hylton-Foster: 'And is it true you said, "But it wasn't me"?'
Alfred Moore: 'Yes.'

If Moore had gone into some detail about why '… it was not possible for you to have one (a solicitor) either there or on the examination of PC Jagger when they took his evidence…', then a little more might be known today about his thinking on this matter. As it was, Mr Hylton-Foster did not want Moore to share details with the court as perhaps he did not know what he might say. If Mr Hylton-Foster and Moore had not discussed this privately, and it was an important point, then it was a sad failure of communication between them, and an issue Mr Hylton-Foster should have had uppermost in his mind.

DCI Edington's deposition said Moore agreed he was satisfied with the way the identity parade had been conducted, which Moore actually denied.

As for Detective Officer Garnett's find of the spent cartridges, Moore said these were old.

Joe Baxter said he saw a Luger revolver in the toolbox, which Moore denied owning (not surprising: as described in an earlier chapter Luger had not manufactured one), and suggested he saw an air pistol or a folded air rifle.

As the interview with the doctor continued Moore told him that he had started his criminal career about three years before, and his last 'job' had been back in the early months of that year: 1951. He went on to say that DCS Metcalfe had twisted all of his statements in order to try and make out that he had been evasive (certainly for example DCS Metcalfe took the opportunity to illustrate Moore's alleged sinister behaviour when he described it at the point of arrest, which demonstrated the police's desire to show him in as bad a light as they could).

In conclusion, Moore told the doctor that he couldn't understand why he was picked out at the identity parade, and it had been someone else who had shot the officers.

The doctor noted that Moore, throughout his remand, had conversed rationally and behaved well; he had been quiet, well-mannered and cooperative. He spent his time reading, but had mixed well with others. There had been no sign of aggression at any stage, verbal or physical. His mood appeared okay and his concentration good. There was no sign of any mental disorder or defect and his intelligence was noted as good. Therefore, there was no reason to assume that at the material time, there was any impediment and he was fit to plead.

This took him up to the third week in October, and he had been on remand for about 14 weeks. Throughout the rest of October and November there were nothing but positive comments about Moore from the hospital staff, which contrasted with the initial assessments.

There are two comments made in the notes from November worthy of discussion. Firstly on the 3rd: '… always seems ready to give other patients advice on how to outwit the police. Obviously is very bitter towards the police'. Assuming Moore was innocent, then in consideration of the way he had been treated by the police there is no wonder he was 'very bitter'. Secondly, a member of the hospital staff had commented 'seems a crafty piece of goods'. However, there is no supporting information or context whereby this can be assessed.

In December, and right up to his trial, the comments in the record of his remand in the hospital wing were as positive as ever. It seemed he was harassed by another patient at one point but dealt with it appropriately. The report for 8th December reads:

> 'Very cheerful. Talked sensibly, and mixed well. Very confident of himself. Says he will be glad to start his case. Since admission here he has shown a big improvement both in his work and mixing. Very adaptable…'

CHAPTER 19

The Trial

The trial took place at Leeds Assizes over three days, from 10th December 1951. The clerk of the assize read out the charge to which Moore entered a plea of not guilty. Mr Hinchcliffe then made the opening speech for the prosecution, which was uneventful save for Mr Hylton-Foster for the defence, who interjected just as Mr Hinchcliffe was about to read PC Jagger's deposition. This seemed to be a taste of what was to come from learned counsel for the defence: 'I suppose I ought to ask if I might see the original deposition'—hardly confidence-inspiring. Mr Hinchcliffe called his first witness.

DCI King had prepared a plan based on the Ordnance Survey map for the whole area he felt was relevant, and it was a true representation; copies were distributed. He was asked a series of questions, mainly about distances between various points around the plan before focusing closely on the footpath south from the farm to the ash-tip and PC Jagger's position; and then further south to the cemetery and on to the village—the route taken by Moore towards the home of his brother Charles. DCI King also described the path east from the ash-tip to Shroggs Bridge, which took in DI Fraser's position.

In cross-examination, the defence focused on what DCI King remembered of the position of various objects around the farm, which didn't meet with clear recollection. He was then asked to clear up any confusion concerning whether footpaths were where he had plotted them in accordance with Ordnance Survey maps; and also what the meaning of 'stile' was in the local vocabulary.

Inspector John Little was a police photographer and presented a collection of photographs for the court. One enlarged aerial photograph demonstrated the accuracy of DCI King's plan but with only the farm and its immediate surroundings illustrated. Also produced were photographs of the murder scene; Insp Little clarified the position in the photograph where DI Fraser and PC Jagger were shot. But the only question about the relationship between that spot and the ash-tip where PC Jagger had been posted was: 'So it is quite close to the tip?' Insp Little answered: 'Yes'.

In cross-examination counsel for the defence ascertained the steep nature of the terrain and asked Insp Little about trees and the chicken pens, and how one of these was actually hidden by a tree.

Moore's brother Charles was called next. He had been at the farm with Moore on the Saturday before the shootings, working on the construction of a pig sty. He had intended to go home by bus at about 10.15 pm but missed the bus and decided to walk. Moore went with him. Counsel for the prosecution took Charles through the journey until he arrived home at 11.35 pm. They parted company some seven to ten minutes earlier when Alfred headed home, although by a different route from which they had come. Charles was also asked about the stepping stones across a stream where Moore claimed he had got his feet wet.

In cross-examination, Mr Hylton-Foster wanted to demonstrate the size of the bulge Moore would have had in his Mac pocket if it contained a torch and a revolver. Charles hadn't seen a revolver in his brother's possession and said he knew nothing about his collection of keys. When asked directly, Charles said he did not know his brother had burgled factories and offices on numerous occasions. Finally, Charles could tell the court there had been no prior arrangement that he would walk home or that Moore would accompany him.

Charles' wife gave evidence next to confirm when her husband had arrived home that night and how she could be so sure. Counsel for the defence did not ask anything in cross-examination.

PC Sellick was the first of the police officers on the cordon to give evidence. Counsel for the prosecution asked for clarification who the other members of the cordon party were and PC Sellick was then invited to discuss the route taken from the brickworks, adjacent to where the officers had parked their cars, up to the individual positions the various officers occupied. This time there was a more focused examination of PC Jagger's position, it being approximately twenty yards to the south-west of the ash-tip. PC Jagger was in position on the night at 11.40 pm. DI Fraser was posted to the east of his position, some eighty-four yards. PC Sellick then went further east to where he was posted and reached his position by 11.45 pm; Sgt Butler then went on alone to Shroggs Bridge.

After a short adjournment, counsel for the prosecution seemed to change the evidence. PC Sellick said he was posted at 11.45 pm, but Mr Hinchcliffe said: 'You had told the jury that you were posted just before 11.40 …'. Regardless of the specific time, nothing happened until approximately 1.55 am when PC Sellick said he heard the report of five shots. He thought the sound of the shots had come from the direction of the postings of DI Fraser and PC Jagger so quickly set off along the path toward their positions. He added that he heard the faint sound of a police whistle. At DI Fraser's post he paused — finding no-one there — but he saw torchlight a short way off so made towards that. He found PC Jagger and DI Fraser lying on the ground and a quick examination of DI Fraser made him think he was dead. PC Sellick then approached PC Jagger, who was alive and conscious. Mr Hinchcliffe prevented PC Sellick from telling the court anything of what PC Jagger said to him, but allowed him to describe the quick reconnaissance he made of the farm; he could see no movement at all. PC Sellick returned to the scene and simultaneously blew his whistle. When he got there, Sgt Butler had arrived.

PC Sellick was asked to plot on the plan the precise location the murder took place. He marked it in pencil and it was handed to the judge. There then followed an odd turn in the examination of his evidence. Instead of the plan being handed to the jury — the judge asked Mr Hinchcliffe if that was what he wished — Mr Hinchcliffe suggested the jury could see it from across the courtroom, so it was held up for them by PC Sellick. The judge told the jury that it was a very small mark showing the actual location.

It does seem strange that Mr Hinchcliffe thought the jury could see so clearly over a few yards, especially when it would only have taken a moment for them to look closely at the map. It may then have been clearer to them that the shootings occurred approximately sixty-six yards to the north-east of PC Jagger's position. Perhaps the jury members would have wondered how, if PC Jagger was posted sixty-six yards from where the shooting took place, it took place where it did.

Mr Hinchcliffe was quick to move things on, and asked PC Sellick to consider two of the photographs of the scene of the shooting to make sure he was plotting things correctly — he thought he was. Mr Hylton-Foster for the defence said the photographs did not show the same point—the judge disagreed, saying they did show '... quite the same point', and that was as far as any challenge or elaboration of PC Sellick's plotting of the scene of the shooting was going to go. Two photographs PC Sellick was shown were taken from slightly differing angles, but they both showed the same bush in the foreground and also the same bungalow with the veranda clearly visible in the distance—the posting place of DCI Jenkins. It was then agreed that the position of the shooting was where PC Sellick plotted it, and no question was raised why the shooting was so far from PC Jagger's posting position on the cordon.

PC Sellick offered some minor details such as lights going on in the farm but, as this was not challenged, it was passed over. He had also checked the timing of the walk Moore was said to have made on the night with Charles, all later agreed as accurate by Alfred. Mr Hylton-Foster in cross-examination seemed keen to know whether the grass had been mown down when PC Sellick made his timed walks—no, it had not.

A white hair had been found on Moore's coat, which the prosecution thought was similar to that of DI Fraser's. It might have been from his head, but Mr Hylton-Foster demonstrated that most of the officers had helped with the moving of the bodies, and had helped search the farm, or were concerned with the collecting of exhibits, so cross-contamination was likely. So the hair couldn't prove anything.

DS Butler was next to give evidence. He was posted to Shroggs Bridge on the far south-eastern extremity of the cordon. DS Butler explained that at approximately 1.54 am he heard shouting (he recognised DI Fraser's voice) and then shots were fired. He made for the scene and, when he got there, he sent PC Taylor to the brickworks to summon an ambulance and to have the superintendent informed. However, later in the examination he says he was sent to the brickworks himself to '... see about an ambulance'. This passed unchallenged. In his evidence earlier, PC Sellick had said he was the only one to flash a torch and blow his whistle, yet DS Butler contradicted this when he said he flashed his torch and blew his whistle too.

Next, PC Taylor took to the stand. He had been posted about 250 yards to the west of the ash-tip and he too heard shots at approximately 1.55 am. Mr Hinchcliffe though cut straight to the fact that PC Taylor had accompanied the two officers to Huddersfield Royal Infirmary in the ambulance. PC Taylor had been present when DI Fraser and PC Jagger's clothing had been removed and he had parcelled it up.

During cross-examination PC Taylor was asked about the knowledge of Moore's appearance and specifically what PC Jagger knew.

Mr Mr Hylton-Foster: '… I am anxious to know to what extent he would have known the appearance of Alfred Moore'.
PC Taylor: 'He did not know him'.

This is hearsay. It is understandable why the five officers who spoke to PC Jagger after the shooting were prevented from telling the court what PC Jagger said, but it is not understandable why the court was allowed to hear PC Taylor's response to this question.

Finally, Mr Hylton-Foster asked if he had been sent to the brickworks to summon the ambulance to which he said he had.

Sgt Lee gave evidence that he had been posted to the west of PC Taylor's position, up towards Daw Knowl on the western-most extremity of the cordon, some 600 yards or so from the farm. As with the other officers he heard shots at 1.55 am followed by the sounding of a police whistle, and made his way to the scene. As with some of the other officers he saw a light on at the farm. Defence counsel did not cross-examine him.

The officer in charge on the night of the shootings was DCI Jenkins. He was called next to give evidence. He told the court that the men on the cordon were carefully positioned with the object to observe the approaches to Whinney Close Farm to see if anyone went to the farm, or if anyone left. As the positioning had been so carefully considered, then anyone using any recognised footpath to or from the farm would have been seen by one of the officers.

DCI Jenkins had taken up his position at 11.45 pm and reported that it had been a moonless night with no wind or rain, and that visibility was about sixty yards. He explained how a person at a distance may have been difficult to observe as he may have just merged into the background.

As with the other officers on the cordon that night, DCI Jenkins heard voices followed by the series of shots at 1.55 am, so went in the general direction of where the shots had come from. As he made his way through the fields he was joined by PC Hopping who had been posted between him and the farm. When they arrived at the scene, PC Sellick and Sgts Butler and Lee were already there.

DCI Jenkins told the court about the recording of the scene; he made a sketch which when he offered it to the court, Mr Hinchcliffe asked him to just leave it 'in case it is needed'. The photographs taken later that morning were also scrutinised. Prosecuting counsel asked him about the positioning of various possessions: hats, a thermos flask, and a walking-stick. DCI Jenkins explained how these represented where the bodies of the officers were and how they were positioned immediately after the shooting. The two photographs showed the scene before and after all the grass and vegetation had been removed. His attention had been drawn by another officer at the scene to the lights showing in the house just as he completed his sketch.

At approximately 2.35 am the ambulance crew arrived; the police officers' main priority for that moment was to assist in getting DI Fraser and PC Jagger into the ambulance and off to hospital—the ambulance could only get as far as the brickworks, he explained, so they had to be carried down over the fields.

DCI Jenkins had remained at the scene. By about 4 am the light had improved sufficiently that the farm was just about visible and he noticed that intermittent puffs of smoke were coming from the chimney. At about this time DCS Metcalfe joined the officers at the scene and, shortly after, DCI Jenkins went around to the north side of the farm. The farm was described then as 'surrounded' by the remaining officers from the cordon duty and also re-enforcements, some of whom were armed.

After Moore had been arrested, DCI Jenkins went into the farmhouse and into the lounge area—he confirmed his position by referring to the plan prepared by DCI King. He discovered evidence of a recent fire in the hearth, so he raked some of the debris out to cool for examination. He said of the debris from the hearth: 'It was obviously paper'.

Prosecuting counsel then switched the court's attention to about 8.15 pm that evening when DCI Jenkins had received from a Police Constable Joseph Clark three keys on a key-ring. These are the slightly rusty keys which examination of the small amount of rust on them proved had only been outside for

24 hours or less. He handed them to the director of the forensic laboratories. More evidence was handed to the chief inspector which he explained to the court: a live round of 9 mm ammunition, a '… copper coloured bullet', all of which were forwarded to the laboratory.

In cross-examination, defence counsel focused on clothes found at the farm, a gabardine raincoat and a jacket. Sgt Sadler and PC Hopping collected evidence at the farm with DCI Jenkins. Defence counsel wished to clarify which police officer had touched which item of clothing and when and where.

DCI Jenkins was asked about his posting on the cordon, which had been on the veranda at a bungalow to the west of the farm. Then, there followed a misunderstanding as to rainfall on the night of the shooting (DCI Jenkins later recorded in the appeal documentation that he had made this mistake). He was asked, or rather it was put to him that he had said it had rained on the night of the observation. Even when defence counsel corrected him about the timing of when the rain fell (at the beginning of the observation and not towards the end) they still did not realise DCI Jenkins had been referring to the Friday/Saturday night and not the Saturday/Sunday night. This shows how a simple mistake can be made, which then risks becoming entrenched as a fact in a trial. There was a detailed weather report for the Saturday/Sunday night provided by the head of the local meteorological station for the weather for Huddersfield, including the Kirkheaton area.

Mr Hylton-Foster wanted to know about the debris pulled from the fireplace, but DCI Jenkins wouldn't be drawn to say anything other than what he had already said: 'It was obviously paper'. A rather bizarre exchange then took place, almost to the point of parody. DCI Jenkins replying to Mr Hylton-Foster:

DCI Jenkins: 'No. I will only say paper.'
Mr Hylton-Foster: 'Paper?'
DCI Jenkins: 'Yes.'
Mr Hylton-Foster: 'No sign of any effort to melt down revolver cartridge cases?'
DCI Jenkins: 'No identification of that at all.'
Mr Hylton-Foster: 'Anything like that?'
DCI Jenkins: 'No.'

Mr Hylton-Foster: 'No doubt a revolver is a tiresome thing to burn in a domestic fireplace, but no signs of an effort to burn anything of that kind?'
DCI Jenkins: 'Not that I saw.'

It seems surprising that counsel would think that a gun would could be burned or melted down in a domestic fireplace. He asked the chief inspector about a raid (unsuccessful) the police had attempted to attribute to Moore at the local brickworks. This didn't take the cross-examination anywhere.

DCI Jenkins then explained that, contrary to what Moore maintained, he had only seen him once in the cell, which was on the Tuesday after the murders, to take his fingerprints. However, DCI Jenkins gave evidence that he had taken a letter from Moore, addressed to his wife on the Sunday night at just after 9 pm. But he remained adamant in cross-examination that he had not seen Moore in the cells apart from when he took his fingerprints and he hadn't interviewed him at all. 'No' was his final word.

PC Hopping was the next witness. So continued the cordon member evidence — he had been posted to a hen hut approximately seventy-five yards to the west of the farm. He had a clear view of the lane approaching the farm. The observation, he said, was uneventful from when he took up his post at about 11.50 pm until 1.55 am on the Sunday morning, when he heard a total of five gunshots. He left the hen hut and moved in the direction the shots had come from, meeting DCI Jenkins in a field on the way. He later saw a light on in the farm. This part of PC Hopping's evidence has already been covered in *Chapter 17*, meantime he helped to search the farm.

PC Hopping found the crepe-soled shoes Moore had worn when he had walked a part of the way to Charles' house the previous night; PC Hopping described the shoes as wet through. He found the shoes shortly after 5 am.

In cross-examination he said he hadn't seen Sgt Sadler with Moore's gabardine raincoat though he confirmed he had been in the bedroom with him. He had left the farm quite early, but whilst he was there he had helped Sgt Sadler start to piece together an inventory. They had found some money and had counted it.

PC Murray gave evidence that he was a member of the cordon and had been posted to a small copse to the north-east of Shroggs Bridge on the eastern extremity of the cordon. He had taken up his position at 11.45 pm and at 1.55

am heard some shouting and five gunshots. From the scene of the shooting he had later seen the light come on in the farm. In cross-examination he said it had been his impression that the light had been on in a lower room and therefore someone (i.e. Moore) was awake in the house for whatever reason.

At that point the police evidence gave way to the medical staff evidence. When the two officers first arrived at the Huddersfield Royal Infirmary they were received by Dr Jessie Beard. Dr Beard confirmed she had been on duty and that the two officers were accompanied by PC Taylor. When she examined DI Fraser he was already dead so she concentrated on PC Jagger. It became clear that the officer was gravely ill so she called for her senior colleague to assess him. But she was able to give the court an outline of the wounds and confirm that the police photographs of the officers were how she had seen them.

Mr Hylton-Foster had no questions in cross-examination.

Mr James Hall Wrigley had been Dr Beard's senior and he was to oversee the treatment of PC Jagger. Mr Wrigley told the court that when he saw PC Jagger he was conscious, and Mr Wrigley was then asked:

'Was he able to give a good history of what had happened?'

At this point for the defence, Mr Hylton-Foster objected that the witness was merely being asked a question in '… support of the credit of a witness'. And he went on to say '… this evidence is not, in my submission, admissible'. Mr Justice Pearson agreed that the objection was '… theoretically sound'. But Mr Justice Pearson emphasised that '… it depends on what line is taken up by the defence'. Mr Hylton-Foster then said: 'I am unable to understand to what relevant issue this evidence is directed'. It has to be remembered that some of the statements had unquestionably been withheld from the defence, but even so, this was only a few hours after PC Jagger had been shot. It doesn't take an awful lot to imagine he is gravely ill and traumatised. PC Jagger, as has been shown in other statements, was inconsistent in what he said.

Why didn't Mr Hylton-Foster get the advice of someone who knew what PC Jagger had gone through and that the reliability of his evidence might have been open to question? There could have been a good defence argument regarding PC Jagger's capacity as a witness but Mr Hylton-Foster insisted of PC Jagger: 'No question arises as to his mental or physical capability to give evidence on oath, at this stage at all events'. It is difficult to believe Moore's own barrister said this, but that is what is recorded.

Mr Justice Pearson said again: '…I suppose it depends on what line is taken up by the defence.' And he later adds: 'On a possible line that the defence may or may not adopt…'. That seems to be as strong a hint as he dared give Mr Hylton-Foster. But Mr Hylton-Foster didn't take the hint. In fact he didn't cross-examine Mr Wrigley and said: 'May I say that to the best of my knowledge, information and belief in anticipation, there will not be any question of needing Mr Wrigley back.'

This was a missed opportunity. By not recognising the element of doubt which could have been introduced if PC Jagger's (Mr Hinchcliffe's examination) '…state of mind…' had been properly considered, Mr Hylton-Foster seemed to put a noose around his client's neck. He then tightened it by saying, 'No question arises to his (PC Jagger's) mental or physical capability to give evidence on oath, at this stage, at all events'. And by not obtaining the relevant medical specialists' advice and considering this 'line' of defence, and in suggesting '…there will not be any question of needing Mr Wrigley back', Mr Hylton-Foster effectively opened the trapdoor.

Dr David Price was the pathologist who performed post-mortem examinations on the deceased officers. There were a series of questions and answers about the bullet wounds and the tracks they had made through the tissues and organs. Dr Price was helpful too insofar as he could give a professional report followed by a summary in non-technical language that the court could understand.

In the case of DI Fraser, death was caused by:

> '…shock and heamopneumothorax…Chest cavity full of blood; that is the heamo side, the pneumo is the perforation of the chest wall and admission of air into the chest leading to collapse of the lung.'

PC Jagger's *post-mortem* explained the track of the bullet and the damage it did and led to. During the operation a great deal of faecal matter was found loose in the abdomen, which would inevitably lead to an infection (peritonitis) and death. Dr Price:

'...the cause of death was shock and toxaemia following peritonitis...inflammation of the lining...of the abdomen...and retro-peritoneal haematoma...a large loss of blood clot and haemorrhage behind the intestines.'

Dr Price concluded that the deaths of both DI Fraser and PC Jagger had been brought about by gunshot wounds.

When Mr Hylton-Foster rose to cross-examine Dr Price, the latter said he took samples of hair from Moore:

'Which as far as one can see, have no significance at all...Very trivial...'.

So concluded the evidence of the medical staff.

The police evidence resumed with PC Earnshaw. He informed the court that he had known both DI Fraser and PC Jagger for a number of years. He was present when PC Jagger was examined by Percy Crowther, who was an examining justice and had taken PC Jagger's deposition at Huddersfield Royal Infirmary on 15th July 1951. This deposition was taken on oath.

On 16th July PC Earnshaw was also present when Insp Little took the photographs of the deceased officers at the mortuary, as he gave guidance as to their identification. PC Earnshaw had also identified the bodies of the deceased officers to the pathologist, Dr David Price, and had stayed present as the *post mortem* examinations took place. Following this he received from Dr Price the bullets from both bodies and later handed these to the director of the forensic laboratories, Lewis Nickolls.

Mr Hylton-Foster had no questions in cross-examination.

Norman Black, counsel for the prosecution, made a submission that the foundation had been laid for the deposition of PC Jagger to be read at the trial, it having been proven and taken under oath. PC Jagger's deposition was then read to the court by Mr Black.

Thereafter, for the prosecution, Mr Hinchcliffe called DCS George Metcalfe. DCS Metcalfe stated that he arrived in the vicinity of the farm to take charge of the operation and investigation at approximately 4 am, and just as he was at a position on the footpath between the ash-tip and Shroggs Bridge he could see smoke coming from the chimney of the farm. From that position he went to the north side of the farm to Cockley Hill

Lane and then, at about 4.40 am, with PC Cleaver as his armed escort, he approached the farm. As discussed earlier there was considerable dispute as to exactly what happened, or rather what was said between Moore and his wife and DCS Metcalfe and PC Cleaver. Alfred and Alice said there was a short conversation about fowls and foxes whereas DCS Metcalfe said this didn't take place. It seems strange that the Moores would make this up, unless the whole scenario is to discredit Moore's evidence; DCS Metcalfe swore blind he said two officers had been shot.

However, in his evidence, PC Cleaver refers to DCS Metcalfe mentioning 'a' police officer which makes one seriously consider the integrity of DCS Metcalfe's evidence: in his summing-up Mr Justice Pearson said DCS Metcalfe's evidence was supported by PC Cleaver, when in fact it was not.

DCS Metcalfe said that when Moore was perceived to drop his guard he took hold of him and PC Cleaver handcuffed him.

Alice was said to be upset and offered to get Moore a solicitor, Mr Eaton-Smith, and Moore allegedly said: 'Eaton-Smith can't help me in this.' He was cautioned and asked: 'Where is the firearm.' To this question there is no quoted verbal response from Moore but non-verbal responses were also not noted, such as shaking of head, surprised facial expression, shrugging of shoulders or such like.

Moore was taken to Huddersfield Police Station. At 8.15 am that morning he was seen by DCS Metcalfe accompanied by DCI Edington. In court, questioning continued:

Mr Hinchcliffe: 'What did you do?'
DCS Metcalfe: 'I cautioned him and I then told him that at about two am that morning Detective Inspector Fraser and Police Constable Jagger were keeping observation in plain clothes in a field adjoining his house and smallholding when they were shot. I told him that the inspector was dead and that the constable was in a critical condition.'
Mr Hinchcliffe: 'Did the prisoner say anything?'
DCS Metcalfe: 'He said, "I went to bed with Mrs Moore... about 12 o'clock within a quarter of an hour each way. I never got up again, lad."'

Moore had been asked to account for the smoke coming from the chimney at approximately 4 am and knew he was stuck there. So he replied, continued DCS Metcalfe, by saying, 'If you must know, I got up to burn some rubbish'. Thereafter Moore refused to answer questions without his solicitor present and complained of a headache.

Moore was seen again by the same two officers at 3.30 pm when they announced they were going to place him on an identity parade, to which he again stated he wanted a solicitor. The two officers returned twenty minutes later to tell him they were unable to contact the solicitor he wanted. Allegedly, so the police claimed Moore was offered another solicitor but declined.

DCS Metcalfe's evidence continued. The clothes Moore had worn on the previous night, as vouched for in evidence by his brother Charles, and obtained by Sgt Sadler were produced and there followed some focus on what he had worn.

After the identity parade Moore was seen again by DCS Metcalfe at about 5.20 pm in Huddersfield Royal Infirmary. He was then formally charged with the murder of DI Fraser to which he responded: 'How could it be me? I've told you I was in bed.'

After the identity parade and makeshift magistrates court Moore was returned to the cells. The items of clothing he had worn for this were officially listed as exhibits and were returned to Sgt Sadler.

DCS Metcalfe explained some of the problems the police encountered in the farmhouse which, he said, was impossible to search properly and thoroughly unless it was pulled down. The same was to be said about the outside, it had numerous difficulties: a copse, ditches and dykes, overgrown hedges and a considerable pile of tippings.

This almost concluded the examination-in-chief of the chief superintendent but before Mr Justice Pearson wrapped up the first day's session, DCS Metcalfe was asked about the role played in the interviewing of Moore, whilst he was in custody, by DCI Jenkins. He emphatically denied DCI Jenkins had any involvement in interviewing Moore.

At the start of the second day of the trial Mr Hylton-Foster, for the defence, commenced his cross-examination. DCS Metcalfe confirmed that he was the officer in charge of the entire enquiry, and that he did not address Moore in the cells as 'Albert'. He also confirmed that nothing was found in the farm that had been stolen on the night of the shootings. Mr Hylton-Foster changed tack at that point and asked about the police's inability to conclude an investigation into the burglaries that had taken place in the Honley area. DCS Metcalfe confirmed this was so, but the specific details about just what had been stolen during this spate of burglaries he couldn't elaborate on.

There followed a series of questions about the searching of the farm; showing that there had been, at any one time, twenty officers — usually arranged in two teams. Local volunteers also helped with the search at the weekends as well as a group of men from the Army Engineering Regiment based at Ripon. The grass had been cut right down to help in the search:

Mr Hylton-Foster: 'And did you demolish a number of dry walls?'
DCS Metcalfe: 'Yes.'
Mr Hylton-Foster: 'And drain feeding troughs?'
DCS Metcalfe: 'Yes.'

The police searched, climbed trees and drained ditches for a fortnight, and all that was found were a few spent cartridge cases, a live bullet, a collection of keys and a number of small metal objects. But the place was full of possible hiding places. Mr Hylton-Foster ridiculed the idea of hiding a live bullet in a pile of rubble, when so many better places were available.

The cross-examination continued about Moore's clothes, before switching the focus back to where the live bullet was found. Counsel pursued the point that the pile of rubble had already been moved or 'raked over' before the search which revealed the bullet.

Counsel wished to consider the events at the point of arrest. DCS Metcalfe confirmed Moore had hidden behind the door. There was a flat denial that anything had been said in conversation after the question about Moore's fowls; there were no questions about foxes or the shooting of them. DCS Metcalfe was asked about his questions to Moore, about the clothes he had been wearing, and at what time he had got back to the farm on the night of the shooting.

Mr Hylton-Foster continued by stating that it must have been unpleasant for Mrs Moore, and how she was not comfortable with stolen property in the house — she wanted it out. DCS Metcalfe said: 'I would not say it is the best of times.'

Mr Hylton-Foster: 'In due course you took him away, and his recollection is, I put to you, not that you said, as you said yesterday, before leaving Whinney Close that you were arresting him in connection with the shooting of two police officers, but that in fact you only mentioned one man at that time as having been hurt?'

DCS Metcalfe: 'Oh, no. I could not make that mistake.'

But he could, and he did.

DCS Metcalfe was then probed again about whether he'd said two officers or one had been shot. Perhaps this question should have been directed to the other officer present, PC Cleaver. This would have cemented some doubt as to DCS Metcalfe's powers of recollection, if the term 'power of recollection' is accurate. As it was, Mr Justice Pearson simply used DCS Metcalfe's version in his summing up.

Mr Hylton-Foster put to DCS Metcalfe that Moore had continued to insist he was at home and in bed at the time of the shooting. Asked if this was his line of response to police questions, the reply was, 'Substantially, yes'.

The clothes Moore had been wearing again became topical as Mr Hylton-Foster started to work his way around to the identity parade. But Mr Hylton-Foster pursued Moore leaving the pair of flannel trousers out for washing and repairing.

The question of Moore's headaches was broached as he was said to have complained of his head being 'bad'. The headaches had been a part of his life since his youth, but they had never warranted medical attention. In the event, in cross-examination, little was gleaned that was helpful.

As for the firearm, there appeared to be a misunderstanding between Moore and DCS Metcalfe, so when it was discussed by a third party in court it seemed more confusing, especially to the jury. It also seems to have been assumed that Moore completely understood DCS Metcalfe's question about the firearm. But as he was (perhaps) not guilty of using the 'firearm', then he might not have completely grasped what DCS Metcalfe was talking about. There is no indication of any non-verbal response to the question such as shaking his head or shrugging his shoulders.

Finally, Mr Hylton-Foster makes the point:

Mr Hylton-Foster: 'And after the parade this is quite clear, is it not, he was insisting "But it was not me" or "It was not me all the same?"'
DCS Metcalfe: 'Yes.'
Mr Hylton-Foster: 'Insisting on that?'

Mr Hinchcliffe then re-examined DCS Metcalfe, asking him again about the identity parade. DCS Metcalfe reiterated that he was not present in the ward when it was held, but that he was in the infirmary. It had been Supt Foster who had conducted the identity parade.

A misunderstanding about the defence's line of questioning revolving around the use of coke brieze at Whinney Close Farm was clarified. The issue became less complicated, but no doubt left the court unnecessarily confused.

The conversation that took place between Moore and DCS Metcalfe at the point of arrest was discussed again, with DCS Metcalfe again denying he made a mistake. He maintained that, because two people had been shot, he felt it was important to get the suspect secured in handcuffs at the earliest possible opportunity. There were yet more questions about the flannel trousers Moore had worn on the night, which DCS Metcalfe acknowledged had been put in the wash.

PC Cleaver was then sworn in to give evidence. He confirmed that he had been with DCS Metcalfe as he went to arrest Moore and he (PC Cleaver) was armed with a revolver. He had first seen the movement of a curtain in an upper storey window of the farm as the two officers approached. It was the south-facing bedroom window. Alice Moore appeared in the window after DCS Metcalfe had called out: 'Come out. We are police officers.'

PC Cleaver was in uniform. Alice asked them what they wanted, to which came the reply that they wished to speak to Moore. After DCS Metcalfe had explained what they wanted, Alice said she would come down. She came out of the door where the two officers were waiting. Moore was following her but he paused to put on his wellington boots. PC Cleaver said: 'Mr Metcalfe then spoke to the man who was hiding behind the door'. 'Are these your fowls?' and so on. Moore was handcuffed, to the alarm of Alice. Alice suggested she contact Mr Eaton-Smith, a solicitor. Moore replied: 'Eaton-Smith can't help me in this'. This might have caused a misunderstanding—with DCS Metcalfe and PC Cleaver assuming it to be a statement of guilt as to the shooting.

But two or three yards away, trying to deal with what was described as Alice Moore's 'hysteria', PC Cleaver could still hear what passed between DCS Metcalfe and Moore, and he was being '… arrested in connection with the shooting of a police officer …'. PC Cleaver said he then went into the house with Alice to take possession of the shot-gun, where he was also shown the evidence of a recent fire in the hearth of the living room by DCI Jenkins.

At cross-examination there is further mention of 'a' police officer having been shot:

Mr Hylton-Foster: 'Was what Mr Metcalfe said to the prisoner after you had moved two or three yards with Mrs Moore that he was being arrested in connection with the shooting of a police officer in Cockley Hill Fields?'
PC Cleaver: 'No, Sir. After I had moved Mrs Moore away, he said that to him then.'
Mr Hylton-Foster: 'But that is what he said, "in connection with the shooting of a police officer?"'
PC Cleaver: 'He said he was being arrested in connection with the shooting of a police officer.'

It is recorded that DCS Metcalfe denied this, and on oath. What PC Cleaver said though was in broad accordance with Moore's version of events. So, what is a mystery is why Mr Justice Pearson, later in his summing-up, claimed that DCS Metcalfe's evidence was supported by PC Cleaver's, when it was not.

PC Hudson gave evidence next. He had arrived at the farm after the shootings; at approximately 4.30 am. DCI Edington had posted him to overlook the house and the driveway. There was some confusion about whether PC Hudson was viewing the back or front of the house so he was asked to mark his position on a map, but this time it seems the jury were allowed to see it. He did observe some movement in the house and described it as 'a figure moving about', but couldn't say whether it was a man or a woman. In cross-examination Mr Hylton-Foster wondered if he had seen anyone putting anything down a slot by the rear window, but PC Hudson could not be sure that he had.

DCI Edington then gave evidence. He had gone with DCS Metcalfe to the cells at about 8.15 am on the Sunday morning, and together they were to interview Moore. During this interview DCI Edington kept notes so had these to refer to. According to his record, Moore had said he had gone to bed at about midnight but didn't get up again. DCS Metcalfe then asked him about the smoke seen coming out of the chimney, Moore knew he was stuck as he had been destroying proceeds of robberies and could only say he had got up to burn some rubbish. DCS Metcalfe quickly moved the interview on and asked Moore about guns and firearms. But Moore didn't answer immediately and said he wanted time to think. It must be noted that Moore's account of this is different, but little of note then happened in this interview.

At about 3.30 pm that afternoon, the two officers went back to Moore's cell. They wanted to discuss the proposed identity parade, but Moore wanted his solicitor present. DCS Metcalfe and DCI Edington explained that they would try to contact the solicitor he had requested. However, after about twenty minutes, they returned to the cell to advise him they had been unable to contact the solicitor. He said he would speak to his solicitor the following day—Monday.

The two officers then listed the clothes Moore had worn on the Saturday night. He agreed with what they said he had been wearing. Thereafter he got dressed ready for the identity parade. They then went to the Huddersfield Royal Infirmary and got there just before 5 pm.

After the identity parade he was formally charged and DCI Edington escorted Moore back to the cells at the police station. When charged he had said: 'How could it be me? I told you I was in bed.'

Mr Hylton-Foster then cross-examined. He asked DCI Edington if that had been Moore's plea throughout, that he had been in the house since he got back from seeing Charles home at around midnight. He said that, substantially, that is what Moore had said. Moore insisted that he had as much right to be believed as PC Jagger.

Mr Hylton-Foster asked a series of questions about the preparation for the identity parade; he especially wanted to discuss the clothes Moore had worn the night before; around the time of the shooting. But, by that time, in the cells, Moore was complaining of headaches. DCI Edington said he observed Moore to be stressed.

Supt Foster next gave evidence. He confirmed he had conducted the identity parade at Huddersfield Royal Infirmary, and with him was DI Bradley. Supt Foster confirmed that Moore wore a raincoat, flannel trousers and a sports jacket. There were eight other men on the parade who were all dressed similarly (this is not wholly confirmed by the Identity Parade Record form). Moore was below average height and balding, but there is no record of how tall the other men were. Supt Foster said that, in the parade, PC Jagger had pointed at the prisoner. There then followed the counting procedure and either of the 'methods' used at the identity parade could be open to abuse, but Moore allegedly said after the parade when asked if he was satisfied with the way it was conducted: 'Yes. But it wasn't me.' Moore always denied saying this or that he was 'happy' with the way the parade had been conducted.

In cross-examination counsel for the defence asked about a photograph the police had of Moore. This was several years old. The superintendent confirmed the West Riding Constabulary had such a photograph, but knew little else about it other than its existence.

Mr Hinchcliffe re-examined the witness but only to ask if Moore had wished to shave before the identity parade and Supt Foster confirmed he would have been allowed to if he had requested it.

DI Bradley was next to give evidence. He confirmed he had been present throughout the identity parade of the Sunday afternoon—15th July 1951. The outcome of this examination-in-chief though was unremarkable. Part of the cross-examination of DI Bradley is confusing:

Mr Hylton-Foster: 'Did you help with trying to get the solicitor, Mr Webb Eaton-Smith?'
DI Bradley: 'Yes.'
Mr Hylton-Foster: 'Did you go into the cell with Mr Metcalfe at the time when it was necessary to tell the accused you had been unable to get hold of Mr Webb?'
DI Bradley: 'I never went in the cell.'
Mr Hylton-Foster: 'Were you standing about the door?'
DI Bradley: 'Part of the time, yes.'
Mr Hylton-Foster: 'Was it to you that the accused suggested you ought to try the Queen Hotel, which is a place where the gentleman might be found?'

DI Bradley: 'I never heard that suggestion at all.'
Mr Hylton-Foster: 'And something about playing tennis?'
DI Bradley: 'I never heard anything about that.'
Mr Hylton-Foster: 'Did you, Mr Bradley, at some stage handle the grey flannel trousers which the accused wore at the parade?'
DI Bradley: 'Never, Sir.'

Mr Hylton-Foster's questions seemed to relate to the evidence of DCI Edington, rather than the man he was questioning.

Sgt Barber in his evidence told the court he had found a bullet at the scene of the shootings on 20th July. He handed this to DCI Jenkins to pass on to the forensic staff. He placed an iron bar at the site of the find; there seemed little that cross-examination would uncover.

Sapper Leslie Gilbert from the 36th Army Engineering Regiment gave evidence next. On 19th July, Sapper Gilbert had been searching with his mine detector when he received a signal indicating metallic objects. Two keys were then found, one broken. Counsel asked if the jury could see the keys. On further examination, Sapper Gilbert said he had found the keys to the south of the farm where there is a small field, more of an enclosure, inside a larger field.

Sapper Gilbert's cross-examination was not very long. It established that there were ten members of the Army Engineering Regiment engaged on the search at Whinney Close Farm, and they were there for thirteen days. The records suggest that all they managed to locate were the keys Sapper Gilbert found. Moore was to say at the time that if they did find anything then it may well have belonged to Julius Caesar.

In his evidence, PC Clarke related that he was involved in the search of the farm and, at about 8.05 pm on the evening of 15th July, in a field to the south of the farm, he found three keys on a ring. The grass had, by now, been cut right down and he had been raking the cut grass over when he found the keys. In cross-examination, Mr Hylton-Foster seemed to spend an inordinate amount of time discussing how far the grass-cutting machine would throw the grass after it had cut it.

PC Clanton was an additional witness and he told the court that on 15th July he found what appeared to him to be an Army-type jack-knife. This was in the same field as the keys above had been found. There was a long discussion as to where, in which field, in which direction *vis-à-vis* Whinney Close Farm he was to make the discovery of an implement which seemed to have no relevance to the case whatever. Needless to say, the cross-examination yielded nothing of note.

On the evening of 19th July, PC Barclay was searching '… an area near to Whinney Close Farm.' At 8.15 pm he found a round of live ammunition. It was discovered just over sixty feet from the front door of the farm. PC Barclay placed a metal pin in the position where he had found the round, and this was photographed. The round had been in a pile of rubble which PC Barclay and Police Sergeant William Brown were searching: the search consisted of them moving the rubble from one place to another and sifting it though; it is unclear as to whether they had any apparatus to do this, or if they just used their hands. As the round was dislodged during the search it was not possible to say exactly where the bullet was when the search began.

Sgt Brown corroborated PC Barclay's evidence in examination-in-chief and cross-examination. This concluded the evidence for the outside searches, and it is strange that the sappers (who were there for 13 days) with mine detectors seemed to find a good deal less than police officers with only their hands and eyes. One reason for this was that the sappers were looking away from the scene of the shootings. Their search took them from the scene, up to the farm, as they were looking for where the gun may have been concealed on the route The Man was said to take.

Detective Officer John Garnett was a part of the farm search team on 15th July 1951. At about a 4.45 pm, DO Garnett, whilst looking in the only bedroom, searched the tallboy. On the middle shelf, at the back, he found a 9 mm cartridge case that had been fired. DO Garnett was very vague about what else he had found on the middle shelf: 'Small tins. A sock or two.' He did not smell the cartridge he found; a characteristic odour could determine if it had been fired recently, or an absence of an odour would suggest the opposite.

He was present when the inner wall downstairs was pulled down, and could detail the list of what was found to counsel. DO Garnett was clear that the items found had not been in the cavity for very long, and among them there were two 9 mm cartridges that had been fired.

When Sgt Sadler entered the witness box and took the oath, Mr Black, for the prosecution, could return the focus of the court to the cordon duty. He said he first heard a whistle being blown at about 2 am. He went off towards where the sound had originated from and finally found himself at the scene of the shooting. When he got there most of the other officers were there so, as they tried to help DI Fraser and PC Jagger, he assisted DCI Jenkins in making the sketch of the scene. As he was doing this he looked momentarily at the farm and saw a light go on.

Later, at about a 4.45 am that morning, together with PC Hopping, he searched the bedroom of the farm. Under the bed he found a pair of brown, crepe-soled shoes which he described as '… drenched' with wet. The shoes were covered in seeds on the top and soles and also there was a residue of a clay-type of substance.

Sgt Sadler also searched the wardrobe where he found a Webley air pistol, a folded brown jacket and the gabardine raincoat. He took the raincoat away and later, at the police station, parcelled it up in brown paper before he handed it to Chief Inspector Verity. It was returned to him shortly after to take to DCS Metcalfe.

There were a number of other things Sgt Sadler found at the farm: a starting pistol, an air rifle and a cycling lamp. He also identified the large black tool box that Joe Baxter (below) allegedly saw the 'revolver' in. He started on the long task of making an inventory of all property at the farm. At cross-examination it was demonstrated that, as he and PC Hopping had helped remove DI Fraser and PC Jagger and later went to the farm, then the likelihood of cross-contamination of evidence was high.

Joe Baxter was next to give his evidence. He had attended the bungalow in Honley where Moore and his family lived prior to moving to the farm. It was Mr Baxter who would organize the removals. This was done over two evenings and, during the first of these he had loaded up the hen huts and also numerous crates containing the poultry. He also took a large black box which Moore kept some of his tools in, but when Moore and Mr Baxter lifted the box, it split. Mr Baxter said he saw the contents of the box: he saw what appeared to him to be a German automatic Luger revolver. Mr Hinchcliffe asked him, as he had received small-arms training in the Navy in the war, if he knew the difference between an automatic pistol and a revolver: 'Yes' and this was 'a revolver'. He went on to describe it as 'dilapidated' and 'rusty'.

In cross-examination, the rapport between Mr Hylton-Foster and Mr Baxter was not good:

Mr Baxter: 'I said it appeared to be a Luger. I have seen Luger revolvers before and it just appeared to be of the similar type as a German Luger revolver. I have not had practice with German Luger revolvers. I was in the British Navy, not the German Navy.'

This was an unfortunate retort to Mr Hylton-Foster asking him why he was sure. It was a shame Mr Hylton-Foster couldn't gently extract where Mr Baxter had seen a Luger revolver instead of the confrontational:

Mr Hylton-Foster: 'This is a serious matter you know.'

Joe Baxter said he did not see the air rifle in the toolbox. So, to summarise Mr Baxter's evidence: he saw a weapon Moore denies having, and which Luger never manufactured; he didn't see an air rifle Moore did say he owned and which had definitely been manufactured, and was a court exhibit.

Dr Alfred Horace Mayes, a Master of Science and a Doctor of Philosophy, worked for the Home Office. He had made a special study of firearms and their projectiles. He had received the bullets recovered from DI Fraser and PC Jagger and also the other bullet that had been found at the scene of the shootings. He also received the spent cartridge cases which had been found in the demolished cavity wall and in the tallboy.

Dr Mayes could confirm all were 9 mm ammunition. He could also tell the court that all four bullets recovered from the deceased officers were fired from the same weapon, which was most probably a revolver; he also described why he concluded the weapon was a revolver. He also said the bullets seemed to have been fired from a gun whose barrel appeared too large for them, and so therefore the bullets had distinctive marks on them.

As for the spent cartridges, Dr Mayes did not think it was possible to say whether the bullets had been fired by the same weapon which had fired the cartridges. With no evidence forthcoming from the defense's expert ballistics witness Major Pollard, Mr Hinchcliffe seemed happy to simply let his witness speak. It is strange that if Ted Hutchinson, Moore's solicitor, had received a report from Major Pollard, that Mr Hylton-Foster didn't object. But Major Pollard had said he intended to tell the defence to '… leave well alone'. In the event, the cross-examination of Dr Mayes was merely used to demonstrate that Joe Baxter had been wrong and that Luger had never manufactured a revolver.

Lewis Charles Nickolls, the director of the forensic laboratories, gave evidence next. On the morning of 15th July he had gone to Whinney Close Farm early, and he was there from about 5 or 6 am. He examined the ashes in the grate in the lounge of the farm and formed the opinion that they were the residue of a hot and fierce fire, probably of paper. He had taken some of the remnants for examination and found them to be postage stamps.

Mr Nickolls then examined the shoes which Sgt Sadler had found upstairs in the bedroom. They were wet and had seeds over the whole of the shoe above the welt, and there was also some light shaley soil on the soles. The seeds could, and probably were, picked up on the path which led up to the farm from the ash-tip, and the shaley soil was characteristic of some soil around the farmhouse, and found in a bank of earth to the south of the house. However, as later highlighted, that soil could have got on the shoes coming over the earth bank after following the path up from the ash-tip when Moore got home. But as Moore claimed he checked his poultry stock on his return to the farm then the soil may have been picked up by his shoes at either end of the earth bank. The prosecution maintained that it was to the western end (when Moore had gone out to hide the live round: although why he hadn't put it in the cavity wall or left it in the revolver were not questions that were addressed). The defence explained it was when Moore climbed the earth bank at the other end of the southern aspect of the house, which was the route from the house to the fields where he kept his stock, that he picked up the soil on his shoes.

Mr Nickolls also examined the keys and the jack-knife found in the enclosure in the field south of the farm. They were, he explained, in about the same condition in court as he had seen them at the scene, with very little rust apparent. Mr Nickolls said the items could only have been in the field for up to about twenty-four hours but no longer.

On 17th July, Mr Nickolls received the clothing of PC Jagger. He identified an entrance hole which was consistent with the entrance wound found in PC Jagger's abdomen. He calculated that the shot was fired between about two and six inches from PC Jagger's body. On that same day, he received the clothing of DI Fraser. There were a number of bullet holes found. The most important was the almost contact shot which entered DI Fraser's body in the region of the left breast. It was seen to penetrate through all of his clothes.

Mr Nickolls also examined Moore's gabardine coat. He found vegetable fibres (cotton) and animal fibres (wool). There was also what appeared to be a human hair which was said to be DI Fraser's, but this couldn't be substantiated. He examined the bullets and cartridges, but had nothing to add to Dr Mayes' assessment; nor did he seek to question any of it. Cross-examination revealed he had found some chicken feathers on the coat. But it was also established by Mr Hylton-Foster that no evidence was found to link Moore's coat to a firearm, either recently discharged or not.

In summary, it was claimed by the prosecution that the evidence of the witnesses all converged to support the central identification of Moore by PC Jagger. However, not only is the identification made by PC Jagger open to question, but there seems little else to justify a guilty verdict. If anything the trial record/transcript, when considered with the statements and the depositions of the witnesses, reinforces the view that it wasn't what the court heard that was significant; it was what the court didn't hear. In the next chapter Moore's own evidence is scrutinised.

CHAPTER 20

Defence Evidence

Although the right to silence meant an accused person could choose whether he or she gave evidence or not, if Edith Thompson[1] had not gone into the witness box, she may well have been acquitted. Conversely, it is said that because Dr John Bodkin Adams[2] did not go into the witness box, he avoided the gallows. The right of silence has its critics and its supporters, but exists to emphasize that someone is innocent until proved guilty. Although in quite recent times the law has changed so that the judge can comment on the accused's silence and inferences can be drawn from it there is still no law that insists that he or she should speak in his or her defence. Under the origins of the original rule, the uneducated were also protected and could not incriminate themselves. So there have been inroads into the rule and maybe the time has come to further review its value, but in the immediate post-war period the rule certainly had its place.

Although at that time Moore was entitled to remain silent, he elected to give evidence, and the jury was given a first-hand study of the prisoner in the dock. It must be remembered that in those days the police were regarded with far more respect than they are today, and if a police officer gave evidence then the likelihood was that the jury would take their word for it. This was something the police were not slow to exploit. But one has to ask whether any police officer ever stopped to think if when convicting whichever suspect they could, it served the needs of justice; did it make the world a safer place? And was there any job satisfaction to a copper in 'banging up' any villain whether guilty or not? If there was, then the satisfaction the police may have gained from this case is definitely that they stopped a burglar, but whether or not they left a dangerous gunman on the loose is also a relevant question.

There was apparently a deposition made by Moore but it isn't in the archives and so couldn't be considered for inconsistencies. Although there

---
1. *R v Bywaters and Thompson*, Graham Hall, Jean, and Smith, Gordon D (1997, Barry Rose).
2. *Easing the Passing: The Trial of Dr John Bodkin Adams*, Devlin, Patrick (1985, Bodleyhead).

is a file still held by the West Yorkshire Police, this wasn't available at the time of writing. However, I believe it has been demonstrated that in this case the police bent the truth, the scientific evidence proved little, if anything; prosecution witnesses left the truth wanting, counsel for the prosecution changed the evidence and the learned judge got his facts wrong. So what can be said of Moore's evidence?

This time it was counsel for the defence who undertook the examination-in-chief. Moore answered a few general questions before Mr Hylton-Foster focused on the war years and Moore's service in the Merchant Navy. Moore had avoided his Army service (he was called up but didn't actually serve until after the War). It appeared that the police placed him under the category of 'wanted' for failing to report for military duty, and his photograph was circulated in police journals. They finally caught up with him and, after a Court Martial, he served a few months in the Army. The military authorities were satisfied that his service in the Merchant Navy was vital to the war effort; it was also probably more dangerous than Army service.

Mr Hylton-Foster asked Moore if he had ever used violence — 'No'. And did he have any information on who shot DI Fraser and PC Jagger? 'No'.

Mr Hylton-Foster: 'Had you anything to do with the shooting of Inspector Fraser or Police Constable Jagger?'
Alfred Moore: 'No.'
Mr Hylton-Foster: 'Do you now know who shot them?'
Alfred Moore: 'I have no idea.'
Mr Hylton-Foster: 'On the night when they were shot, were you yourself concerned with any crime at all?'
Alfred Moore: 'No.'

These are fairly straightforward questions, but even though Moore might not have had anything to do with the shooting of the two officers, his counsel may have been leading him onto dangerous ground. The scene was simple: an individual, in the early hours of Sunday morning, is on a path which leads to Moore's farm, and he is armed with a revolver. So the questions are obvious ones: where was he going? And why was he going there? Moore claimed not to have left the farm for three weeks until that night, and hadn't performed a burglary for several months, so had no new 'goods'. So it is doubtful it was a fence — a dealer in stolen goods — who was coming up to the farm. Assuming then, that the farm had been his destination, other questions present themselves. As I said earlier in this book I am not going to speculate on the actual identity of The Man but the question unavoidably arises about whether it was someone other than Moore. And why was he armed? Had there been other visitors in the early hours? Even though Mrs Woodhead from the bungalow overlooking the farm had kept a note of comings and goings during the weeks leading up to the shootings, even she might not have observed into the early hours. Although nobody had approached the farm on the previous night, or the Friday and Saturday night of the previous week, no-one knows whether or not The Man had been to the farm before.

Mr Hylton-Foster continued his examination of Moore, who briefly described his criminal career. He had burgled approximately twelve mill offices. His collection of keys was noted, and he was willing to admit that he had studied keys and knew how to modify a key's composition so it could be used as a skeleton key. He also had a large collection of tools in various places around the farm.

Moving on, counsel asked him about 9 mm ammunition. He said he had never bought any, nor had he ever been in the possession of a revolver. He had acquired some 9 mm cartridge cases at Malvern, an army base, about four years before. As he hadn't used the cartridge cases for any specific or intended purpose, they had circulated throughout the house. And Moore even thought that the majority of the cartridge cases were in the large toolbox where Joe Baxter said he saw a revolver. He described the two weapons that he had stored in the box — an air rifle and an air pistol, which had later been recovered from the farm. There was no attempt to conceal or camouflage this evidence.

Counsel and Moore focussed on his farming and he described his stock; he felt confident that he could make a living from farming. Moore explained how they had come to acquire the farm and that they were settled in the 'habitable' part of the farmhouse. The keys had been kept in a cardboard box in the kitchen, under the table, which was a place his children often played.

Moore confirmed that the jack-knife was his and he used it as a tool for maintenance, mainly for re-felting the roofs of the chicken huts. He was not quite aware of where it was on the night of the shootings, but assumed it was in one of the poultry huts.

They moved on to Charles' presence on the Saturday. That night Moore said he had not planned to leave the farm but thought he would walk with Charles '… just to stretch my legs'.

He had not taken a weapon out with him, but had taken a torch. The route, as Charles described it, was correct, and Moore left him, he said, at about 11.20 pm. He described his route back to the farm which took him a different way, but he had stumbled on some stepping stones across a stream on the walk with Charles so wished to avoid this on the return journey (he didn't actually say this, but its inference is apparent); avoiding a hazard would make sense. But largely, once he got up as far as the farm pathways, then the route back had been the same as the route out. He followed the paths up to the farm; he did not make a detour across any field. If he had taken a detour across the field it would have made his Mac wet around the hem, and there was no trace of this the following morning. This does support Moore's version of events. There is no avoiding the fact that Moore returned to the farm and in the absence of other evidence by the route he said—although at what time is something to be considered.

Moore said he had no idea that the police had put a cordon around his premises. He said he had met no one on his return journey, and he had nothing on his person he would not have wanted the police to see. He got back to the farm, checked on his hen-houses, which he did every night, and went into the house. He had a wash, put his trousers into the wash and went to bed. He would put the time of this at between 11.45 pm and midnight. Moore had put the rest of his clothing in his wardrobe. He got into bed and went to sleep.

He was awakened by Alice, as she could hear a whistle being blown outside; it was a 'shrill' whistle and he said Alice wondered what it was. She pulled back the curtains to look outside. They could not see much, just a light in the general direction of the south-west, towards the cemetery and brickworks. Moore said he went downstairs and out, but he could not see anything out of the ordinary. He put on his wellington boots and checked his stock, fearing poultry thieves. Satisfied that all seemed well he returned to the house, but both he and Alice wondered what was happening.

Alice was aware that there was stolen property in the house and, with the activity outside, her feeling of unease appears to have been exacerbated. Mr Hylton-Foster wondered what Moore did with it:

Mr Hylton-Foster: 'Did the question of police arise in this conversation between you and your wife?'
Alfred Moore: 'Well, yes, it did. With seeing all the lights and hearing the whistles, we had assumed there was something amiss.'
Mr Hylton-Foster: 'Ultimately, did you decide to do something about your stolen property?'
Alfred Moore: 'Yes.'
Mr Hylton-Foster: 'I do not know at what time you started on that.'
Alfred Moore: 'No, but it was lightening slightly.'

Moore went downstairs to start to conceal the traceable stolen goods he had acquired. He had no definite plan and he just happened to remember the crack in the wall by the window sill. He started to put the keys in there. He was unsure if there were any cartridge cases among the keys in the cardboard box; he was certain that he didn't put any of the cartridge cases into the crack individually. Moore described how he collected various items from around the home (watches, cigarette boxes) to put down the crack in the wall. Finally he put the box in which he had kept the keys on the fire.

Mr Hylton-Foster mentioned the stamps, which Moore said he had accumulated over time, and he had burnt them together with about $100 in notes. He said the whole exercise had taken only about a quarter of an hour. But then he said he started to think that he was perhaps acting hastily; after all, the police weren't 'bothering' him. He smoked a cigarette and as things outside had appeared to settle, Moore settled too. He looked out and could see no activity.

There was nothing so far in Moore's evidence where there was doubt about his accuracy and truthfulness. His assertion that it was 'lightening slightly' as he completed his concealment of the stolen property ties in with when the police officers saw the smoke issuing from his chimney.

The next that Moore and his wife become aware of any activity outside the farm was when Alice heard someone call out. It was DCS Metcalfe and

PC Cleaver who had come to arrest Moore. He said that at this point he had no idea that the policemen had been shot. They went downstairs and Moore paused at the doorway to put on his wellington boots. This does make sense if taking Moore's point of view, but if taking the police's position then they let a dangerous, armed man conceal part of his body—and surely that does not make sense?

There followed a short conversation. This is a list of the questions Moore claimed that DCS Metcalfe asked him:

'Is this your poultry?'
'Are these your pullets?'
'Have you had any foxes?', or, 'Do you have any trouble with foxes?'
'Have you been shooting foxes lately?'
'Were you shooting them last night?' The answer to that was, 'No'.
'Did you go out last night?'
'What clothes had you on?'
'What time was it you went out last night?'
'Have you a gun?'
'There has been an accident. Somebody has been hurt.'
'In your field. Have you a gun?'

Moore's answer to each question was confirmatory, or informative and not evasive. However, DCS Metcalfe later gave quite a different version but as explained elsewhere showed himself to be unreliable witness. So is there any basis to challenge Moore's version of events?

Mr Hylton-Foster then took Moore forward to about 8.15 am in the cells at the police station. DCS Metcalfe and DCI Edington had interviewed him. Moore said he agreed with the account given of that interview. In brief, he had said that on the night of the shootings he had gone to bed with his wife at about midnight; their children also slept in that sole-occupied bedroom. As regards the timing of Moore's return to the farm that night he said that the police officers suggested 'a quarter of an hour each way' vis-à-vis midnight, and he agreed this was as likely as not. He also quickly admitted he had initially lied about getting up again, trying to cover up for concealing or burning evidence or residue of the robberies which were in the house. He was not aware, or it simply didn't occur to him that smoke had been seen from the outside, but as soon as this came to light he admitted getting up again. As to the other interviews, Moore said he '... more or less agreed...' with what had been said about them in court. He described to the court the clothes he had worn on the night, which were not exactly the same clothes he wore for the identification parade—the trousers were different.

Moore said that through that morning in the cells he had three interviews—DCS Metcalfe was present for all three, but on a couple of the interviews he had different officers with him. Moore also said he had two interviews with DCI Jenkins, which DCI Jenkins denied. But it can be confirmed that DCI Jenkins saw him in the cells on the Sunday night—he took a letter from him, and also he saw him the following Tuesday to take his fingerprints. So, Moore did see DCI Jenkins twice.

The next topic for examination was the identity parade. Mr Hylton-Foster emphasised that Moore had been without legal representation both at the identity parade and afterwards at the taking of PC Jagger's deposition. But Moore was willing to go along with the arrangements as he had no idea at all that PC Jagger would pick him out.

Mr Hylton-Foster then had to back-track and discuss the lights that had been switched on in the farm shortly after the shooting. 'Yes', Moore had switched on the lights, as whistles had been heard; Moore and his wife were not sure of what was happening. Moore had got dressed, gone downstairs and put his wellington boots on. This line of examination petered out here.

Counsel went on to ask about Moore's brother Charles, talking about the children playing around the large beech tree to the south of the farm where some keys had been found. Moore said he didn't put the keys there or drop them, and the children did play with keys in the house as they were accessible in the box under the kitchen table. In answers to further questions Moore said he was not aware that there was a live 9 mm bullet on the farm and he certainly did not go to the pile of bricks and rubble and drop the bullet there.

There was still no absence of logic, plausibility or continuity to be found in Moore's evidence. Mr Hylton-Foster brought the examination-in-chief to its conclusion:

Mr Hylton-Foster: 'Have you done what you can in all your thinking to think of anything which would help to track down the killer of these two police officers?'

Alfred Moore: 'I have done all I can, Sir.'

Mr Hylton-Foster: 'Is it true that you said that you yourself were entitled to be believed as much as PC Jagger?'

Alfred Moore: 'I may have said words to that effect, Sir.'

Mr Hylton-Foster: 'Do you desire here on oath to protest your innocence of this shooting?'

Alfred Moore: 'I do, Sir.'

Counsel for the prosecution, Mr Hinchcliffe then rose to cross-examine. Moore said he had no sense of guilt in regard to firearms. Mr Hinchcliffe went on to suggest that, according to DCS Metcalfe when asked what firearms he possessed, Moore had said: 'Oh, my head is bad. Don't talk about it. It is awful.' But he had no recollection of saying his head was bad, and was clear that he did not say: 'Don't talk about it. It is awful.' He had told DCS Metcalfe what firearms he possessed and when Mr Hinchcliffe persisted, Moore retorted: 'I have just referred to that'.

Mr Hinchcliffe wasn't going to let it go, if Moore had no sense of guilt in relation to firearms then why hadn't he told DCS Metcalfe exactly what firearms he possessed? He had, in the cells. So Mr Hinchcliffe then asked him why he hadn't told DCS Metcalfe that at the house; to which Moore replied it was because he wasn't asked.

Mr Hinchcliffe: 'What did he ask you?'
Alfred Moore: 'Had I a gun?'
Mr Hinchcliffe: 'Is that all?'
Alfred Moore: 'Yes.'

The prosecution's role is to test the evidence. There seems little that Moore said that would not stand up to this testing. Mr Hinchcliffe moved on to discuss Joe Baxter. This witness said he had seen a revolver in a toolbox Moore possessed, but Moore did not possess a revolver; he tried in vain to get Moore to say he had a revolver but he would not. Moore would not be browbeaten.

This is a short section of the cross-examination. Mr Hinchcliffe couldn't move him:

Mr Hinchcliffe: 'If you please. Now let me ask you something else. You have listened carefully to the evidence, have you, Moore?'
Alfred Moore: 'As near as possible, Sir.'
Mr Hinchcliffe: 'It would seem that five rounds were fired by someone at these two police officers. Is that your understanding?'
Alfred Moore: 'I gather that from the evidence.'
Mr Hinchcliffe: 'If you please. Three shots fired at Fraser, and a fourth shot fired at Fraser that misfired?'
Alfred Moore: 'That is the evidence, Sir.'
Mr Hinchcliffe: 'One shot fired at Jagger?'
Alfred Moore: 'I believe that is the evidence, Sir.'
Mr Hinchcliffe: 'You know, do you not that 9 mm bullets have been recovered?'
Alfred Moore: 'I believe that is in the evidence, Sir.'
Mr Hinchcliffe: 'In all probability fired from the same weapon?'
Alfred Moore: 'I believe that is the suggestion.'
Mr Hinchcliffe: 'And a weapon that was not personally adapted for firing such bullets?'
Alfred Moore: 'I believe that has been said, Sir.'
Mr Hinchcliffe: 'Two 9 mm cartridge cases were found in your cavity wall, were they not?'
Alfred Moore: 'That is the suggestion.'
Mr Hinchcliffe: 'Is it true?'
Alfred Moore: 'It may be.'
Mr Hinchcliffe: 'Is it true?'
Alfred Moore: 'It may be.'
Mr Hinchcliffe: 'What do you mean when you say it may be true?'
Alfred Moore: 'There is just that possibility, Sir.'
Mr Hinchcliffe: 'Possibility of what?'
Alfred Moore: 'Of them being there.'
Mr Hinchcliffe: 'But they were picked out of the cavity wall by a police officer.'
Alfred Moore: 'Yes.'

Mr Hinchcliffe: 'What do you mean by saying there is just a possibility that they were there?'
Alfred Moore: 'I mean that at one time I did possess some spent rounds of that—of Sten-gun bullets.'
Mr Hinchcliffe: 'Were they in the cavity wall?'
Alfred Moore: 'Not to my knowledge, Sir.'
Mr Hinchcliffe: 'And a third spent 9 mm cartridge case was found in the tallboy in your bedroom, was it not?'
Alfred Moore: 'That is said.'
Mr Hinchcliffe: 'Is it true?'
Alfred Moore: 'It is possible, Sir.'

Moore wasn't present when the farm was searched. This was the general tone of the cross-examination, and the more Mr Hinchcliffe tried to make Moore say things, the more he simply retorted: 'That is the evidence' or 'That is said' or 'That is the suggestion'. It is possible that this did not make a favourable impression on the jury, but that will never be known.

There are a number of clearly identifiable examples of where Mr Hinchcliffe stated the obvious, in that he wanted to focus the jury's attention onto a specific point. Discussing with him the live 9 mm round:

Mr Hinchcliffe: 'Where had you kept that round of ammunition?'
Alfred Moore: 'I do not account for it.'
Mr Hinchcliffe: 'Are you saying to the jury that you did not know you had it?'

Mr Hinchcliffe had a number of ways to focus the jury's attention. This one seems to be legitimate. Another quite legitimate point was:

Mr Hinchcliffe: 'What are you asking the jury to believe today, that you did get up or that you did not?'

However, it pulled the jury's attention to the next few questions. Moore's lie, which he corrected as soon as he realised that DCS Metcalfe knew that he had got up and out of bed again, was about to be exposed. And Mr Hinchcliffe wanted the full impact.

Mr Hinchcliffe: 'Why then did you lie to Mr Metcalfe?'

He then changed tack quickly and completely. There followed a series of fact-probing questions, which Moore dealt with in a straightforward manner; the questions were largely about Charles' walk home. But it developed into a question of whether Moore had a gun.

Mr Hinchcliffe: 'And did you have with you the revolver that Mr Baxter says he saw?'
Alfred Moore: 'I have no such weapon, sir.'

It is surprising Mr Hinchcliffe would ask this when it had been exposed as incorrect, and more to the point, when Mr Hinchcliffe knew it was incorrect. But Moore wasn't fazed.

Mr Hinchcliffe then took Moore back to the return journey at the point when he and Charles parted. He left his brother at 11.25 pm to make a walk that took '… not less than 31 minutes …' back to the farm. Moore would have passed PC Jagger's position a good ten minutes after he had taken up his cordon posting, but he did not see him.

Mr Hinchcliffe: 'How did you get through the police cordon?'
Alfred Moore: 'I saw no-one.'
Mr Hinchcliffe: 'I hear you say that; but all the normal routes to the farm were covered?'
Alfred Moore: 'That is the evidence.'
Mr Hinchcliffe: 'And the route that you took was covered by Inspector Fraser and PC Jagger?

Actually this is not true; the area in question was not covered by DI Fraser. And from his position, in the darkness, he couldn't have seen the footpath Moore had been on.

Alfred Moore: 'That is the evidence. Sir.'
Mr Hinchcliffe: 'How did you pass through those two police officers?'
Alfred Moore: 'I did not see any police officers, Sir.'

Mr Hinchcliffe: 'Could you fail to have seen them?'

Alfred Moore: 'It is obvious that I failed to see them, Sir.'

Mr Hinchcliffe: 'Were you using your torch?'

Alfred Moore: 'No.'

Mr Hinchcliffe: 'Were you so familiar with the footpath that you knew exactly its line?'

Alfred Moore: 'Well, it is hard to miss, Sir.'

Mr Hinchcliffe: 'The police, you know, or some of them, certainly Mr Fraser and PC Jagger had taken the same route as you to the point where they took up their positions?'

Alfred Moore: 'I could not say, Sir.'

Mr Hinchcliffe: 'You heard that evidence?'

Mr Hylton-Foster: 'My Lord, I do not accept that is true.'

Mr Hinchcliffe: 'You heard the evidence given, did you not?'

Alfred Moore: 'I heard the evidence given, yes.'

Mr Hinchcliffe: 'Is there anyone that is living today that knows the time that you arrived at your farmhouse?'

Alfred Moore: 'Two people.'

Mr Hinchcliffe: 'Who are they?'

Alfred Moore: 'Mrs Moore and my... daughter.'

It is well worth noting the line, 'It is obvious I failed to see them, Sir'. Mr Hinchcliffe was not going to get Moore to say something incriminating. Moore knew what they had tried and failed to get his wife and daughter to say against him at the magistrates' court about the time that he had got back from Charles' and later about the (police) whistles and the lights flashing in the field below. So here Moore might be throwing down the gauntlet, and it doesn't seem a reckless act at all.

Then, at counsel's request, Moore put on the gabardine Mac and placed the air pistol (this was an exhibit in court) in the pocket. He then opened the coat and slipped the air pistol into his jacket pocket. It isn't clear what purpose Mr Hinchcliffe had in mind when he asked Moore to do any of this.

There followed a series of questions or points on the suede shoes, which didn't seem to establish anything. It certainly didn't establish that Moore's evidence was unreliable.

Moore said he later got up, at about 3.30 am for a cup of tea. Mr Hinchcliffe was keen to remind the jury that a fire had been lit in the sitting room. But he didn't think this would establish anything more incriminating than that Moore, by his own admission, had got up to burn some paper items from the burglaries. It transpired that a fire hadn't been freshly lit in the lounge but had simply been rekindled by him throwing on the box in which he had kept the keys. He also said he had later burned the postage stamps.

Slowly, Mr Hinchcliffe was moving around to the incidents at the point of arrest. But not before suggesting that as the time by then was about 4.40 am Moore had had time to 'play with', which didn't seem to have any effect, it merely drew a little more pedantic accuracy from Moore. The Moores thought that the police had come about poultry thieves. There had been some mention of the word 'serious' between the police and Moore, but Moore couldn't quite remember what the 'serious' actually referred to. Mr Hinchcliffe was now darting around from place to place in the evidence and from one time to another, but Moore still didn't seem to be fazed by this. He went on to explain that as the policemen reached the farmhouse, it had been Alice who went downstairs first. Mr Hinchcliffe continued, did she ask DCS Metcalfe what he wanted her husband for?

Alfred Moore: 'I suppose that would be the usual question to put, Sir.'

Alice had gone out to the two officers whilst Moore put on his boots behind the door, not deliberately shielding himself.

Mr Hinchcliffe: 'With the rest of your body shielded by the door?'
Alfred Moore: 'Yes.'

He had to put something on his feet.

Mr Hinchcliffe: 'I see. Did Mr Metcalfe say something like this: "Are those your poultry?"?'
Alfred Moore: 'He did.'
Mr Hinchcliffe: 'Did he then advance towards you, saying, "Come here"?'
Alfred Moore: 'No.'

Mr Hinchcliffe: 'Is that untrue?'
Alfred Moore: 'It is.'
Mr Hinchcliffe: 'Did Mr Metcalfe quickly seize you?'
Alfred Moore: 'After a conversation he put some handcuffs on.'
Mr Hinchcliffe: 'Who did?'
Alfred Moore: 'Mr Metcalfe and PC Cleaver. They both held the handcuffs. I believe Mr Metcalfe actually put them on.'
Mr Hinchcliffe: 'You say Mr Metcalfe put them on?'
Alfred Moore: 'To the best of my belief.'
Mr Hinchcliffe: 'Moore, you appreciate that, whatever you knew, the police by then knew that two police officers had been shot?'
Alfred Moore: 'I assumed that they knew that, yes.'
Mr Hinchcliffe: 'And you know, do you not, that that is what they had come to your farm about?'
Alfred Moore: 'I know that now, yes.'
Mr Hinchcliffe: 'Are you asking the jury to believe that Mr Metcalfe had a conversation with you about foxes and poultry before you were handcuffed?'
Alfred Moore: 'Yes.'
Mr Hinchcliffe: 'Where did the conversation take place?'
Alfred Moore: 'About 50 feet from the front of the house.'
Mr Hinchcliffe: 'Quite a friendly conversation?'
Alfred Moore: 'Quite, shall I say, a casual conversation.'

Moore said he had no idea that he was being arrested until the handcuffs were put on him. His recollection of his conversation with DCS Metcalfe at the point of arrest is different to that of DCS Metcalfe and PC Cleaver. But if the two police officers wanted to discredit Moore's evidence then this method would appear efficient.

The question and answer 'Is it serious?' and 'It's serious enough' were credited to Alice and Alfred respectively at the point of arrest. Though it is hard to see what if any conclusions can be drawn from this.

Mr Hinchcliffe: 'What was it that was serious?'
Alfred Moore: 'The fact that I had jewellery in the house.'

Mr Hinchcliffe moved on to DCI Jenkins' interviews.

Mr Hinchcliffe: 'When you went to the police station, I gathered from the questions that you're [sic] learned counsel was putting yesterday that you are telling the jury that you had a long interview with Chief Inspector Jenkins.'
Alfred Moore: 'There was [a] long interview. To the best of my belief, it was Superintendent Jenkins.'
Mr Hinchcliffe: 'When you say to the best of your belief, you know Mr Jenkins now perfectly well, do you not?'
Alfred Moore: 'Yes.'
Mr Hinchcliffe: 'Do you still say that you had an interview with Mr Jenkins?'
Alfred Moore: 'It is because of that interview, Sir, that I am able to recognise him.'
Mr Hinchcliffe: 'Are you making a mistake, do you think, between Mr Jenkins and Mr Edington?'
Alfred Moore: 'No.'
Mr Hinchcliffe: 'Mr Jenkins told the jury that he was not at the Huddersfield Police Station on the 17th of July. Is that untrue?'
Alfred Moore: 'I am not referring to the 17th of July.'
Mr Hinchcliffe: 'What date are you referring to?'
Alfred Moore: 'The 15th.'
Mr Hinchcliffe: 'Mr Jenkins told the jury that no such interview ever took place.'
Alfred Moore: 'Yes, he did.'
Mr Hinchcliffe: 'Is that untrue?'

DCI Jenkins did not tell the jury this: he did not say he did not go to the police station on the 17th. Mr Hinchcliffe got this wrong, which is more charitable than suggesting that he made it up, or Mr Hinchcliffe was changing the evidence (again). DCI Jenkins did not even mention 17th July or the Tuesday after the shooting in court except:

'I only saw the prisoner on one occasion when I took his fingerprints.'

This was on oath.

The 17th July or Tuesday are not mentioned in DCI Jenkins' sworn deposition for the court either. But interestingly, in his original statement, DCI Jenkins stated:

> 'On Tuesday, 17th July 1951, at 9 a.m. I took the fingerprints of the prisoner Moore. He signed his name on the form with his right hand'.

It is documented in DCI Jenkins statement that Moore gave him a letter addressed to his wife in the cells on the Sunday night, the 15th.

So it seems that, as well as Mr Hinchcliffe conjuring up some of the evidence, DCI Jenkins was mistaken, possibly being untruthful, he did see Moore twice.

Cross-examination is supposed to be based on facts; but more freedom is afforded to counsel in cross-examination than in examination-in-chief. But counsel can neither change evidence nor create it. Of course, if challenged, a simple 'I beg your pardon' usually gets them off the hook. But this is exploiting the jury's lack of experience in the mechanisms of criminal trials. It is therefore unfair on the jury, and is grossly unfair on the accused, and it does not serve the interests of justice.

Not surprisingly then, when Mr Hinchcliffe asked Moore if PC Jagger was mistaken in his evidence, he answered 'Yes'. And when Mr Hinchcliffe asked Moore if it was some other man who shot the officers: 'It must have been some other man, Sir.' Mr Hinchcliffe goes on to say that the man answered to the name of 'Moore', he whipped out a revolver, and twice police torches were shone in his face. Mr Hylton-Foster for the defence then objected, but Mr Justice Pearson allowed Mr Hinchcliffe to continue. But between bouts of changing the evidence, Mr Hinchcliffe led Moore through a series of questions thus:

Mr Hinchcliffe: 'It is true, is it not, Moore, that in the Huddersfield Royal Infirmary an identification parade was held?'
Alfred Moore: 'Yes.'
Mr Hinchcliffe: 'Were you given the opportunity of seeing the eight other men paraded with you?'
Alfred Moore: 'Yes.'

Mr Hinchcliffe: 'Was each wearing a mackintosh?'
Alfred Moore: 'Of various types, yes.'
Mr Hinchcliffe: 'Were you given the opportunity of objecting to any one of them?'
Alfred Moore: 'Yes, Sir.'
Mr Hinchcliffe: 'Did you object?'
Alfred Moore: 'No, Sir.'
Mr Hinchcliffe: 'Were you given the opportunity of taking up a position in a parade where ever you wished?'
Alfred Moore: 'Yes.'
Mr Hinchcliffe: 'Which position did you take up?'
Alfred Moore: 'Third man from the left, Sir.'
Mr Hinchcliffe: 'Was PC Jagger then asked to see if he could pick out the man that had shot him and Inspector Fraser?'
Alfred Moore: 'No; we first filed into the ward.'
Mr Hinchcliffe: 'After you have filed in the ward and were paraded before PC Jagger?'
Alfred Moore: 'Yes.'
Mr Hinchcliffe: 'Who did he pick out?'
Alfred Moore: 'Me, Sir.'
Mr Hinchcliffe: 'Were you given an opportunity of cross-examining him?'
Alfred Moore: 'Yes.'
Mr Hinchcliffe: 'Was the question you put, "Are you quite sure?"?'
Alfred Moore: 'It was, Sir.'
Mr Hinchcliffe: 'And was the answer, "I am quite sure"?'
Alfred Moore: 'Yes.'

There ended the cross-examination. Of course, the idea that Mr Hinchcliffe wanted to 'win' his case by fair means or foul is mere conjecture, as is the thought that the real killer may have been free to kill again.

But that wasn't quite the end of Moore's evidence. There followed a brief re-examination by Mr Hylton-Foster. He asked Moore about the growing apprehension Alice had, her feelings related to the stolen goods in the house and to the police. This was what convinced Moore that this property should be concealed.

Mr Hylton-Foster was also keen to try and get some idea of what Moore's Mac would look like carrying both a torch and a revolver. Finally, it was proved that the path Moore had walked up that night, the path on which The Man had shot DI Fraser and PC Jagger, the path on which the latter was posted, did not just go up to Whinney Close Farm, but went further north to Cockley Hill Lane.

My checking and re-checking of Moore's evidence did not show any examples where he told anything to the court that was not the truth.

CHAPTER 21

The Prosecution

The case for the prosecution was put by Mr G Raymond Hinchcliffe and Mr Norman Black. Mr Hinchcliffe was to go on to become a judge of some distinction who presided over some of the Thalidomide damages cases and was said to be rich in criminal judicial experience. In Moore's case he was pleasant and courteous, but it might not have been his finest hour.

In the opening speech for the prosecution, Mr Hinchcliffe said: 'The prosecution submit that the person who committed this murder is the prisoner in the dock.' So what evidence did the prosecution produce to support this?

There was a query surrounding the times that Moore said he arrived back at the farm (around midnight) and when the two police officers were shot (about two hours later); however, no evidence was offered as to Moore's whereabouts during this two-hour period; there were no burglaries nor reports of illegal activity. There were a few people around Kirkheaton at that late hour, but no sightings were made of a man of Moore's description lurking about the town.

There is no doubt that the material times for Moore and his brother parting, and Moore's arrival home placed him back at the farm after the police cordon had been set up, but there is a strong suggestion that a highlighted weak point in the cordon was where PC Jagger was posted. It is to be expected that Mr Hinchcliffe would argue that the police would tell the whole truth, but that could have been challenged by asking how in the world he got back to his farm through that police cordon. The answer would seem to be that PC Jagger was off position at least once and therefore only saw The Man after he had passed through the cordon. So it can be suggested that he didn't see Moore two hours earlier when he passed through, because he was off position then too. PC Jagger made a deposition but even that says, 'As I got near to him...', but the idea of a cordon is to lie in wait and stop people as they arrive at the cordon boundary, not go after them after they have passed through it. 'As I got near to him...' suggests a journey from the place PC Jagger was and the whereabouts of The Man at that time—it is a description PC Jagger gave as he made the journey from (his posting or) wherever he was, to the point The Man had got to. It does not prove PC Jagger was where he was supposed to be (in position in a cordon), if anything, it suggests the opposite.

As for the identity parade held at PC Jagger's bedside Mr Hinchcliffe said: 'You will hear that PC Jagger looked along the line of the nine men and without any hesitation picked out the prisoner.' As described earlier in this book he had to count along the line, so there was possibly some hesitation, although the police would no doubt argue this was merely for the purposes of confirmation. Whatever, Mr Hinchcliffe never mentioned the counting rigmarole in his final speech.

There was no doubt that when Moore was faced with the fact of the light going on and off in the farm and the smoke seen coming from the chimney a couple of hours after the shootings, that he held up his hands and conceded. The one time Moore did lie, he admitted it as soon as it was put to him. Yet this proved only that he was destroying the evidence of the burglaries. It seems strange he would use up so much time doing this, if what he really needed to do was hide the gun. That is, if he ever had one—and that was never proved.

Mr Hinchcliffe went on to say that, at the point of arrest, Moore was cautioned and informed that he was being arrested in connection with the shooting of two policemen. This was not proved and there is a suggestion that one of the officers present at the point of arrest can be shown to have lied under oath.

Circumstantial evidence, such as the three keys found in a field with little rust, suggesting they had lain there only a short time, invited Mr Hinchcliffe to suggest Moore had thrown them there; one possibility is that one of Moore's children left them there. The unfired round of 9 mm ammunition raised the question of why it was hidden in such a strange place; and there is some question as to whether it *was* hidden and what its origins were. The demolished wall revealed, among other things, the bulk of his huge collection of keys used in burglaries and spent ammunition cartridges. If keys were said to have been thrown into the field then it didn't make sense to do a detour on his way back to the farm, surely Moore would have put them down the cavity wall with the others? It is possible the keys were from another job, but there was no evidence of this. There was also no proof that any of the spent ammunition or the live round had any connection with the murder.

It was also not proved that the clay-type soil found on Moore's shoes was picked up when he went out to 'conceal the live round'. He said the soil had become encrusted when he checked his poultry before he went in at midnight. The white hair was not proved to have come from the head of DI Fraser. What was established though, was that some cross-contamination of evidence could have occurred.

Finally, Mr Hinchcliffe introduced evidence of a revolver-type gun being in Moore's possession. Not only was this disproved but also credibility and reliability of the witness were not evident either.

So little of what Mr Hinchcliffe said in his opening speech was proved to have happened. But what of his final speech, what evidence had come up during the trial to support the contention that Moore was the killer?

Moore certainly had the opportunity to commit the murders as he passed through the cordon after it was set. He definitely passed the point of PC Jagger's posting in the cordon, but Mr Hinchcliffe says he passed the posting point of DI Fraser. However, if moving north from the cemetery up to Whinney Close Farm then he wouldn't pass DI Fraser's point.

One of the police officers measured PC Jagger's posting position as sixty-six yards from the scene of the shootings—a fact which wasn't shared with the jury. That puts the murder location a good distance inside the cordon boundary. No wonder he had to say 'As I got near to him' in his deposition, because PC Jagger might have had a good few yards to make up. In his dying declaration, of course, PC Jagger phrased things slightly differently and actually said, 'Saw a man going up a field. I went after him. As I got near to him he...' But this still suggests a time-lapse from 'I went after him...' to 'As I got near to him.' If it is taken as the minimum of 30 yards visibility then the obvious questions are: How did The Man get inside the cordon boundary before he was seen? And: Where was PC Jagger when he first caught sight of him?

DCI Jenkins explained to Mr Hinchcliffe that the cordon had been set up so that if anyone approached the farm by any recognised path then they would be seen by one of the officers on the cordon. But the murder happened at approximately the place PC Jagger caught up with The Man. If PC Jagger was positioned where he was evidenced to have been positioned, then how did the murder happen where it happened? None of this proved that Moore was guilty, what it does prove is that the police evidence given to the jury doesn't fit the facts.

Mr Hinchcliffe's answer for the prosecution was simple and apparently effective. If the evidence doesn't fit, then change it: 'Again I remind you that PC Jagger was posted in this position a little to the *east* of the tip at a few minutes before 11.40.' That is what Mr Hinchcliffe for the prosecution said in his final speech. To say 'Again I remind you' means he has reminded them previously and so he would have had to tell them in the first place that PC Jagger '… was posted in his position a little to the east of the tip …' In the trial transcript there is no such informing or reminding.

PC Sellick, in evidence, said PC Jagger was posted elsewhere. The following is the court transcript from the first day of the trial, Monday, 10th December 1951:

Mr Hinchcliffe: 'When you got to the tip, would you tell My Lord and the jury whereabouts PC Jagger was posted?'
PC Sellick: 'He was posted within the vicinity of the tip.'
Mr Hinchcliffe: 'Can you be a little more precise than that?'
PC Sellick: 'I should say where the three paths actually meet; approximately there.'
Mr Hinchcliffe: 'That is just to the south of the tip?'
PC Sellick: 'Yes.'
Mr Hinchcliffe: '*It is south-west?*'
PC Sellick: 'It would probably be about 20 yards below the tip. There is a stile and there is three pathways join there [sic].'

It's quite clear, PC Jagger's position according to the evidence as given by PC Sellick was twenty yards to the south-west of the tip. So when Mr Hinchcliffe said to the jury in his final speech, 'Again I remind you that PC Jagger was posted in this position a little to the *east* of the tip at a few minutes before 11.40' was he intentionally misleading them? And DCI King's map clearly shows PC Jagger's posting was to the south-west of the ash-tip.

Can it have been a mistake? It is unlikely as Mr Hinchcliffe's professional task involved remembering evidence and formulating arguments, sometimes two or three days after evidence had been given in court. He pursued the point of PC Jagger's specific cordon posting position with PC Sellick, and there was also DCI King's map. Not forgetting Mr Hinchcliffe's odd behaviour when PC Sellick marked the map (he kept the map on the opposite side of the court from the jury while this question was discussed—see *Chapter 4*), and his apparent disinterest in DCI Jenkins' sketch of the murder scene. So the thought arises that this mistake was no accident.

However, Mr Hinchcliffe was not on his own in the role as counsel for the prosecution as he had a junior, Mr Norman Black. Between them they shared the examination of the witnesses far more than the defence. One such witness was DS Butler. Mr Black elicited the position of DS Butler and then pursued the action he took after he heard the shots. As he had heard shouting before the shots, DS Butler was already running in the direction of where the shots came from. He ran past PC Sellick's position—he wasn't in position as he too had heard the commotion—and went on to DI Fraser's position, he was also not at his position. DS Butler then ran to PC Jagger's posting position and he also wasn't there. What seems strange is that DS Butler got to PC Jagger's position at all, but when he did get there, he said in response to Mr Black:

> 'On the right diagonally from me I saw the light of a torch lying in the grass and when I got to the spot I saw Inspector Fraser lying on his back and Police Constable Jagger was lying on his left side with his knees pulled up towards his stomach.'

Anyone moving on from DI Fraser's posting position would soon have had a head-on view of the scene of the shooting. So it is unlikely that either officer to the east of DI Fraser coming through his position would go to PC Jagger's posting position because according to the map they would have been moving past the scene. So:

Mr Black: 'Did you then run towards Police Constable Jagger's position?'
DS Butler: 'Yes.'

Mr Black: 'What did you see when you got there?'

Arguably DS Butler's continuation to PC Jagger's position was unnecessary and possibly it didn't even happen once he saw the torchlight in the field. But perhaps this is an indication that 'lines' for answers were practised, and DS Butler was a little ahead of himself.

Moreover, Mr Black asked DS Butler if he had measured the distance between various points of the police postings. He said he had done, but he had also measured the distance from PC Jagger's position to the point of the shooting and this information was not asked for in court. Mr Black already knew, as there is a note on DS Butler's statement, and it is in Mr Black's handwriting. There was no need for him to ask the witness something he already knew but this would have occurred so that the jury could hear this from the witness in question. The point is that not asking a question is also a method by which evidence can be concealed; Mr Black wouldn't have wanted the jury to be aware what the distance was, and he certainly didn't want counsel for the defence to know either, that might well have led to a few questions and answers the prosecution didn't want the court to hear.

Returning to Mr Hinchcliffe, there is the question as to whether, in changing PC Jagger's position, he misled the jury or was simply mistaken. The important thing here is the effect Mr Hinchcliffe's moving of PC Jagger's posting position had on the jury. How many of them noticed and thought they might have missed something and how many of the jury members questioned the reliability of their own memories—'Did PC Sellick say it was to the south-west of the ash-tip? I was sure he did. But he can't have. Can he?' Whether it was deliberately misleading or a simple mistake, if Mr Black knew (which he did) it is inconceivable the two prosecution lawyers wouldn't have discussed it. One can consider the whys and the wherefores, but it is almost certain that moving the position of a posting and failing to clarify the distance between PC Jagger's proper posting and the scene of the shooting, did not help the jury reach a true verdict.

It is interesting to compare the introduction to the court of DCI King's map and Insp Little's photographs (which were at the prosecution's request shown at once to the judge and the jury), with DCI Jenkins' sketch of the scene of the shootings which was given hardly any attention when it was produced. DCI Jenkins giving evidence:

Mr Hinchcliffe: 'You produce that sketch, Exhibit No.11.'
DCI Jenkins: (Producing notebook) 'Here.'
Mr Hinchcliffe: 'Perhaps you could leave it there in case it should be required. When you were [sic] finished that sketch, was your attention directed to something at the farmhouse?'

It must have been a shock to the police and the prosecution to discover that PC Jagger was about sixty-six yards as the crow flies, but more like one hundred as the policeman runs from his position of posting, but it seemed that they managed to dupe the judge and jury easily enough.[1] The simple fact which cannot be escaped is this: The Man was already inside the cordon when he was seen. How he got past PC Jagger's position is another question. PC Jagger went after The Man and shouted; DI Fraser joined them and The Man shot them. What is clear is that the cordon was demonstrably passable.

But then why was this not picked up by counsel for the defence? The posting of PC Jagger, as the court heard, was twenty yards to the south-west of the tip. In his sketch, DCI Jenkins clearly shows the scene of the crime was a number of yards to the east of the tip. Why counsel for the defence didn't pick this up is a mystery.

To return to Mr Hinchcliffe's opening speech:

'The prosecution submit to you on that evidence that the overwhelming probability is that the prisoner was returning by that footpath to his farmhouse, not at midnight, but at 1.55 in the morning when he was seen and spoken to first by PC Jagger and then by Detective Inspector Fraser.'

The prosecution submitted this but they did not prove it. Mr Hinchcliffe then provided the jury with a motive for the killing, to buy time to hide the evidence of his previous crimes. But this doesn't establish a plausible motive or prove that Moore was at the scene of the shootings at the time of the shootings, nor does it prove that he was in possession of a gun.

Short of hard facts, Mr Hinchcliffe went on to ask the jury to assess

---

1. Based on measurements that can be made on DCI King's map—see *Chapter 17*.

Moore's behaviour at the point of arrest and in custody too. But that assumed that DCS Metcalfe told the truth when it is plain that in part of his description about the discussion — and particularly the cautioning which took place at the point of arrest — he was contradicted by the other police officer present. So, if DCS Metcalfe lied or was simply mistaken, then it begs the question what other lies did he tell, or was he mistaken about? Regardless, his evidence appears to be unreliable. So when Moore was asked, 'What firearms do you possess?' and DCS Metcalfe claimed he gave the bizarre answer, 'Oh, my head is bad. Don't talk about it. It's awful.' this remains open to question as does his assertion that Moore hid behind the door as discussed earlier.

The prosecution invited the jury to consider the evidence of the removals man, Joe Baxter, about whether he saw a gun that was never manufactured or whether he saw something else. In his statements, deposition and evidence in court, Mr Baxter is sure he had seen an object that started off as an automatic, became a revolver and ended up as an automatic revolver, made by the Luger company. So he saw a gun that was never in fact made. It is surprising that this evidence ever reached the court; the selection of this witness for the prosecution doesn't simply seem a mistake — it seems bizarre.

The white hair that was found on Moore's coat might not have been from the head of DI Fraser, and even if it was there is the possibility of cross-contamination. It goes further than showing a reasonable doubt about the white hair; it suggests that the whole of the police handling of the exhibits might have been clumsy. It is surprising that the introduction of DI Fraser's hair in the opening speech was also a point in the closing speech as it only really demonstrated the police's ineptitude with some of the evidence.

Still nothing seemed to have been proven beyond reasonable doubt by the prosecution. But Mr Hinchcliffe then argued that the whole catalogue of poor quality evidence or mistaken or lied about circumstantial evidence supported the central point of the evidence for the prosecution: PC Jagger's deposition. What PC Jagger's deposition proves beyond reasonable doubt, even without the points he made in his verbal comments to other officers, or in his earlier dying declaration, is that the purpose of the cordon of police around Whinney Close Farm that night was to place officers on or near to paths so they would see anyone coming up the path, not see them after they had passed, and have to go after them.

Another difficulty is the evidence Moore was questioned about by the prosecution in court. He dealt with all the evidence on fact competently, but when Mr Hinchcliffe pulled the stunt of asking Moore about evidence that had not been presented to the court—evidence he seems to have dreamed up—Moore dealt with this too but the effect on the jury of asking him these questions may not have been lost on them. What Mr Hinchcliffe asked him was part of DCI Jenkins' evidence that he (DCI Jenkins) was *not* at the Huddersfield Police Station on 17th July, 'Is that not true?' DCI Jenkins didn't say this, and he *was* at the Huddersfield Police Station on 17th July; he took Moore's fingerprints.

In summary, what the prosecution offered the court fell short of what a jury would require to find a murder charge proved beyond reasonable doubt. But the verdict was still guilty.

Chapter 22

The Defence

The defence was presented by Mr Harry Hylton-Foster KC and Mr C Raymond Dean. Mr Hylton-Foster was 46 at the time of the trial and had been made a 'silk' four years before. He was said to have the 'saving grace of not taking himself too seriously', which may account for some of the comments he made during the trial. But Mr Hylton-Foster was saddled with the pressure to follow in his father's footsteps, as he had also been a barrister. Whether he had lost interest at this point in his career it would be unfair to assume, it was just that the year before he had been elected as the Member of Parliament for York. He was a conservative, and two senior members of the party in power were Winston Churchill and David Maxwell-Fyfe, both of whom had a fierce dislike of police killers: not unreasonable, provided the police get the right man.

The main criticism of Mr Hylton-Foster is in not pursuing the possibility that PC Jagger, through no fault of his own, was an unreliable witness. On the hillside he may not have got a clear view of The Man and almost certainly he would have been influenced by what was said by DI Fraser and the responses of The Man immediately prior to the shooting. At the time PC Jagger gave his dying declaration, whatever time it was, he would have been deeply traumatised. Later at the identification parade he was only a couple of hours post-anaesthesia and would have remained traumatised, which may have affected the accuracy of his recollection. If PC Jagger was an unreliable witness did Mr Hylton-Foster completely ignore the implications of this when he made objection to Mr Hinchcliffe's examination of Mr Wrigley, the surgeon? There may have been abundant evidence from the medical staff to render PC Jagger's evidence inadmissible or unreliable.

But Mr Hylton-Foster was not without his argument. He began his closing speech by throwing down the gauntlet to the prosecution by raising the issue that on the night of the shootings not a single premises was broken into, nor was any report made of any attempted break in. However, the prosecution was never challenged either directly or indirectly to account for the time-lapse from when Moore parted from his brother, at about 11.25 pm, until the shootings at 1.55 am. Considering the time to get from the vicinity of his brother's house, that would leave at least two hours that were unaccounted for.

He did point out the prosecution's case was nothing more than mere suspicion. This is a difficult assertion to deal with, because apart from saying Moore wasn't at the scene of the shootings at the material time there appears to be little else that can be said. He didn't make as much of Moore's cooperation as he might insofar as he seemed to agree to participate in the identity parade with little prompting; though, of course, it was a dire shock to Moore when he was picked out. With the description the police officers had been given, leaving aside the photograph for a moment, it might have been fairly easy for PC Jagger to pick out Moore; whether he was able to pick out the killer is another question. This might have depended on what DI Fraser had said to The Man in PC Jagger's presence. But Moore had no legal representation at the identity parade, and a lawyer and a proper cross-examination of PC Jagger might have produced quite different results. It was also unfortunate that Supt Foster wasn't asked in court just how many of the other eight men on the identity parade were aged thirty-six, balding and only 5' 6" tall. PC Jagger might have identified Moore from the description he was given in the briefing, taken with what DI Fraser and The Man had said, and considering he probably knew by the time of the identity parade that Moore was the only suspect, it might not be too surprising that PC Jagger picked him out. PC Jagger could have put out of his mind what he saw on the night, but brought into his mind only what he heard then, and at the briefing, and simply applied that to the identity parade. It is difficult to assess what was in the mind of PC Jagger at the time of the identity parade, but with the effects of injury, trauma and anaesthesia, it would be difficult to support the assertion that he was as mentally alert as his surgeon had said.

It was what PC Jagger possibly didn't know that the defence seemed to get bogged down with, and the photograph of Moore that the police had, tended to hinder rather than help. The identity of the killer was the point in question — the defence was pursuing what PC Jagger didn't know rather than what DI Fraser did. DI Fraser, through the connections he had, was working on an up-to-date description of Moore. The problem was that it was unclear just how much DI Fraser had established in his own mind about the identity of Moore. But when he had been staking out the bus stop he would have needed to know who he was observing; in short, Moore's identity. What he said to The Man in the presence of PC Jagger will only ever be known via what PC Jagger says was said — and this seems to have fluctuated. If PC Jagger's evidence was unreliable then what about the accuracy of what he said The Man said? Should Mr Hylton-Foster have made an argument that when The Man said he was Moore on the hill it was false, or at any rate, dubious? Was he likely to give his true identity to someone claiming to be a police officer? He was armed and in a strange place at 2 am, and being asked if he was Moore may have put the words into his mouth. Considering the description PC Jagger had been given of Moore, and what The Man said with reference to what DI Fraser said, it is apparent that PC Jagger may have based his identification on what he heard as much as on what he saw.

With the level of ill-feeling towards Moore it is of no surprise that the police were totally unshakeable in their evidence. If they believed Moore was guilty they were certainly steadfast in attempting to help the prosecution prove it. So it would have been expected that their individual accounts about the timing of the forming of the cordon would tally but there are plenty of discrepancies apparent elsewhere in the evidence.

The defence quite properly drew attention to the poor quality of the evidence surrounding the cartridge cases found at the farm. Mr Hylton-Foster argued that '… there is not a shred of evidence …' that the cartridges had anything to do with any of the recovered bullets from the bodies of the dead officers. He wondered whether a cartridge case found in the tallboy in the bedroom — and therefore that couldn't have been dropped from clothing — demonstrated Moore wasn't hiding the cartridges to avoid a murder charge, but was hiding the keys to avoid burglary charges. It seems, from reading the archived documents, that the cartridges found in the cavity wall with the main bulk of the keys just happened to have been in the box in which the keys were kept.

It didn't help the defence that some of the exhibits were presented in the way they were. For instance the keys were carefully presented on a board, which probably didn't help the jury understand that the keys and spent cartridges were found together inside the cavity wall. It tended to promote the illusion that the keys were isolated from the cartridges.

Mr Hylton-Foster highlighted the clumsiness of the police in dealing with the evidence insofar as a list of small bits of miscellaneous metal objects, as found around the farm, was vague. The evidence tying the cartridges to the murder was non-existent, particularly when the argument is offered that any cartridge recently discharged in a gun had a particular smell about it for several hours. There was also evidence, which would have supported the defence, that appears to have been suppressed. The examination that Major Pollard made of the bullets recovered from the two officers and the cartridge cases found on the farm led him to his conclusion that the two were probably not related.

Mr Hylton-Foster argued that the word 'conceal' used by the prosecution when discussing the live round found on the farm, was inaccurate. It was not made clear, nor probably could it have been, just where in the pile of building debris the bullet was found, in relation to where it was before the search commenced. So linking the bullet with the arsenal Moore was said to have, didn't quite gel.

After a lengthy discussion about the possible times that Moore left his brother Charles, in relation to when the police cordon was said to be complete, Mr Hylton-Foster considered the possibility of PC Jagger being slightly off his position. He discussed the 'orientation' of the officers to their patch on the cordon. He suggested they had a quick look around their immediate posting position; this strongly indicates that Mr Hylton-Foster was unaware this was not the first night of the cordon. So it became apparent again that evidence, and potentially quite important evidence too, was withheld from the defence. Mr Hylton-Foster didn't know, for example, that this was the fourth night that the cordon was set.

It was unfortunate that a significant amount of time was taken by Mr Hylton-Foster to discuss the white hair found on Moore's coat. It may or may not have come from the head of DI Fraser, but the prosecution had already alluded to the fact that this couldn't be proven. It might have been more helpful to the jury to just explain in his closing speech about cross-contamination of evidence. But this was left until later. Mr Hylton-Foster tended to jump from one topic to another in his closing speech, and this might not have helped the jury focus on his arguments.

In his closing speech, Mr Hylton-Foster spent a fair amount of time discussing the coat Moore was wearing on the night and how the rain may have affected it, as he had elicited from DCI Jenkins precisely when the rain had fallen and for how long. The unfortunate part was that DCI Jenkins was caught at cross-purposes because it was the previous night that there had been quite a prolonged downpour just after midnight. But in court DCI Jenkins had confused the two nights. DCI Jenkins later tried to correct his error or at least let it be known, and a report by the Met Office which would confirm the lack of rain on the night was not presented to the court.

Not enough consideration was given to the various points noted at the time Moore was arrested. Moore's use of the words 'serious enough', when asked by Alice whether his arrest was for something serious, rendered their conversation open to assumptions—assumptions the police were more than willing to make.

Mr Hylton-Foster then picked up on what he described as the prosecution's '… trifling inaccuracy' about the question of the firearm. It was a shame that his sharp legal mind only picked up on a trifling inaccuracy rather than a blatant changing of the evidence, i.e. Mr Hinchdcliffe asking Moore whether he had the revolver Mr Baxter said he saw, even though it had been proved such a weapon never existed.

Something Mr Hylton-Foster could have raised but didn't was the prosecution changing the precise positioning of PC Jagger's cordon posting. And not just there—Mr Hinchcliffe, in the examination of PC Sellick much earlier, established that the officer had been posted at 'a quarter to 12', but after a short adjournment Mr Hinchcliffe said: 'You had told the jury that you were posted just before 11.40 …' It wasn't subtle enough to say 11.40, it had to be '… just before.' Now, it may not be relevant what time PC Sellick took up his position but what is relevant is that Mr Hinchcliffe changed the evidence to suit.

From there Mr Hylton-Foster dealt with yet more trifling inaccuracies about a prisoner's right to silence, but didn't say that the police had made a damning inference about Moore's inability to discuss the 'firearm'. Though he did say the police tricked him into things and then complained he didn't want to answer questions when in custody.

Regarding the matter of Moore throwing, or being accused of throwing, keys into a field, it may have helped the jury if Mr Hylton-Foster had suggested that it would have made more sense if, instead of throwing the keys into a field Moore would simply have dumped them with the others, down the cavity wall. Otherwise, he would have had to cross a field and not leave a track in the long, damp grass. It might have been more effective if Mr Hylton-Foster had simply told the jury that as there was no track through the grass then no-one could have walked through it. Either way, a link between the keys and the shooting wasn't established but for some reason defence counsel didn't make more of how tenuous and circumstantial the evidence was.

Mr Hylton-Foster was confrontational with the witness Joe Baxter about the gun, and this probably did more harm than good — he was hard on the man and not hard on the issue i.e. that there never was made such a gun as a Luger revolver and that the witness was therefore unreliable.

Just like everyone else involved with the case, Mr Hylton-Foster did not see the folly of the police's behaviour — as explained by them — at the point of arrest. This supposedly hellishly dangerous man was allowed to hide behind a door where he could have had anything in his hands.

Mr Hylton-Foster claimed that the final point to clinch Moore's innocence was the fact that the gun wasn't found anywhere on the farm.

It is easy to criticise Mr Hylton-Foster and how he handled the case but the tragedy of Moore's defence is four-fold. Firstly, it is apparent that evidence was withheld, which clearly demonstrates that the trial was unfair or imbalanced. Secondly, more could have been done with the evidence surrounding the medical staff and what happened in Huddersfield Royal Infirmary, not only with the post-operative period but also with what happened before — if it happened before — PC Jagger's surgery. Thirdly, the support, or specifically lack of it, afforded to DCS Metcalfe at the point of arrest by PC Cleaver — the central point was missed that PC Cleaver's evidence did not support DCS Metcalfe's — this could have exposed a leading prosecution witness as a fraud. But talking of fraud leads to a fourth point: Mr Hylton-Foster also missed the fact that his learned friend for the prosecution moved the scene of PC Jagger's position in the cordon. This does not even take into account the factual errors Mr Justice Pearson made in his summing-up.

As I mentioned earlier Mr Hylton-Foster had recently became an MP and that is where his strengths lay. As counsel for the defence in Moore's case he was uninspiring. In the case of the murder of Mary Hackett two years later his poor handling of the prosecution was only slightly better than a poor defence.[1] But as a conservative MP he did become a successful politician and was Speaker of the House.

---

1. *R v. Albert Hall*, 1953. See http://www.yorkshirepost.co.uk/news/main-topics/local-stories/hanged-but-was-he-really-a-killer-1-2483020

CHAPTER 23

Withheld or Ignored Evidence

It is one thing to demonstrate that evidence was withheld from the defence, it is quite another to think what might have happened if that evidence been disclosed to them or heard in court. Another thing that seems to have disappeared is a statement Moore said he made, which he gave to his own solicitor, Mr Hutchinson. One can only hope that one day this will surface. There is information about this case in the National Archives to demonstrate that evidence was withheld. Indeed, the bulk of the official documents are in the National Archives.

The West Yorkshire Police have confirmed to me that they also have documents relating to the case, but say they are exempt from disclosure under the Freedom of Information Act, so therefore are unavailable. Sadly it seems that the individual police officers' pocket books are not available for scrutiny.

To demonstrate that some of the evidence was withheld, changed, edited or ignored, it is worth comparing some of what was presented in court with what appears in individual statements. This is not a complete assessment but merely a short review. It might be helpful to consider what effect a few of the 'hidden' issues might have had on the court if they had been raised.

In the final speech for the defence, Mr Hylton-Foster made it clear he was disappointed with the evidence of the removals man employed for the move from Gynn Lane to Whinney Close Farm, Joe Baxter. He actually felt Mr Baxter had been '… impertinent' with his reply to the question of where he had seen a Luger revolver. But Mr Baxter didn't only answer to Mr Hylton-Foster, he also discussed the Luger revolver in cross-examination and re-examination. It was a '… Luger revolver' he had seen, and he recognised it as he had also seen one whilst serving in the Navy at Davenport. Two key things here; one of which was brought out in court and one that was not. Firstly, it was proved by the ballistics expert that the gun used in the crime was a revolver, but as explained in earlier chapters Luger never manufactured a revolver. And, secondly, was Mr Baxter consistent in what he claimed? He did say it five or six times in court so it would be fair to assume he said this to the police in his statements. But, in a statement made by Mr Baxter to DCI Jenkins in the presence of Sgt Sadler and DO Naldrett on 28th July, Mr Baxter said '… an automatic pistol like a Luger'. He continues: 'It was an automatic pistol like I had seen and used in the Navy'. In examination Mr Baxter was asked about his training in the Navy and did he '… know the difference between a revolver and an automatic pistol?' 'Yes,' he replied. So, in this case, Mr Baxter's evidence was changed before it was presented in court. But, whoever changed it didn't do their homework as, in changing his story to accommodate the weapon being a revolver rather than an automatic, it wasn't checked that such a weapon ever existed. If Mr Hylton-Foster had known that Mr Baxter initially thought the gun was a Luger automatic and later 'reviewed' this observation to claim it was a revolver he'd seen, possibly to fit with other evidence, then it is likely Mr Hylton-Foster would have used this.

Another change in the evidence was made by DCI Jenkins concerning his activities in the police cells on 15th July. He said in court that he only saw Moore once in the cells, and that was when he took his fingerprints; this happened on Tuesday 17th July at 9 am. However, in a statement, DCI Jenkins said that he was in contact with Moore and he, DCI Jenkins, was '… in the cell corridor'. Moore called out to him and asked him to take a letter to his wife, which DCI Jenkins agreed to do. It is unclear why DCI Jenkins was in the cell corridor at 9 pm and later claimed he was only in the police station from 9 pm to 9.15 pm. It means, in simple terms, that he saw Moore at the police station on 15th July at 9 pm and again on 17th July to take his fingerprints. DCI Jenkins may not have had prolonged contact with Moore on the evening of 15th July, but what he said was misleading as he had seen Moore on more than one occasion, yet under oath he said he only saw him the once. Without this documentation Mr Hylton-Foster could not challenge this.

Mr Hylton-Foster did query whether in the first few minutes of the cordon the officers would have just been scouting around to see the make up of their 'patch'. He was unaware it was the fourth night of the cordon. It becomes clear in his closing speech he didn't know — a statement (not used) by Mrs Lucy Woodhead who lived in the bungalow adjacent to Whinney Close

Farm describes the cordon formation and the previous three nights it had been in place. These days the rules of disclosure would ensure the defence received all such documents.

Moore was also observed in his previous home. If Mr Hylton-Foster had known this then a line of defence could have been DI Fraser knew Moore, so why ask who he was? He could simply have addressed him as Moore Moore or Mr Moore. DCI Jenkins claimed the description from an earlier reported burglary sounded like Moore, although which burglary he referred to was not recorded.

The defence didn't appear conversant with the statements(s) the daughter made—said to hear a police whistle and later say she had never heard a police whistle in her life. So not only does this demonstrate police coercion it also shows how some possible lines of defence were denied Moore.

Insp Knapton made a statement to say he was at Huddersfield Royal Infirmary with Supt Foster at just after 4 am on the morning of the shooting, that is just over two hours after the shooting. In the Emergency Department, Dr Baird started PC Jagger on a saline solution which was infused intravenously to replace fluid he had lost as a result of his injury. It is highly unlikely that, as PC Jagger didn't get to the hospital before about 3 am, his blood could have been matched and a blood transfusion commenced in as short a time as an hour. The blood would also usually be given after surgery; PC Jagger's would have been tested for its haemoglobin levels and there appeared to be no medical need for a blood transfusion before his operation. Yet Insp Knapton said that PC Jagger couldn't sign his dying declaration with his right hand (and therefore signed it with his left) at 4.20 am as he had a 'blood transfusion' going into his right arm. This cannot be supported by the facts, and counsel for the defence would have wanted to establish what Insp Knapton saw, what the doctors gave and when, and then questioned what time Insp Knapton saw what he said he saw. But counsel for the defence cannot have seen Insp Knapton's statement (or they might not have realised there was any significance in it.)

All of the police officers on duty on the cordon that night made statements and gave evidence in court. The problem with one of the officers was that he liked to measure distances. For instance, he measured the distance between PC Jagger's position and DI Fraser's and made it eighty-four yards, and then measured the distance from DI Fraser's position to PC Sellick's position, which was 199 yards. However, he also measured the distance from PC Jagger's posting position to the scene of the shootings, thus demonstrating that his colleague was certainly off position at the time of the shootings. In the original statement, Mr Black for the prosecution highlights this, so in court the matter isn't broached.

The jury didn't hear evidence from Major Pollard of Churchill's the Gunsmiths in London. He suggested that the bullets recovered from the officers and the cartridges recovered from the farm were not related. But this evidence may not have been withheld by the police or the prosecution; this might have been an example of poor communication within the defence team.

In the appeal against conviction it was said that at the trial Mr Justice Pearson had suggested that Moore might have been 'inside' somewhere, which may have affected the way the jury felt and that this was misdirection. In the event this contention was rejected.

Did the police actually withhold evidence? Moore Moore was said to be a very dangerous man who shot two police officers and casually went back to his farm. At the point of arrest Moore had stood in the doorway of the farm, a door behind which he was said to be hiding; DCS Metcalfe said: 'His body was partly shielded by the door, around which he was peeping'. At this point, his armed escort, PC Cleaver, was a few feet to DCS Metcalfe's rear. So much effort was put into making this point about Moore 'hiding' and 'peeping' and generally acting in a sinister manner, but the one thing that any sensible person would expect to have been said wasn't said, which would have been PC Cleaver, with a gun pointed at Moore, saying 'Stick 'em up' or 'Hands up'. Instead they let what they must have believed was a police killer partly shield his body behind a door. This might have been sheer lunacy, or it might have been recklessness; or it might not have happened as described by the officers. Their story certainly raises questions.

The one thing that is certain is that PC Jagger told DCI Jenkins what had happened, DCI Jenkins later told DCS Metcalfe and the latter went to arrest Moore. This brings us to the question of who knew what? If DI Fraser shone his torch into The Man's face then he would have been expected to know whether it was Moore or not, which deepens the mystery because of what he was said to have asked him. Then he was shot dead and could not make his observations known, other than what can be gleaned from his questions immediately prior to the shooting, and then only in the presence of PC Jagger. So did the police know it wasn't dangerous to approach the farm? With the evidence given, it certainly looks as though DCS Metcalfe was the hero, but what did he know that he didn't share, or has remained hidden? In evidence, Moore said he was putting on his wellington boots at this point, which would mean his arms, hands, legs and feet would have been out of sight of the two officers; they later said he was wearing wellington boots at the point of arrest so this goes some way to corroborating what Moore said. But as they made much of the fact that his body was partly hidden and did not mention at that time that he was putting on his wellington boots, then the activity was hidden, so too then were the fingers that supposedly had so recently pulled the trigger of the gun that had just mortally wounded two police officers. If DCS Metcalfe knew it wasn't Moore who had shot his colleagues and knew Moore had never used violence then it explains why he didn't ask Moore to show his hands were empty. Of course it is possible there were other officers, armed and with their weapons pointed directly at Moore but no evidence was ever given to this effect. It seems strange that this whole charade at the point of arrest wasn't analysed at the time.

There are a couple of minor points from the identification parade which didn't come out in the evidence. Part of the information was not sworn on oath or taken from a police statement but was the subject of a report in a newspaper forty years later. In court, Moore said he was '… third from the left' in the identification parade. If this is correct, then counting from one direction he would be number four, and counting from the other direction he would be number six. However, both Supt Foster and Insp Bradley, who were the officers conducting the parade, said Moore was in the centre; and further stated that when PC Jagger counted from one end he stopped at number five, the accused; and when he counted from the other end he came to rest on number five, the accused. What seems strange is, if Moore was picked out without hesitation as both Supt Foster and Insp Bradley say he was, what was the purpose of the 'counting'. They had their suspect and they could now charge him. If one accepts what the police officers said as the counting being just a confirmation of identification, then the parade seems to have established the identity of the accused. But, in a newspaper in 1991, one member of the identity parade spoke out. He said that PC Jagger's finger wavered between him and the man stood next to him, who was Moore. This was why Supt Foster asked him to count from either end. In his statement, Supt Foster said PC Jagger '… pointed to the accused, Moore'. Insp Bradley said that 'without hesitation Police Constable Jagger immediately pointed to the accused'. It seems that this was not the case.

Each murder trial is made up of much tedious evidence and it must be difficult for all jury members to follow the proceedings. They rely on the lawyers and their final speeches in particular must be reassuring. One can't help almost hearing them sighing with relief when Mr Hinchcliffe says in his final speech that they have now heard the '… whole of the evidence'. But even though they had not heard the whole of the evidence, he didn't tell them that some of the evidence didn't quite suit the prosecution's case, so it needed a few minor changes. Because it has to be asked—what if someone noticed the distance between PC Jagger's position and the murder scene? It's possible the prosecution might have claimed that he crawled there before the other running officers could arrive. Of course, PC Jagger would have had to carry DI Fraser over his shoulder, which is not quite plausible, so the prosecution decides to move PC Jagger's position in the cordon. That seems to suit all concerned, except truth and justice.

In a brief compass, the evidence the jury heard was far from complete and was heavily biased towards the prosecution's argument. But where the evidence was inconvenient to the case against Moore, it seems to have been withheld, ignored or distorted. If the wrong man was convicted of this crime then the real killer was free to kill again.

In modern times the law requires that all unused evidence must be made known to the defence unless the judge rules that it can be withheld on a very limited number if grounds.

Chapter 24

Some Thoughts on the Summing-up

Rather than reproduce long, detailed parts of the summing-up, it might be better to focus on a few things in the final directions to the jury which seemed to go a bit awry. The idea behind a summing-up is not to go into the minutiae but to cover the salient points. A jury properly directed, so the theory goes, will arrive at a true verdict. But a jury can also be misdirected: as to the law or as to the facts. It is only misdirections of fact that seemed to raise their head in Moore's trial. But it must also be emphasised that a judge can share an opinion with the jury and if that opinion is wrong or misleading then it might not necessarily constitute a misdirection.

So a few observations. Generally speaking, a person approaching a point or person, is said to be *coming*; and a person moving away from a point or person is said to be *going*. But it is in the use of these words that the jury could first have been misled in Mr Justice Pearson's summing-up, although he used the same words PC Jagger used. PC Jagger's posting position is shown in *Figure 1* in *Chapter 3*.

Mr Justice Pearson said: '... nothing had happened for a considerable time and then someone was seen coming in'. If PC Jagger was in his rightful position he would have observed The Man *coming* up the footpath which runs up to that position from the cemetery. But The Man wasn't seen until he was '... *going* up a hill', and PC Jagger had to go after him. So telling the jury The Man was '... coming in' suggests The Man was approaching the cordon boundary, when he appears to have passed through it. This leads to the inevitable question that if The Man was able to pass through the cordon at 1.55 am, then had Moore been able to pass through at about midnight?

So as The Man had clearly passed the boundary of the cordon, PC Jagger approached him. It is assumed The Man kept to the paths around the farm. The path the murder took place on was obscured by trees and undergrowth from the direction of PC Jagger's posting position, so PC Jagger could only have observed him from a different position. Even if PC Jagger was near his posting position and 'went after him' and if he moved twice as fast as The Man, it would still suggest that The Man had passed the boundary of the cordon by about thirty yards or so before he was seen. This is complicated by the visibility that night. PC Sellick judged vision to be about thirty yards. DCI Jenkins said sixty yards, but PC Sellick was lower down the hill than DCI Jenkins, which might have made a difference.

Backtracking slightly, the time of the cordon becoming operational has been questioned by other commentators.[1] Thinking about the various timings, that is the actual timings and not what Mr Hinchcliffe would want them to be, then it does seem reasonable to accept that the cordon was in place, by and large by 11.45 pm. So Mr Justice Pearson seemed satisfied that the timings did not allow Moore to pass the cordon before 11.50 pm and if it is accepted that the cordon was in place by 11.45 then this fits. What doesn't fit is that there is no suggestion of where Moore might have been between midnight and 2 am. And where was PC Jagger at around midnight? It cannot be denied that he was off position when The Man passed at 1.55 pm, so where was he at midnight when Moore claimed he passed?

Mr Justice Pearson made an error in describing PC Jagger's posting position as being '20 feet' from the ash-tip—it was actually twenty yards. But that pales into insignificance when Mr Hinchcliffe moved the posting position about sixty yards to the other side of the ash-tip.

Moving forward to the scene of the arrest, Mr Justice Pearson said that PC Cleaver's evidence supported that of DCS Metcalfe; Moore claimed DCS Metcalfe said that *one* officer had been *hurt*. But DCS Metcalfe was adamant. Under oath he said *two* officers had been *shot*. But PC Cleaver said 'a police officer'. PC Cleaver leaned more towards Moore's version of events rather than DCS Metcalfe's. At that point in the evidence his Lordship had even highlighted that it might '… have some bearing of the reliability of the evidence one way or another.' But he seems to have forgotten this when he came to deliver his summing up. If a conversation took place at the point of arrest about fowls and foxes and their shooting then any discussion and consideration of the events around the scene of Moore's arrest may now

---

1. Fenton Bresler, *Scales of Justice: Reconsideration of Twenty Court Cases of This Century* (Littlehampton Book Services Ltd, 1973). Steve Lawson, *Wrong Neck in the Noose* (Amazon Kindle Publishing, 2012).

be tainted with the phrase: '… the evidence of Superintendent Metcalfe confirmed by PC Cleaver.'

But it might be that this was preparation for the misquoting of Moore, and there were a number of comments attributed to him which he later denied saying. For example Alice Moore asked about the reason for arrest: 'Is it serious?', and DCS Metcalfe said "… the prisoner said, 'It is serious enough'."

Mr Justice Pearson went on to say that DCS Metcalfe had given in evidence:

> 'Mrs Moore said to the prisoner, "Shall I get Eaton Smith for you?" The prisoner said, "Eaton Smith can't help me in this."'

Mr Eaton Smith was a Huddersfield solicitor. Moore denied saying 'Eaton Smith can't help me with this.' Mr Justice Pearson quoted further from DCS Metcalfe's evidence:

> 'Mrs Moore was quite hysterical. She tried to pull me from the prisoner. Police Constable Cleaver took her away to the house door. I then cautioned Moore. I told him that he was being arrested in connection with the shooting of two police officers about two a.m. that morning in Cockley Hill Fields.'

PC Cleaver said he was about three yards away, and in earshot. He heard 'a' police officer, so did not confirm DCS Metcalfe at all. So what was the impact on the jury of hearing Mr Justice Pearson say PC Cleaver supported DCS Metcalfe when it was not completely true?

The fact that the weapon wasn't found was unfortunate, but it should be noted that Mr Justice Pearson did mention the ballistics question. However it is conjecture whether, if he had known what Major Pollard had said, he would have quoted Dr Mayes verbatim:

> 'It is not possible to say whether or not the spent cartridges were fired from the same weapon as the spent bullets'.

Major Pollard's evidence was not heard by the court, so it wasn't just the jury who were excluded from this evidence. A jury properly directed will reach a true verdict but can a judge properly direct a jury if he has not heard the full evidence?

Mr Justice Pearson also said of Mr Baxter's evidence:

> 'He said he did see a revolver and it was a Luger, that is to say a German make of revolver. Of course, there are several possibilities, members of the jury. He may not have seen anything at all. He may have seen one of the two exhibits 24 and 25 and mistaken it for a revolver. He may have seen a revolver which was not a Luger, or he may have seen a Luger revolver and it has disappeared since.'

This raises several points, e.g.:

1. No-one saw Moore with a revolver at any other time.
2. The make and type of gun Joe Baxter claims to have seen was never manufactured.
3. It was never found. With the concentrated search, had the revolver remained on the farm or in its immediate surroundings, then the likelihood is that it would have been found.
4. Had Mr Baxter just seen Moore's air pistol?

Is it acceptable that Mr Justice Pearson commented '… or he may have seen a Luger revolver that has since disappeared'? The jury were being asked to consider the possibility that something impossible occurred.

To end at the beginning. Before the officers were shot the question of identity came up. At the beginning of the summing-up identity was discussed — Alfred or Albert Moore. It is quite incredible that it was accepted as fact by the court that a man brandishing a gun and acknowledging he is Al**** Moore was truly Alfred Moore. What was not addressed was the point that if The Man was a villain, would he have been likely to have given his real name or would he have been more likely to have said 'Yes' when given the opportunity to say he was someone else?

Mr Justice Pearson said the case was a matter of identification, but he didn't tell the jury that the crucial question of the identification of Moore on the hillside rested quite heavily, if not entirely, on what The Man himself said and following the events PC Jagger related. As this pre-dated the Turnbull direction (see *Chapter 16*) by many years then this can't be part of the argument as such, but Lord Devlin did say after his committee had reported in the late 1970s that the recommendations vis-à-vis the Turnbull direction were what was being done by '… sensible judges anyway'. So did Mr Justice Pearson fall into that category?

CHAPTER 25

The Run Up to the Appeal and its Aftermath

The murder of police officers in any way or form is a strike against freedom and democracy itself, and appeal court judges were not reputed to show much compassion to their killers. That might be considered reasonable and when Mr Hylton-Foster commenced his address to their Lordships in the Court of Appeal he did at least have some fresh evidence which we will come to, but first he considered errors in the trial.

Mr Hylton-Foster wished their Lordships to consider that Mr Justice Pearson had misdirected the jury in suggesting that as Moore's raincoat was dry then he had been '… inside somewhere', when in actual fact it hadn't rained on the night of the shootings. Whether Mr Justice Pearson had been suggesting Moore had been in a premises burgling somewhere isn't quite clear: but there was no such activity noted in Huddersfield that night. The appeal court judges—the Lord Chief Justice, Lord Goddard sat with Mr Justice Byrne and Mr Justice Parker—were not perceivably impressed.

Some keys had been found which the prosecution said had been thrown by Moore to where they had landed. Quite where this was taking the appeal is a mystery.

It was explained that although Moore said he had gone to bed at around midnight and that he didn't get up again, once he knew the seriousness of the situation he admitted he got up again to burn some paper money and stamps. He hadn't said this at the point of arrest because he quite simply didn't see the relevance: all he had been told was that *an* officer had been *hurt*. DCS Metcalfe swore to the court he told Moore *two* officers had been *shot*. This was not supported by PC Cleaver's evidence, despite what Mr Justice Pearson said: PC Cleaver said 'an officer'. More may have been made of this in the appeal if the defence had scrutinised PC Cleaver's evidence and Mr Justice Pearson's summing-up. Exposing the head of the CID as giving misleading evidence could have (there was no guarantee) swayed the jury. But it was all there in the trial transcript. In summary, PC Cleaver and

DCS Metcalfe's evidence not tallying was not raised. Neither therefore was the fact that the judge had misdirected the jury to consider that Metcalfe's evidence was corroborated by Cleaver's.

The prosecution laboured Moore's lie quite intensively. In the dock he could only stand by and watch as Mr Hinchcliffe's catalogue of incorrect assertions grew:

1. The posting time of PC Sellick (which Hinchcliffe changed).
2. DCI Jenkins claiming he'd only seen Moore once at Huddersfield Divisional Headquarters.
3. The position of PC Jagger's posting (it was changed).

So that is DCS Metcalfe, the head of the CID, counsel for the Crown and the original trial judge misleading the jury—anything else seems anti-climatic. But there were various points the other police officers made that were arguably incorrect—as an example, Insp Knapton claimed to have seen blood being transfused before the surgery.

The second part of the appeal centred around fresh evidence not available at the time of the original trial, which suggested that DI Fraser had arrived later:

> 'That evidence is now available...Which materially effects the time when Inspector Fraser took up his post in the cordon around Whinney Close Farm on the material night...'

It didn't actually prove anything, it was merely a suggestion that he'd spent the evening with Ben Stafford.

There were considerable issues about whether DI Fraser addressed Moore as Albert. The identification made by PC Jagger seems to have been made by an amalgam of what The Man said in response to the questions of both DI Fraser and PC Jagger, coupled with the attire, age and size of Moore on the identification parade, and the doubtful integrity of the identification parade. The appeal court was told that it was unlikely that the photograph of the appellant, Moore, which members of the police cordon carried in the days running up to the murder could have helped PC Jagger in his identification because when he flashed (or shone) his torch into the face of The Man, he would most likely have screwed his face up in response to the sudden exposure to light. But DI Fraser should have known if it was Moore or not, as this would be recognition not identification.

'Are you Moore, Albert Moore.' When DI Fraser said this then the only two people who heard it were The Man and PC Jagger. After he was shot, when in shock and all the accompanying difficulties PC Jagger recited that DI Fraser said 'Albert Moore'. For a professional like a detective inspector to make this mistake is unlikely, however for anyone who has just been shot and has witnessed the murder of a colleague, confusion about what had been said: Albert Moore, Alfred Moore, whatever — would not be surprising. So it is highly significant. Lord Goddard, Lord Chief Justice at the appeal was quoted as saying that PC Jagger gave evidence '… in the most clear and convincing way…' He may have given evidence in the most clear and convincing way, but was it reliable? In fact the Lord Chief Justice was reputed to have dismissed the appeal without conferring with his two fellow judges. He got it horribly wrong just about a year later when Derek Bentley was denied a fair trial, one over which Lord Goddard presided. Whether one takes his evidence at face value or one probes the deeper recesses of the mind where the night's events demonstrably muddied the water, PC Jagger did not give *reliable* evidence in the most clear and convincing way. Lord Goddard's view is too simplistic and therefore unacceptable.

The appeal was dismissed without ceremony. Three weeks into 1952 the question was how long Moore would survive into the new year. He was said to look strained at the Court of Appeal, and so he might for one who had witnessed the futility of a not guilty plea, had shown all due respect to the mechanisms of the law, then he was left high and dry by the Assize Court verdict and the dismissal of his appeal.

The 'system' had convicted him with reliance on questionable identification evidence held together with dubious prosecution evidence where the integrity of the ministrations of law had been shaky. There was not one piece of evidence in the trial that pointed to Moore's guilt without reasonable doubt.

So, back at Armley Prison, Moore was given all the usual comforts of one in the condemned cell. The twenty-four hour attendance of two prison officers who, in the circumstances, would often create a less rigid and strict regime. There would be activities to relieve the boredom with board games, cards, dominoes and Moore's speciality, chess. There could be books and newspapers too with an allowance of a pint of beer a day and tobacco. The Governor and medical officer would keep a close eye on things and it was the Governor who delivered the letter to Moore that his appeal to the Home Secretary to commute his death sentence had been rejected. It was Moore who broke the news to Alice when she next visited — and visiting for the condemned was far more amenable. But it was only a short while before the state was going to kill him.

Moore could spend his exercise periods no doubt contemplating his doom but where were his thoughts? In the *Epilogue* I discuss, albeit briefly The Man who may have occupied his thoughts, but his thoughts were not to be shared with anyone, at any rate as far as we know. The two officers were gunned down within a stone's throw of the farm. One has to ask if the carrying of guns in the rural areas surrounding Huddersfield in the early 1950s was for the defensive or for the offensive-minded. But in the clandestine world of crime many disputes are not settled by ordinary discussion and appeal to reason.

Moore was a crook and he'd be the last to deny this and there is plenty of weight in the suggestion that he was more than just a burglar. As he was always said to have worked alone it does pose the question of how some of the recovered stolen goods found at the farm actually got there. Some of it was bulky, so for a man on foot careful to take the route home under cover of darkness and helped by the shadows, then it doesn't quite gel that he could have stolen some of the goods himself. Money, yes, and small items of jewellery. So, if some of his other activities were linked to the criminal fraternity, and if he dealt with stolen goods then this relied on trust and goodwill with the crooks in his network — this begs the question was there anyone in that network who could possibly have murdered two police officers? Maybe there was as I mention in the *Epilogue*. If Moore knew of such a person it seems he had decided to take such knowledge to the grave. If someone was coming to see him in the dead of night and shot two police officers then was he fearful of what that person might do if he were to name him? He had a wife and four children to think of.

One of the last people to see the condemned man is the executioner: Steve Wade was the executioner with Harry Smith as his assistant. As Moore exercised they could observe him and make calculations, confirmed by other details of weight and build and calculate what length of 'drop' would best serve their gruesome task.

Moore had free access to the prison chaplain. I don't get the impression that religion played a part in Moore's life and the arrangement may have been on a 'Don't call me. I'll call you' sort of basis. But this is secondary to the thought that part of the chaplain's role would be to help the condemned make peace with God before the execution, and as I am convinced Moore didn't need to make peace because he didn't murder the officers, then the role of the chaplain in this instance would be superfluous. But the chaplain would be there purely for the condemned and not to bring some legitimacy to the state to remove a citizen from its midst by killing him.

Alice made her final visit with their eldest daughter. This would have been highly charged, and it is said both were strong for each other and the children. After Alice had gone, Moore sat and wrote his last letter, addressing it merely as 'Sir' it was to be held by the prison Governor but eventually became part of the archived records.

The letter is quoted in full with observations interspersed. It is exactly as Moore wrote it.

5.2.52

'Sir,

I Alfred Moore still maintain that I was not the person in the crime committed on Sunday July 14th 1951, at Whinney Close, Kirkheaton.

After the death sentence the prisoner is given three Sundays to make his peace with God. Most, if not all confess at some stage. Moore didn't, my view is he had nothing to confess.

I maintain that the evidence of arrest given by Supt Metcalfe was entirely a figment of his own imagination, untruthfully supported by Inspector Cleaver.

This can be demonstrated by the trial transcript, and the judges summing-up. It seems that even Moore started to think that Cleaver supported Metcalfe's version of events (whereas he didn't).

> I maintain that I gave the police all the information as set out in my original deposition which is in my own handwriting on prison paper, and was given to my solicitor.

This document is not in the National Archives and I was unable to find a copy through other channels.

> That Inspector Jenkins was given my raincoat at 5.15 am that morning, this he denies. That time I state is correct by Metcalfe's watch. I saw it and later asked him the time.

If DCI Jenkins was given his coat it seems strange that he'd deny it. The lack of forensic evidence is, in fact, forensic evidence—and indisputable—a gun had not been in the pocket of that raincoat.

> That I continually asked for legal aid and secured only abuse. That I did NOT SAY at the time of arrest: "Eaton Smith can't help me now" that is typical of the way Supt Metcalfe talked during his short interviews that day. That I was only told somebody had been hurt. See my deposition in my handwriting on prison paper. Mr Hutchinson has this. That the depositions of all the police witnesses gave an entirely wrong account of what happened and appear to have been manufactured and are mainly untruthful in their contents. That Supt. Metcalfe made suggestions such as "you don't like the police Albert, do you" "You are confused Albert can't you think", they're things he has put down as untruthful to make it appear that I said such things as "Oh my head" and "Give me time to think" and "I never did like the police". These above phrases are entirely Metcalfe's own sayings rephrased and falsely collaborated by other police witnesses. I did not say these things. All that happened until after the identity parade was that I was asked what guns I had. This was also asked before my arrest and I told them.

DCS Metcalfe wanted a conviction and he got one. This paragraph needs re-reading several times because there is much in what was not said. Some of DCS Metcalfe's evidence was not collaborated [sic] at all—it was just believed, despite evidence to the contrary. When evidence was given that did contradict DCS Metcalfe, i.e. PC Cleaver's, it didn't seem to register.

> That Inspector Jenkins and Eddington [sic] subjected me to cross-examination from about 8 pm to 1 o'clock Sunday night. This Jenkins denies, that the police were told everything before the time of the arrest, such as clothes I wore and time I came back. That when I said I didn't go out again it was meant to imply that I didn't set off anywhere, which is perfectly true. This was said to Jenkins during cross-examination Sunday night. And not to Metcalfe as he implies and as his witnesses falsely support, see original deposition in my own handwriting on prison paper, Mr Hutchinson has this.

'I didn't go out again' meant he didn't leave the farm, not that he didn't go out and check his poultry. A misunderstanding but it helped the prosecution because they could make much of this 'untruth'.

> I feel that I was systematically obstructed from getting a solicitor for about twelve hours before the identity parade.

The evidence would support this, but one problem was that the police said they could not contact anyone. He declined to have a solicitor he did not know and this was presented to the jury as a refusal. In the event Mr Eaton Smith declined to represent him, but Mr Hutchinson did not.

> I feel that the 9 MM cartridge cases found on the farm are not the ones I had, but may have been picked up by the children in or around the out-buildings. That there were bullet holes through top bedroom window in unfinished part of the house when we first bought it as an unfinished structure because of this I feel that there is some person near Kirkheaton who has a weapon and was in the habit of going into the farm building when it was unoccupied for a considerable period.

Who was taking pot shots at the farm?

Mr Harthouse [Hartly: author's note] of Messrs Mays Ltd. Builders, Huddersfield can vouch for what I say about bullet holes in windows.

Only hours before his death and he still wanted to argue his innocence, nobody listened to him say DCS Metcalfe had lied — Moore and his defence team didn't seem to notice the prosecution's actions nor the judge's.

The above statement is true.

Alfred Moore 6/2/52'

Epilogue

The Rest of February 1952 and On

There isn't much else one can say about Alfred Moore, who died on the same day as King George VI, 6 February 1952. All the main characters are now passed, Mr Justice Pearson as Baron Pearson passed away in 1980. Sir Harry Hylton-Foster died in 1965, and Sir (George) Raymond Hinchcliffe followed in 1973. DCS George Metcalfe became plain Mr in 1970 and met his maker in 1984. DCI Arthur Jenkins passed in 1978 and PC Sydney Cleaver in 1987.

Alice Moore died in 1990 and one of the children in 2003. Little is known of DI Fraser's widow and child. I hope they found future happiness. PC Jagger's widow joined him in 1993. Both of PC Jagger's children have lived on: I wish them well and hope they too have recovered as best they may. There remain a couple of issues to conclude — the gun and who pulled the trigger.

In theory it is possible it was Moore, and that he did go up the paths to the farm. But I think it far more likely The Man reversed and went back down the path and past the ash-tip to the cemetery and away into the night. I believe Moore was in bed and this also convinces me The Man retraced his steps.

The gun could have finished up anywhere, and we know where it didn't finish up. Stafford Hill Lane is about a five minute walk from the farm and it is possible that *knowledge* of the gun had got that far by the late 1950s. When a young lad found a gun, he showed it to his father: there was a reaction! His father could well be described as a gangster who had little regard for the law or for other people. The gun was a revolver. The lad's father had actually bragged later that he had the gun that had done the deed.

When two former policemen from Huddersfield — Steve Lawson and Colin van Bellen started to study the case they used the local paper the *Huddersfield Examiner* to publicise it. This paid dividends and a lot of people gave them the name of that lad's father. He had been a criminal associate of Moore so it might make sense that he was out to get him. Especially as Moore wanted to go straight. Colin passed away unfortunately, but Steve is still active and wrote his own book *Wrong Neck in the Noose*.[1] He named a local man who was renowned for his crimes and brutality. Clifford Mead was an associate of Moore and he'd used and would use firearms again—in broad daylight he threatened a man with a shotgun. Later he'd bragged that he had the gun that had shot the 'two coppers'. Young DC Lawson felt the police could act on firearm offences and search his house—one wonders what they might have found. As it was, more senior police officers didn't think it was a wise move.

Another modern commentator is former barrister and Judge Patrick Robertshaw, he also feels the case had the wrong outcome. His book *No Smoking Gun* is a rewarding read.[2]

༄

In the event though the police didn't actually prove that Moore had done it and neither did the lawyers, but the jury thought that they had. The clinching factor was probably PC Jagger's evidence—evidence given in such dire circumstances that no-one could say for sure that there was no chance of error. Thankfully, we don't hang offenders anymore, and please God may we never return to that.

The fact remains that Alfred Moore was identified as The Man who on the hillside shot both DI Fraser and PC Jagger. But whether that identification came about because PC Jagger clearly saw him or because of suggestion, pleading, coercion, argument, injury, trauma, lies, or general mistake is not clear. As for the court proceedings, they fell short of accuracy, let alone proof; and the appeal was before a dogmatic and dominant, if not dangerous Lord Chief Justice.

On the hill in Huddersfield in the dead of night two policemen were shot and killed. A dangerous and armed man was at large. If the account of the arrest and trial of Alfred Moore shared in this book is correct then it means that a dangerous and armed man remained at large.

---

1. Steve Lawson, *Wrong Neck in the Noose* (Amazon Kindle Publishing, 2012)..
2. Patrick E. Robertshaw, *No Smoking Gun: The Story of the Kirkheaton Police Killings* (New Generation Publishing, 2012).

Index

A
accident *51–52, 180*
air pistol/rifle *89, 115, 147, 170, 177, 186*
alibi *86, 127*
Almondbury *27*
ambulance *47, 152–154*
ammunition *27, 89, 102, 169, 184, 194*
anaesthetic *61, 117*
antibiotics *59*
armed police, etc. *54, 154, 164*
Army *97, 107, 162, 168*
arrest *19, 49, 116, 147, 162, 188, 194*
arrogance *115, 157*
ash-tip *10, 35, 43, 51, 122, 149, 218*
assizes
    Leeds Assizes *11, 149*

B
ballistics *11, 97, 107, 111, 219*
Barber, Sgt *72, 168*
Barclay, PC *109, 169*
Bark Hill Council School *15*
Baxter, Joe *99, 111, 147, 170, 208, 211*
Beard, Dr Jessie *57, 157*
Beck, Adolph *128*
Bentley, Derek *225*
B & J Whitman's *18*
black market *23, 30*
Black, Norman *70, 135, 193, 197*

blood *11, 57, 73*
    blood transfusion *60, 213*
blood pressure *58, 59, 117*
blood transfusion *59–61, 117, 213*
Bodkin Adams, Dr John *175*
Bottoms Farm *18, 19*
Bradley, Det Insp *65*
Bradley, DI *167*
break-ins *19, 21, 24*
Bressler, Fenton *81*
brickworks *10, 152, 178*
    brickworks raid *156*
briefings *10*
Brockholes *25*
broken windows *130*
Brown, Sgt *109, 169*
bullets *72, 105, 107, 110, 155, 171, 205*
    bullet holes *130*
burglary *9, 20, 23, 31, 162, 177*
Butler, Det Sgt *46, 70, 132, 150, 152, 197*
Byrne, Mr Justice *223*

C
Canada *12*
cartridges *11, 97, 105, 109, 110, 147*
    cartridge cases *169, 177, 205*
cash *23–25*
cavity wall *109–110, 179, 183, 205*
cemetery *36, 149, 178, 217*
chaplain *227*

Churchill's Gunsmiths *104, 214*
civilians *98*
Clanton, PC *110, 168*
Clarke, PC *168*
Clark, PC *154*
Cleaver, PC *49, 71, 116, 164, 180*
clothes *161*
cobbler *139*
Cockley Hill Lane *32, 192*
coercion *81, 101, 213, 232*
coke brieze *164*
communication *71*
   non-verbal, etc. signals *65, 67*
condemned cell *225*
contradictions *94, 101, 200*
cordon *9–11, 32, 37, 67, 70, 123, 150, 178, 193, 205, 224*
cornfield *135–137*
counsel *119*
court *31*
   Court Martial *176*
   Court of Appeal *125*
   makeshift court *11*
   Military Court *20*
credibility *55*
crepe-soled shoes *156, 170*
crime prevention *23*
Criminal Procedures and Investigations Act 1996 *128*
cross-examination *119, 120, 182*
Crowther, Percy *159*

D

Dalton *17*
David Brown & Sons *19, 20*

Daw Knowl *153*
Dean, C Raymond *203*
death sentence *12, 143*
debt *144*
'denial' *46, 77*
depositions *11, 39, 45, 63, 69, 79, 98, 112, 149*
depression *92*
Devlin, Lord *127*
disclosure *126, 128, 213*
discrepancies *53, 205*
ditches *97*
doubt *12, 125*
   reasonable doubt *12, 127, 200*
dry stone walls *97, 162*
dying declaration *39, 45, 58, 60, 79, 195*

E

Earnshaw, PC *62, 72, 159*
Edington, DCI *73, 86, 101, 147, 165*
employment *18*
errors *218*
ethics *123*
evidence *97, 175, 208*
   circumstantial evidence *194, 200*
   concealed evidence *70, 119, 198*
   cross-contamination *104, 152, 170, 195*
   manufactured evidence *95*
   missing evidence *206*
   'not used' *100, 130*
   police evidence *69*
   prosecution evidence *111*
   suppressed evidence *46, 125*
   tampering with *69*
   withheld evidence *211*

examination-in-chief *119*
'extractor marks' *105*

F
fairness *65*
family *81, 99, 144*
fear *116*
fingerprints *71, 156, 181*
fire *187*
   fire brigade *97*
   fire in the hearth *154*
First World War *15*
flannel trousers *164*
flashbacks *78*
footpaths *33, 98, 132, 133, 149*
foreign currency *82, 88, 179*
forensics *12, 71, 103, 104, 155, 228*
Foster, Supt *57, 166*
fowls and foxes *160, 218*
Fraser, DI *9, 31, 45, 224*

G
Garnett, DO *108, 147, 169*
Gilbert, Sapper *168*
Goddard, Lord *223, 225*
Goitfield Council School *15*
Golcar *15, 28*
Grimsby *19*
gun *10, 38, 39, 47, 77, 85, 97, 111, 194, 231*

H
haemoglobin levels *59, 117, 213*
hair *73, 104, 108, 152, 159, 173, 195, 200*
Hallis, Rex *34*
Hall Wrigley, James *57, 157*

handcuffs *89, 160, 188*
hanging *9, 12, 232*
Hartley, Arthur *99, 130–131*
headaches *73, 163, 166*
hearsay *45, 48, 153*
Heath Hill *19*
Heckmondwicke *93, 143*
hen hut *133, 134, 156, 170*
Hinchcliffe, George Raymond KC *11, 149, 193, 231*
Hirst and Mallinsons *18*
hobbies *15*
Home Office *102, 171*
Home Secretary *226*
Honley *9, 25, 26, 27, 29, 162*
Hopping, PC *47, 70, 108, 132, 145, 156*
hospital *65*
Houses Hill *34*
Huddersfield *9, 17, 226*
   Huddersfield Borough Police *65, 68*
   Huddersfield CID *31*
   Huddersfield Magistrates' Court *19*
   Huddersfield Police Station *160*
   Huddersfield Registry Office *18*
   Huddersfield Royal Infirmary *11, 47, 57, 70, 153, 159, 208*
Hudson, PC *72, 165*
Hull *19*
Hutchinson, George (Ted) *104, 172, 211, 228*
Hylton-Foster, Harry KC *11, 72, 146, 149, 176, 203, 231*
hypervigilance *78*
'hysteria' *219*

I

identification *37, 39, 49, 65, 74, 111, 128, 133, 173, 220, 224, 232*
   identity parade *11, 41, 65, 74, 117, 163, 190, 194, 204*
   mistaken identity *145*
   reliability *79*
innocence *94, 143*
   protests of innocence *12*
integrity *65*
interview *139, 189*
inventory *156*
investigation *69*

J

jacket *155*
jack-knife *103, 110, 168, 172, 177*
Jagger, PC *9, 45, 77, 97, 132, 150, 193*
Jenkins, DCI *10, 42–43, 47, 49, 71, 115, 129, 145, 152, 195, 228*
Jenkins, Roy *127*
jury *12, 119, 151, 184, 207, 219*

K

keys *103, 108, 110, 115, 154, 168, 172, 177, 194, 223*
King, DCI *70, 131, 149*
King George VI *9, 12, 231*
Kirkheaton *9, 29, 62, 193, 229*
Knapton, DCI *57, 74*

L

Lawson, Steve *231*
Leeds
   Leeds Assizes *11, 149*

Lee, DS *132, 135*
Linthwaite *24*
Little, Insp *70, 103, 149*
live round *155*
locksmith *24, 110*
Lockwood *16*
Lodge, Michael *130*
logic *82*
Longwood *15, 18, 25*

M

magistrate/court *11, 58, 81, 83, 145, 186*
   makeshift magistrates' court *161*
Mallinson's *18*
map *34, 42, 131–133, 197*
Maxwell-Fyfe, David *12*
Mayes, Dr Alfred Horace *102, 112, 171, 219*
Mead, Clifford *232*
media *69*
medical staff *159, 203, 208*
memory *69, 78*
mental illness *75*
Merchant Navy *19, 20, 24, 31, 90, 139, 176*
metal detectors *97*
Metcalfe, DCS *10, 45, 49, 71, 101, 115, 145, 159, 179, 230*
meteorologist *155*
Met Office *100, 207*
military detention *20*
Milnsbridge *18, 24, 25*
mine detector *107, 168*
misdirection *217, 223*
mistake *155, 163, 190*

Moore, Alfred *9, 231*
  behaviour in prison *140*
  calmness *139*
  character *139*
  evidence at his trial *175*
  intelligence *142*
  'lazy' (in prison) *140*
  'sinister character' *72*
  temper *15, 90, 94, 144*
Moore, Alice *9, 18, 50, 87, 143, 164, 178, 231*
Moore, Charles *98, 145, 150, 181*
  Uncle Charles *81, 83*
Moore, Mahala *98*
Moore, Mr and Mrs David *15*
murder *9, 11, 69, 223*
Murray, PC *47, 156*

N
nail scrapings *73*
Naldrett, DO *212*
National Archives *211, 228*
nerves *92*
Nickolls, Lewis *103, 159, 172*
nurses *57*

O
observation *9, 32, 37, 100, 115, 153*

P
Parker, Mr Justice *223*
pathology *158–159*
pathways *36, 42, 178, 196*
Pearson, Mr Justice *11, 54, 114, 158, 217, 231*
peritonitis *159*
photographs *130, 149, 198*
pig sty *150*
Pioneer Corps *20*
pistol *97, 99, 102, 111, 170, 212*
plan *70, 149, 154*
pocket books *49, 211*
police *69, 98, 175*
  armed police *71*
  Police and Criminal Evidence Act 1984 *128*
political pressure *69*
Pollard, Major *104, 172, 206, 219*
post-traumatic stress disorder *78*
Price, Dr David *158*
prison *139*
  Armley Prison *12, 225*
  hospital wing *139*
  prison hospital *93*
  prison officers *139*
prosecution *11, 193*
psychiatry *75*
psychology *75*
public *69*
putting on an act *140*

R
rain *207*
raincoat (gabardine) *103, 155, 173, 186*
rationing *23*
reading *15*
recall *69, 78*
re-experiences *78*
revolver *11, 85, 89, 97, 102, 231*
  'Luger revolver' *11, 111, 170, 211*

rights of way *33*
Robertshaw, Patrick *232*
rubble pile *109, 162, 169, 181*

S

Saddleworth *18*
Sadler, Sgt *108, 212*
saline infusion/solution *57, 117, 213*
Scapegoat Hill *19*
science *98, 102*
search *162, 169*
Second World War *33*
self-incrimination *121*
Sellick, PC *42, 46, 48, 70, 103, 132, 145, 150, 196*
shock *66*
shoes *103*
shooting *9, 10, 37, 39, 45, 77, 122, 129, 133, 151, 197*
shortages *23*
shot gun *89, 115*
Shroggs Bridge *34, 149–152, 156*
silence
  right to silence *73, 125, 175, 207*
sinister behaviour *147*
sketch *43, 198*
Slaithwaite *18*
Smith, Harry *226*
smoke *11, 23, 71, 145, 159–160, 166, 179, 194*
soil traces *103*
solicitor *74, 80, 142, 145, 160, 164, 229*
Stafford, Ben *33, 37, 100, 224*
Stafford Hill Lane *231*
stake-out *38*

stamps *82, 88, 91, 103, 172, 179, 187, 223*
Stancliffe, Frank *129*
statements *69, 83, 98, 130*
  non-disclosure *74*
stress *78, 166*
summing-up *72, 160*
surgeon *57*
surgery *60, 117*
Swallow, Jack *130*

T

tallboy *109, 169, 184, 205*
Taylor, PC *132, 152, 157*
testimony *98*
'The Man' *10, 13, 40, 45, 177, 225, 226, 231*
'The Mountain' *33*
Thompson, Edith *175*
Thongsbridge *26*
timings *218*
toolbox *111, 115, 170, 177*
torch/torchlight *70, 132, 136, 151, 197, 225*
transcript *45*
trauma *46, 77, 116, 157, 203*
trial *149*
Turnbull case/direction *125, 220*
twilight world *23*

V

Van Bellen, Colin *231*
veranda *155*
verdict *173, 198, 217*
Verity, CI *170*
violence *16, 20, 92, 94, 144, 176*

visibility *63, 153, 195, 218*

W
Wade, Steve *226*
Ward, Dr Crispian *58*
Waterloo *87*
weapon *97, 107, 140.* See also *revolver*
weather *115*
West Riding *9, 18*
   West Riding Constabulary *11, 57, 167*
West Yorkshire Police *111, 176*
Whinney Close Farm *9, 21, 24, 32, 70,*
   107, 143, 169, 195
  lights at *194*
whistle *10, 82, 84, 88, 90, 100, 133, 151,*
   178
witness *69, 81, 111, 119*
  witness coercion *81, 86*
  witness statements *45*
Woodhead, Arthur and Lucy *33, 129,*
   212
Woodhouse, Herbert *66*
wounds *58*

X
X-rays *58, 107*

Y
Yeates, DO *101*

Putting justice into words

Murderers or Martyrs
by George Skelly, With a Foreword by Lord Goldsmith

A spell-binding account of an appalling miscarriage of justice. Charged with the 'Cranborne Road murder' of Wavertree widow Alice Rimmer, two Manchester youths were hastily condemned by a Liverpool jury on the police-orchestrated lies of a criminal and two malleable young prostitutes. George Skelly's detailed account of the warped trial, predictable appeal result courtesy of 'hanging judge' Lord Goddard and the whitewash secret inquiry will enrage all who believe in justice. And if the men's prison letters (including from the condemned cells) sometimes make you laugh, they will make you weep far longer.

Paperback & ebook | ISBN 978-1-904380-80-1
2012 | 480 + 8 pages of photos

The Cameo Conspiracy: A Shocking True Story of Murder and Injustice
by George Skelly

The true story of Liverpool's Cameo Cinema murders vividly demonstrates the need to guard against police corruption and legal manipulation. George Kelly was hanged in 1950 for shooting dead two men early in 1949: the manager of the Cameo Cinema, Wavertree and his assistant. Undeniably from the wrong side of the tracks and involved in petty crimes of the post-Second World War era, Kelly and his coaccused Charles Connolly (who went to prison for ten years) found themselves expertly 'fitted-up' as riff-raff in a Kafkaesque nightmare.

Paperback & ebook | ISBN 978-1-904380-72-6
3rd edn. | 2011 | 368 pages

The Cardiff Five:
Innocent Beyond Any Doubt
by Satish Sekar, With a Foreword by Michael Mansfield QC

Satish Sekar shows how a miscarriage of justice destroyed families, divided communities and undermined confidence in the criminal justice system. *The Cardiff Five* case is the first example in the UK of a homicide in which the original suspects were vindicated by the conviction of the true killer in the DNA age. By then, they had shared 16 years in prison for a crime they did not commit.

'One of the most important books ever written about criminal justice': Michael Mansfield QC

Paperback & ebook | ISBN 978-1-904380-76-4
2012 | 208 pages

www.WatersidePress.co.uk

The Colour of Injustice:
The Mysterious Murder of the Daughter of a High Court Judge
by John Hostettler

Based on actual (sometimes exclusive) materials, *The Colour of Injustice* raises questions about politics and the judiciary in post Second World War Northern Ireland. Describing parallel worlds of power and influence, this book—the first on the case—shows corruption at its most disturbing, justice at its most deficient. The case of Ian Hay Gordon involves a miscarriage of justice brought about in circumstances of privilege, patronage and the social and religious divides existing in Northern Ireland in the decades following World War II.

Paperback & ebook | ISBN 978-1-904380-94-8
2013 | 170 pages

**Rough Justice:
Citizens' Experiences of
Mistreatment and Injustice
in the Early Stages of Law
Enforcement**
by Roger Williams
With a Foreword by David Wilson

Recounts the experiences of victims of police and criminal justice failings through the stories of some who fought back, often with amazing commitment and courage. Their feelings encompass frustration, confusion, helplessness and anger. Their encounters affected their trust, certainty and confidence in British justice, sometimes for a lifetime.

It could it happen to you.
Will anything ever change?
When will politicians face up to the need for action?

Paperback & ebook | ISBN 978-1-909976-18-4
2015 | 272 pages

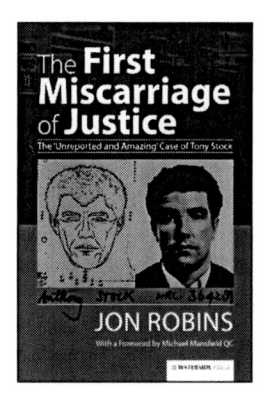

**The First Miscarriage of Justice:
The 'Unreported and Amazing'
Case of Tony Stock**
by Jon Robins, With a Foreword by Michael Mansfield QC

The story of Tony Stock is astonishing: deeply disturbing it sent out ripples of disquiet when he was sentenced to ten years for robbery at Leeds Assizes in 1970. Over the next 40 years the case went to the Court of Appeal four times and has the distinction of being the first to have been referred to that court twice by the Criminal Cases Review Commission. Stock died in 2012 still fighting to clear his name: spending from his meagre savings to hire private investigators and hoping beyond hope to see justice. Jon Robins uses Stock's epic campaign as a way of exploring the treatment of miscarriages of justice over the last four decades

Paperback & ebook | ISBN 978-1-909976-12-2
2014 | 256 pages